Lacan and Cassirer

Value Inquiry Book Series

VOLUME 321

Philosophy and Psychology

Edited by

Arunas Germanavicius (*Vilnius University*)

The titles published in this series are listed at *brill.com/vibs* and *brill.com/pap*

Lacan and Cassirer

An Essay on Symbolisation

By

Antoine Mooij

Translated by

Peter van Nieuwkoop

BRILL
RODOPI

LEIDEN | BOSTON

Cover illustration: Carel Blotkamp, NO, 2011, acrylic on fabric stitched with sequins, 20x40 cm, collection of the artist.

Library of Congress Cataloging-in-Publication Data

Names: Mooij, Antoine, 1944- author.
Title: Lacan and Cassirer : an essay on symbolisation / by Antoine Mooij.
Description: Leiden ; Boston : Brill Rodopi, [2018] | Series: Value inquiry book series. Philosophy and psychology, ISSN 0929-8436 ; volume 321 | Includes bibliographical references and index.
Identifiers: LCCN 2018033035 (print) | LCCN 2018044457 (ebook) | ISBN 9789004373662 (E-book) | ISBN 9789004373426 (paperback :alk. paper)
Subjects: LCSH: Symbolism (Psychology) | Lacan, Jacques, 1901-1981. | Cassirer, Ernst, 1874-1945.
Classification: LCC BF458 (ebook) | LCC BF458 .M66 2018 (print) | DDC 302.2/223--dc23
LC record available at https://lccn.loc.gov/2018033035

This is an English translation and revised edition from: Antoine Mooij, *In de greep van de taal. Symbolisering en betekenisgeving: Lacan en Cassirer.* © 2015, 2017, Uitgeverij Sjibbolet, Amsterdam. Translated from the Dutch by Peter van Nieuwkoop.

Typeface for the Latin, Greek, and Cyrillic scripts: "Brill". See and download: brill.com/brill-typeface.

ISSN 0929-8436
ISBN 978-90-04-37342-6 (paperback)
ISBN 978-90-04-37366-2 (e-book)

This book is printed on acid-free paper and produced in a sustainable manner.

Contents

Introduction

This book aims to present an image of man as a symbolising being that is able to interpret itself and is thus endowed with the capacity of self-determination. However, any image of man has to be substantiated in human and cultural sciences, as well as being founded in a philosophical tradition. Without such substantiation it will be just an empty shell, while lack of foundation will make it an arbitrary effort. Consequently, a philosophical anthropology is composed of three constitutive elements: (1) the basic outline of the view of man itself, (2) its philosophical foundation, and (3) a detailed substantiation in terms of 'empirical knowledge of man'. Reasoned though a choice for a particular concept of man may be, it will always remain a choice. The fundamental choice made in this book is to regard man as a symbolising being. This thesis will be proposed, scrutinized, and discussed, which may result in a contribution to a philosophical anthropology made concrete.

The emphasis in this book is on the second element: its foundation, which defines the concept of man as a symbolising being. What does that mean? Symbolisation or representation means, by way of introduction, that nothing can 'be' unless it is something else too or represents this *other* thing. Something is red if it has the properties of a red colour, thus representing red. For example, an official represents a particular authority, deriving his authority from this representation (rather than from what else he may be). In the course of the past century, two thinkers offered major contributions to the inherent field of research: the Neo-Kantian philosopher Cassirer (1874–1945) and psychoanalyst Lacan (1901–1981). Juxtaposing the two may raise a few eyebrows, as Cassirer and Lacan at first glance seem to have very little in common, whilst holding quite disparate views. Cassirer (1874–1945) was a quintessentially academic philosopher, and is hardly a household name in the world of philosophy. One of the last of the philosophers of culture, the name Cassirer smacks of bygone days, of pre-World War I Neo-Kantianism. And yet his chef d'oeuvre, his philosophy of culture, was written in the 1920s, in the midst of the exciting and fascinating years that followed the Great War. Cassirer is also known for his famous Davos debate with Heidegger. However, his forced exile from Germany in 1933 relegated him to the margins of history. And then there is Lacan (1901–1981), a famous psychoanalyst, a man with a complex character and a mixed reputation. Some worship Lacan, while others abhor his ideas. In that sense he is the typical French master-thinker. And yet Lacan's work did stand the test of time, earning its place in history thanks to his specific theory of culture, of the symbolic order. In doing so he returned to Freud, to Freud's theory of culture and its

 | DOI:10.1163/9789004373662_002

notion of an inevitable discontent with culture. Whereas Lacan is inspired by Freud, Cassirer owes much to Kant's work, and so their perspectives are fundamentally different. Yet they find common ground in their treatment of Kant's and Freud's work, respectively. In his philosophy of the symbolic forms, Cassirer demonstrates how Kant's ideas can be developed into a theory of symbolisation. In his turn, Lacan adopts a similar approach as Freud in his theory of the symbolic order. Here, in the theme of symbolisation, is where we recognise their mutual relationship. Man represents brutal reality through images, words and formulas, relying on symbolic systems in which language plays a key role. And yet each of these systems are characterised by the same *lack*: being limited to representing or symbolising reality as something else, they can never truly reflect or duplicate reality itself. Their capacity to represent is based on this lack, on this inability to duplicate. Nonetheless, this lack works out positively rather than negatively. Indeed, it enables representation, or productive representation, as well as the creation of a wide variety of symbolic systems. The very inadequacy of any symbolic system creates the need for more symbolic systems, a need that can in fact be addressed. The lack left (and created) by a particular type of symbolisation can be filled by another, complementary or corrective type of symbolisation. This symbolisation will take a variety of shapes and can be substantiated through a wide range of media (language, science, art, religion, etcetera). While none of these will show reality in its true form, each will use their own unique 'refractive index' to project reality. Thus, reality is only given as one single manifestation out of a pluriform range of manifestations: *as* a rock or rock formation, *as* food on the table; *as* radiation, *as* $e=mc^2$; or *as* fascinating or terrifying – while none of these manifestations can be singled out as the 'one and only true' manifestation.

Brutal reality or the real itself eludes any such attempt. This describes the second characteristic they have in common. The real is processed symbolically – through images, languages or formulas – but reality itself is excluded from this process. As a result, man does not coincide with his natural body, nor does perceived nature coincide with nature itself, while knowledge of the other is charged with misunderstanding. Thus, man is denied access to immediacy – to life, brutal reality, to the Other. Inevitably, any type of mediation, of symbolisation, leaves a gap, one that can manifest itself in all kinds of ways: maybe as an experience that does not match theory, or as an unexpected, indefinable impulsive act, or as an event that cannot be dealt with or symbolised in one's own life, ultimately leading to a trauma.

Obviously, this fundamental view of pluriform disclosure of reality may not appeal to all, or indeed provoke fierce criticism. After all, science, most notably the world of physics, only knows reality as it is. The fields of natural sciences, life sciences and neurosciences tell us exactly what nature is, what life is, what the mind is, and will undoubtedly continue to do so. And religion is a thing of the past, isn't it? Criticisms such as these are typical of the dominant discourse: man *is* an animal, man *is* his brain. Sweeping though these statements may seem, they do reflect a type of sentiment commonly conveyed using more elegant turns of phrase. The representation philosophy challenges and actually opposes such ideas. Arguments supporting this philosophy will not be offered by engaging in debate with contemporary thinkers of a naturalist persuasion. Instead, they will come to the fore through the discussion and elaboration of Cassirer's and Lacan's lines of thought.

In this context, Cassirer is particularly relevant. He was a great and versatile scholar and Neo-Kantian and, true to form, a champion of the Enlightenment. Cassirer elaborated the tenet of a pluriform access to reality into a broad philosophy of culture, which encompasses a host of symbolic forms (myth, religion and art, language, law, science, etcetera). Each of these forms can represent or symbolise reality or the real in a specific way, but in doing so it also highlights an intrinsic deficiency. This deficiency or limitation of a representing system tends to be overlooked, however, whenever a specific type of representation claims to offer a comprehensive view. This may lead people to believe that modern science is the sole purveyor of the ultimate truth, that human rights are the greatest good, or that myth and religion are nothing more than fallacies. While Cassirer works out his vision in a broad historical perspective, Lacan chooses to put man itself centre stage by positing that man, the state of human existence, is specifically defined by this lack, by the inadequacy of language, of symbolic systems. In man, this leads to subjective dividedness, to drives circling around a void, which may also bring into being a specific type of anxiety (occurring when symbolisation fails and the unfiltered real looms ahead). Again, this deficiency or fragmented state can be overlooked or ignored, leading to the suppression of inner dividedness and an inability to deal with emptiness.

Lacan and Cassirer may see eye to eye on these points, but their views on the nature of symbolisation are quite different. Cassirer's views are rather outspoken, as he gives primacy to meaning, to signification. When I see a cow, I will already know what a cow is, which means that based on this knowledge I can go on to distinguish and identify a cow as such. The primacy of signification also finds broad support within the philosophical community – from Husserl's phenomenology to Russell's analytical philosophy. Therefore, 'Cassirer' also represents a commonly accepted view that gives primacy to signification. Lacan's view differs in the sense that he first asks another question: How can anyone, for example a child, know what a cow is? The child will hear people talk about things like 'cows', 'heifers', 'horses', 'milking', 'slaughterhouse', 'quota' and 'Brussels'. What is it supposed to make of all these mysterious words? It is not until the child has been given some degree of explanation that it will be able to attribute meaning to these different terms and identify the objects to which these meanings or significations may or may not refer. In this way, Lacan draws attention to material terms, to meaningless letters, to the symbolising 'signifiers' even before a meaning has been established. We could say that Lacan thus complements *and* corrects Cassirer. Their divergent views create a whole range of other considerable differences, for example in terms of ultimate accessibility of reality, of being able to know reality. Cassirer is much more the optimist than Lacan, whose deep scepticism leads him to point out the inevitability of deadlocks occurring. It all goes back to their different points of departure: 'the signification' *or* 'the signifier'. Yet there is more to it than just a comparison between a theory of representation based on the signification (Cassirer) or the signifier (Lacan), respectively. On closer inspection it turns out that their opposing views are in fact mutually complementary, indeed correcting each other in essential ways. This leads to a third theory of representation, one that offers a synthesis of the key elements taken from Lacan's and Cassirer's views (based on the notion that they mutually complement and correct each other). It highlights the issues associated with symbolisation itself, which is essential to be able to understand man, going on to substantiate these insights in the field of 'empirical humanities'.

This explains why the present book was designed as follows. Chapter 1 offers an outline of the human condition in hermeneutical terms: man as a creature that interprets itself and the world. The topics in this introductory chapter, which have been structured in a specific way, are based on earlier work (Mooij 2010, 2012). It provides a necessary historical and systematic background for a fruitful discussion of problems associated with the concept and the process of symbolisation. If we assume that man interprets himself and the world, what then is the nature of this 'self', and how exactly does the 'world' that needs explaining take shape? To answer this question, the basic tenets of the philosophy of Cassirer (Chapter 2) and Lacan (Chapter 3) as well as their mutual relationships will be discussed, with the focus being put in both chapters on symbolisation. Indeed, the proposed mutual relationship had already been pointed out in the earlier work mentioned, while the present work, by contrast, offers a fully-fledged substantiation, which constitutes its very nucleus. The closing chapter (Chapter 4) introduces a synthesis of Cassirer's and Lacan's views on symbolisation – a third form. Above it offers a substantiation of this concept of symbolisation for a number of subdivisions of the humanities. In conclusion, this book is made up of three parts: (1) a view of man, (2) elements for a theory of symbolisation, and (3) its substantiation. Guided by Cassirer and Lacan, the notion of man as a symbolising creature or *animal symbolicum* is thus underpinned and substantiated, whilst contributing to a contemporary philosophical anthropology made concrete.

This approach inevitably leads to some degree of repetition, which offers the advantage of selective reading. Chapter 1 does not contain much that is new to the philosophically versed reader, while those to which Lacan's ideas hold little appeal may want to skip Chapter 3 and focus on the chapter that discusses Cassirer, or vice versa. Chapters 1 and 4 are particularly relevant to those who take a particular interest in the global contours of the view of man as a symbolising being and its substantiation in an 'empirical study of man'. This diversity is very much in line with the subject matter at hand and its approach: offering building blocks to produce a view of man as a representing living creature, as a symbolising animal. Prior knowledge of Lacan or Cassirer is not presupposed, but the chapter on Lacan does address the 'technical' aspect at a somewhat advanced level. Indeed, the work of Lacan has been embraced by a considerable number of French, Anglo-Saxon, German (and Spanish) and Dutch-speaking people (particularly in Belgium), which had given rise to an abundant literature. The magnitude hereof is so extensive that, because of unavoidable arbitrariness, any explicit references to secondary literature will be of a very limited nature. In addition, we have seen the emergence of a post-Lacan reception, elaborating the later Lacan towards 'the real' ('the Lacanian Real'). Indeed, this post-Lacanian development will be referred to and criticised, albeit briefly, because it presents a clear challenge to the interpretation of Lacan's work offered here. By contrast, such an internal discussion would be less relevant with regard to Cassirer's work, because it never gave rise to the forming of different schools of thought. Nonetheless, this would not preclude a divergence in interpretations of his work today. Whilst focusing on its main theses, a broader discussion of these interpretation issues will be left out. The scope of this book, however, does reach beyond outlining both Lacan's and Cassirer's views. Taking their bodies of work as a basis, it is aimed at gaining more insight into the problems associated with symbolisation, while advocating the notion of man as an *animal symbolicum*.

CHAPTER 1

An Outline of the Human Condition

There can be little doubt that modern science undermines the traditional image of man, as a spiritual being with the capacity for freedom and self-determination. Although classical philosophers did devote a section to man, it remained secondary to the story of nature, cosmos and world order. The main challenge was to assign man a position within this structure, which was not essentially problematic. The advent of modernity introduced a new problem – Descartes, Newton and the mechanisation of the world image effectively relegated the traditional concept of man to history. The problem of man has been high on the agenda ever since, owing to the fact that the physical order determined by laws of nature does not afford any conceptual space for the traditional constituting qualities of man – meaning fulfilment, self-determination. In the final analysis, the ongoing debate about the (im)possibility of free will and other phenomena of consciousness – 'man is his brain' – is little more than a rekindling of this debate, triggered by new research data that do not necessarily lead to new conceptualisation.

Once again, the idea is not to engage in a fresh debate on naturalism, but only to refer to it indirectly, where relevant. Besides, the naturalistic view of man has 'strong academic' overtones, as was pointed out by the British philosopher P.F. Strawson (1974, 1–15) in a very influential article. He argues that a person may decide to reject the freedom of will and all that goes with it, but will never actually live by this decision. People live in mutual relationships and do not consistently regard each other as objects – which would be a prerequisite for validating the theories of determinism and physicalism. Yet people do not look upon each other this way, nor do the proponents of this thesis. Moreover, people couldn't even if they tried. Life cannot well be imagined and be worth living without the notions of mutuality or autonomy, of a ratio-driven existence. People will find themselves unable to maintain consistent objectivity in their interpersonal attitudes or to accept the state of isolation this would bring. Even the classical deterministic systems (like those proposed by the Stoics and Spinoza) leave some margin for freedom in the sense of affirming the way things are.

The idea of this book is to outline and make a case for the traditional view of man, as well as to qualify it from Lacan's and Cassirer's perspectives, respectively. Here, the emphasis will be on the latter. This qualification does not result

 | DOI:10.1163/9789004373662_003

in the elimination of the traditional view of man, which would be reflected in concepts such as 'we are our brain' or 'the death of man as a subject'. This traditional view of man remains sustained, with man as a creature that is able to explain both reality and itself and is thus capable of self-determination. It is grounded in the view of man as a being endowed with the gift of reason and language. Man is a speaking and rational being that has 'reason' and 'language' as reference points. This view of humanity goes back as far as Aristotle, who believed only one type of reason and language existed. For example, he derived the fundamental categories of reality from the grammar of the Greek language. A champion of modernity, Kant interiorised reason – 'reason is found inside man' – while also supporting the notion of a single reason. However, the notion of a uniform pattern, there being one valid form of access to reality, one single form of reason, came under increasing pressure in the post-Kantian period. The idea of a single reason gave way to the notion that there are multiple ways of disclosing or symbolising reality. Science as well as religion and law offer various modes of access to reality, of symbolisation, each of which could rightfully claim being 'reasonable'.

Within this qualification of reason, language retains its central role, in the sense that any type of symbolisation will rely on (some form of) 'language' – in mythical stories, to support rites and bans, to express formulas, etcetera. Cassirer elaborated this notion in the first half of the 20th century. Moreover, man may be a creature endowed with reason, but even more so it is a symbolising being or *animal symbolicum*. Indeed, more than a rational creature – according to Aristotle – and symbolising – according to Cassirer – man is part of a community. In Aristotle's times, this community was the city or city state. Just like Kant modified the traditional concept of reason, so did Hegel elaborate the social dimension. Indeed, even the depth structure of knowledge is of a social nature (Brandon 2000, 32–35). Any type of access to reality will take place within a cultural community and is therefore socially embedded. As an individual being, man is a 'subjective mind' whilst being part of an 'objective mind' as well – the mind and mindset of a community and its associated cultural domains such as customs and habits, the legal system, science, and above all language. Indeed, any type of cultural domain relies on language. Once again the significance of language is highlighted, not as a central medium for gaining access to reality but as a social institution. Language as a common vehicle of communication, is defined by an inherent autonomy, by historical inertia and a unique structure or system. When speaking, man must obey the rules and structure of the language he uses. Or, to phrase it differently: Man *owns* language, but to the extent that language is a common asset he is also *owned* by language. Man has language at his disposal, but the reverse is also true, a viewpoint which gained prominence in the later forms of hermeneutics (the later Heidegger). Later on, Lacan would embrace it as his main theme. His thesis was that the mode of existence of man itself is essentially determined by this state of submission to language, which limits his capacity for self-determination quite dramatically.

This thesis poses a challenge to hermeneutics. Why introduce hermeneutics here? Well, there is a very good reason to do so, considering that hermeneutics takes as its starting point the Aristotelian conception of man as a being that interprets both itself and the worlds and is thus capable of self-determination. Hermeneutics would go on to cast this notion into an actualised frame. And this is where it gets problematic. Hermeneutics is capable of processing the widening scope of allowed forms of interpretation and that is actually its founding principle. Nor does hermeneutics object to recognising the social and historical embedding of interpretation, in whatever form. However, it does come up hard against the notion that an external structure (such as language) would determine both the interpretation and the interpreter, effectively dismissing his contribution as being minor or even irrelevant. Thus, we could say that Lacan's structuralist views are diametrically opposed to the basic tenets of hermeneutics. Lacan would have been the first to admit this. Then again, we could also say that Lacan added a deeper level and maybe even a new chapter to hermeneutics. As a result, hermeneutics would take on a broader and indeed added meaning.

Design of this chapter. Before going on to discuss the various types of hermeneutics, first of all we will offer a brief and general outline of the hermeneutical view of man presented here, as a mode of the human condition. For this purpose, three levels of the human condition need to be distinguished. As a second step, three corresponding forms of hermeneutics will be outlined. The distinguishing characteristics of the three levels and three types of hermeneutics constitute the framework of this book (see also Annex). It also throws into relief the views of Cassirer and Lacan, who each address the themes at hand in their own way (as will be explained in Chapters 2 and 3). Next, the applicability of this model will be illustrated by highlighting the field a scientific discipline: psychopathology. This elaboration does offer the possibility of deepening the (three-level) model outlined, while the status of the human body will also be discussed separately and briefly. The final section serves as an overture to the following two chapters by inquiring into the essence of the state of human existence. The answer to this question – the capacity to symbolise – which the present chapter discusses only in passing, will be the central theme of the two subsequent chapters.

1.1 Three Levels of the Human Condition: From Intentionality to Structure

The underlying principle of a hermeneutical anthropology is that man explains both himself and the world. To this we could add that explanation unfolds at multiple levels. This addition implies that it would be meaningful to distinguish levels within the present context. No justification will be offered at this point, as the elaboration of this hypothesis is supposed to bring out its relevance. Consequently, a brief and schematic outline should suffice here. This may come across as somewhat presumptuous, but the design of this book makes this inevitable. To put it succinctly: Man experiences all that happens around and inside himself, while acting on account of insights thus accumulated; he finds himself in a world, at a particular time and place, and therefore in a particular situation; he uses a predefined language to articulate his experiences and actions. Summarising, man is (1) an intentionally living being (2) that finds itself in a world or a multitude of situations and (3) relies on language. The levels at which man interprets himself and the world reflect the three levels of the human state of existence: the living being that interprets both itself and the world.

The *first* level concerns experience (perceiving, thinking, feeling) *and* action (well-considered, immediate, impulsive, etcetera). To experience is not the same as being stimulated, while taking action differs from being moved. A person who experiences and takes action, will both experience and do something; *and* is aware of what he is experiencing and doing. Experience and action are both characterised by what is commonly referred to as intentionality, which should be conceived as focus on an object as well as an awareness of being focused. I see, do, want, desire, remember, or expect something, *and* I have knowledge of this somehow. When describing an intentional relationship the emphasis is on how the experience conveys something to me (in form of a memory or perception, etcetera), or on how an action puts me into a relationship with something (intentionally, unwittingly, by premeditation, etcetera). The emphasis is on the I-pole or subject pole, in which an active role is assigned to me. This intentional relationship can be described as centrifugal, as an arrow departing from the subject and aimed at objects. These objects also have a certain duration, may or may not take place in a space and may also be experienced by others. Which leads us to the next level: the embedding of phenomena in a world.

This *second* level is about the world. All I experience and do is embedded within a coherent set of references that forms a unity: a world. This world is arranged in a categorical fashion. It includes juxtaposed or consecutive relationships (of space and time), of cause-and-effect, of thing-property, of causality, of mutual relationships (intersubjectivity). Thus, man finds himself in a world that always was, that he finds and into which he is 'thrown', in a temporospatial situation that is not of his own choosing. Even though within this situation he 'designs' his own world – the world of a toddler is very different from that of an adult – its margins remain narrow. No one is offered the choice to live in the 21st century or the Middle Ages, it is simply the time that he lives in. Apparently, rather than on the subject pole the emphasis is on the object pole – on the world that a person finds himself in, with the associated categorical definition in space and time, as well as in cause-and-effect. More than space, time and causality, it is also the presence of others that shapes this world. People find themselves in a temporospatial situation that was also – and even essentially – determined by others, being thrown into this situation by others at birth. 'Intersubjectivity' thus becomes an intrinsic part of the world. 'The Other' (all others taken together), however, is assigned a specific role. The others relate to each other by relying on specific and culturally defined means of understanding, including language and its structure. A close relationship exists not only between the world and the Other, but also between language and the Other. This explains why the category of the Other will be discussed from the third level.

The *third* level is that of language and culture. With culture relying on language, language can be described as its universal medium. The unique structure of language gives it an autonomous status vis-a-vis the language user. People may be able to change their situation to some degree, but they have no means of changing language. In this sense, man is fundamentally dependent on language, and this state of dependence is structurally defined. The new-born child is biologically dependent on the care provided by others, but is also dependent on language, which at first will be completely incomprehensible and alien to this child. Notwithstanding, others will attempt to use this language to explain things to the child, like maybe it's thirsty or has an ear problem. As it listens, the child is gradually being introduced into the order of language and its associated cultural habits. From the child's perspective this language comes from outside and is overwhelmingly powerful. We could therefore say that language works retroactively, adding a linguistic quality to the intentional phenomena (of the first level) and the world (of the second level) – a name, an identity, being counted. What is, will now appear as being countable and nameable.

So how exactly do these three levels relate to each other? Obviously, they are not distinct but are interconnected, with language fulfilling a unique role. At the first level, the emphasis is on the intentional relationship and consequently on the subject pole, whereas at the level of the world the emphasis will be on the object pole. We could say that language is the intermediary between the two poles, because language – by virtue of naming alone – adds identity and consistency to the inner world as well as what is happening in the outside world. The connection could be called dialectic, with the opposition between subject pole and object pole being mediated by a third figure: language. Besides, these three poles or levels of the human condition have one element in common, namely that of interpretation or explanation. Thus we have offered a brief outline of man as being capable of explaining himself and the world. Sweeping and broad though this description of the state of human existence may be, it does convey the image of man as a hermeneutical being. A brief explanation of the term 'hermeneutics' might be in order.

Hermeneutics. Hermeneutics is the original, technical name for the art of understanding. Understanding refers to human experiences, actions and linguistic utterances and their results in cultural products such as texts and social institutions. When does a demand for interpretation presents itself? Whenever something is experienced as strange or, in more general terms, in situations where things are not altogether clear. This may occur in everyday life as well as in scientific environments. It is the latter from which hermeneutics emerged in the early 19th century. As society had moved away from its religious traditions the need arose for explaining and reinventing one's own tradition for it to be reappropriated. Moreover, contacts had been established with other cultures, which were also experienced as strange and needed an explanation. It appears that interpretation takes place within the field of tension that exists between 'strangeness and familiarity'. Indeed interpretation will not be possible for things that are considered utterly strange or that cannot be related to. By contrast, things that are completely familiar and self-evident need no interpretation at all. Therefore, hermeneutics has secured a place in the scientific world within the field of the humanities, which are predominantly interpretative in nature: What is the relevance of a legal text in this particular situation, what function does rhyme have in this poem, what is the meaning of this dream, etcetera? At its time of birth, in the early 19th century, hermeneutics had yet another raison d'être, being born from the idea that a natural-scientific mode of experience does not suffice to gain proper understanding of man, of human reality. The latter point of view may need clarification and correction by a perspective that takes sense and meaning into account. Contrary to Kant's beliefs, there is no such thing as a single legitimate – natural-scientific – form of knowledge. No, it is diversity what we see. Thus, in the course of the 19th century, hermeneutics was soon welcomed to the ranks of philosophy to complement or correct Kant's views – much like what was at stake with Neo-Kantianism (e.g. that of Cassirer). Acknowledged also is the influence of Hegel and his notion of the objective mind and of the social context of all knowledge. This would put the hermeneutical philosophy directly in the lineage of German idealism: a type of idealism that is continued with more modest means and a limited ambition (human finiteness itself).

Three types of hermeneutics may be distinguished. The first type closely meets the requirement of objectivity. The central question is: What is the signification of an experience or action that, despite its value aspects, should be answered in the most objective and unbiased manner possible. In light of the ambition of objectivity and neutrality we could speak of a 'hermeneutics of the signification'. The second type calls its possibility into question by arguing that any interpretation takes place within a situation that will bias the question, which means that interpretations are invariably 'prejudiced' to some extent: the hermeneutics of the situation. The third type of hermeneutics focuses on language and its formal structure. It conforms to the notion that man is tied to a situation, while adding language and culture as external structures. Man expresses himself through language and signifiers, but something is left behind. The very fact that these representations, these signifiers come from the outside makes that 'something' (on the subject and object poles) will not find currency. This can be referred to as a 'hermeneutics of the signifier'.

Consolidating these three modes of thought under the umbrella of hermeneutics might be frowned upon. Obviously, there are significant differences within each movement, and even more significant differences between the three movements. And yet this does not necessarily pose an obstacle to introducing such an arrangement, considering that the relevance of a difference is also determined by the perspectival context. Is it historical and specialised, or maybe more general? In search of a general objective – designing an image of man – the choice for uniting what is in many ways diverse, would be much more justifiable than adopting a purely historical and comparative approach, highlighting the differences. In the first case, a *global* structure would be preferable. Another point that argues in favour of this global tripartition is that it ties in well with the three levels of human condition outlined before: intentionality, being-in-the-world and language dependence. We could say that they are congruous. The hermeneutics of the signification refers to the level of intentionality, the hermeneutics of the situation addresses the level of the world and the hermeneutics of the signifier deals with language and its structure. The dialectical relationship established between the three levels of the human condition (of subject pole, object pole and language) returns in the three types of hermeneutics, which engage in a similar dialectical relationship. This puts an intentional analysis opposite a situational analysis, both of which are being brought together by the overarching perspective of structural analysis. Thus, the history of hermeneutics and its three manifestations is progressing in a dialectical fashion, we might argue.

1.2 Three Types of Hermeneutics: From Signification to Signifier

Hermeneutics of the signification. Phenomenology could be regarded as the first representative of the hermeneutics of the signification, although a caveat may be in order. Essentially, phenomenology is a tree with many branches, with the material phenomenology of life (developed by Michel Henry) as its most recent sprout. In this tangle of diversity, reference is invariably made to Husserl (1859–1938), who founded this movement and give it its name. His work covers a wide field to include many areas of study, such as a descriptive psychology and a transcendental philosophy (which in its turn includes static, genetic and genealogical orientations). For all the diversity of interpretations it spawned, a 'standard image' did emerge (Welton 2000, 113–131). The aim was to offer an unbiased and generally valid description of phenomena. In his work, Husserl attempted to steer well clear of any current philosophical tradition, to which end he developed a whole new and complex set of concepts. In fact, he did everything 'himself' – unlike Cassirer and Lacan, who stood on the shoulders of Kant and Freud, respectively. Within the current framework, only a few notions are relevant (in respect of the later discussion of Cassirer and Lacan).

What Husserl discovered was the meaning-giving activity of consciousness, which he defined as intentionality. Rather than just 'record what is', consciousness 'conceives what is', which means an object is not given in its bareness but is part of an 'as structure'. I will not perceive just anything, but I perceive a thing as something else (as a house, or a shed). Even the most elementary perception is charged with meaning, involving a 'sense of knowing', which knowledge is part of the act itself. When I see a house, knowing this becomes part of the act of seeing: I know that I see it. This led Husserl to look at all modifications of consciousness (perceiving, remembering, expecting, etcetera). Yet there is more to consciousness than the part that actively involves me: There is also a lot going on at a pre-conscious level, quite automatically, without any involvement from the 'I'. Underlying conscious perception is a pre-conscious awareness of the world. The process of purposefully moving towards a place is underpinned by walking without thinking. This would become the second major field of study for phenomenology: customs and habits, corporeality, the self-evident (Husserl 1966, 1989). In the 1920s this theme was taken up by Husserl and later also by Heidegger and Merleau-Ponty, in a number of ways (see below). It is worth noting that the distinction mentioned does *not* run parallel to the psychoanalytical conscious/unconscious distinction. The unconscious as interpreted by psychoanalysis refers to a process of repression and exclusion, which is quite distinct from the two ways of being present: conscious and pre-conscious. This point will be discussed in more detail later.

The phenomenological study of two fields – of what is conscious or pre-conscious, respectively – cannot be approached in a similar way, because that which is conscious is not given in the same way as the pre-conscious, which is in a sense non-conscious. 'How this should be approached' will turn out to be a key issue, but will not be considered here. However, what both cases have in common is the ambition of phenomenology to indicate what would be essential or typical of a particular field of experience, in order to develop adequate concepts. To this end, it does not study experiences of an actual consciousness in the sense of an introspective psychology, but rather looks at modifications of the consciousness per se: perceiving a thing, hearing a tone, remembering the past, holding on to the present. Instead of engaging in empirical (introspective) psychology its ambition is to define the nature of phenomena, a descriptive brand of psychology. It strives to identify the essential characteristics of a consciousness performance as well exactly how its object is given. For instance, in external perception a thing will never appear in its entirety, from all sides at once, but only from one side. It is known only perspectivally, inviting or indeed forcing us to walk around us to appreciate it in its entirety. In the case of internal perception (of an emotion) a different process is at work. Inner perception, Husserl would say, is not restricted by perspectival limitation. The perception of the inner state (of an emotion) has no front or back, and is given with the emotion itself, without any adumbrations. Obviously, this resume serves merely to clarify the type of inquiry, the question whether Husserl was right or wrong will not be addressed. What is essential is that experience itself reveals its essential characteristics through exploration of its boundaries. Husserl regards this 'intuitive' moment as essential, thus eliminating the prerequisite of establishing empirical facts. The psychic is eminently suited to this purpose, seeing that we stay 'at home', close to ourselves. This type of phenomenology leads to a philosophical psychology, if you will, describing the essence of psychic phenomena: perception, memory, imagination, as well as hallucination and delusion. In fact, it also led to a phenomenological brand of psychopathology, which was highly prolific and still resonates in the established definitions of psychopathological phenomena (e.g., anxiety, compulsion, urge). This type of phenomenology may not offer an empirical psychology itself, but it does enable an empirical phenomenological psychology and psychopathology. This brand of psychology could rightfully claim its place, and interestingly it was in this field that phenomenology made its strongest impact (Waldenfels 2000; 2004). We could even say that the essential contribution of phenomenology lies in the limited field of descriptive psychology, even today and in the future. Husserl went even one big step further, by proposing consciousness as the very source of being, of the validation of being, rather than simply describing the essential structures of consciousness. Indeed, these essential structures would build the map of reality and its domains, to create a regional ontology. This resulted in a philosophical idealism taken to its extreme (De Boer 1976) that attracted little following, although there is still ongoing debate about the exact remit of his philosophy (Bernet 1994, 392–395; 2004). The universal pretensions of phenomenology met with fierce criticism from hermeneutical quarters. One criticism was that any description cannot aspire to be more than an interpretation that will not have any lasting 'apodictic' validity (Mooij 2010, 93–165).

Historically, the significance of interpretation and its inherent uncertainty was highlighted particularly by Dilthey (1833–1911). Interpretation is the central motif: How to gain access to the experiences of others, of life forms that appear as unfamiliar to us (De Mul 2004). At first glance, moving from Husserl to Dilthey, from essential structures of consciousness to historic factuality, from philosophy of consciousness to a philosophy of life, may seem like a huge leap. Yet the consciousness as interpreted by Husserl also includes deeper, preconscious layers, while life according to Dilthey 'shows itself' or expresses itself. This will become the central theme of Dilthey's work: the inner quality of life that expresses itself and can only be understood through expression, which he describes as *Leben, Ausdruck, Verstehen* ('Life, Expression, Understanding') (Dilthey 1961, 230–239). This has a definite impact on society, on human science. Again we see a 'dialectical of the interior and exterior' at work, with the interior not being understandable without expression, and the expression representing the interior. The interior may be conceived in two ways, namely as referring to the state of mind of an individual (as in the case of the early Dilthey) or in relation to a tendency, a focus seen in a culture or cultural community (the later Dilthey). In Hegelian terms this would be the subjective *or* the objective mind, respectively. In both cases, the interior can be known and therefore exist only through its interpretation. In fact, Husserl also attaches importance to interpretation, arguing that perception gives meaning (is interpretative), which would also apply to consciousness as a whole. Thus, we could say that phenomenology is the basis for hermeneutics, and hermeneutics in its turn presupposes phenomenology (Ricoeur 2001, 101–130; Grondin 2003). This means that phenomenology can be transformed or reduced to a hermeneutical phenomenology. Consequently, both movements can be placed under the heading of hermeneutics of the signification, which is driven by a desire for objectivity and neutrality, unlike the type of hermeneutics introduced below.

Hermeneutics of the situation. Interpretation does not solely refer to intentional phenomena such experience and action, but also applies the situation in which experience and action take place. Moreover, each person will be shaped in a fundamental way by the situation in which he lives and grows up, in which he has been 'thrown'. This term aptly describes the element of chance that comes with being, with being where we are and what we are: our fate or destiny in life, which we did not choose ourselves. In that sense, people will always be children of their time, of their age. The value that is attributed to fate, to coincidence, to life events, the absurdity that comes with it, actually reflects a watershed between the pre- and post-World War I philosophy. While in the 19th century the emphasis was on developing rationality, the horrors of World War I brought home starkly the lack of reasonability of events, the absurdity of people's actions and the role of coincidence and contingency. This would have a dramatic impact on the worlds of religion, art and philosophy. Rational religion, which includes natural theology, has run its course, and Karl Barth (2010) now proposes a fundamentally different concept of Christian religion, e.g. a belief that relies on a naked and contingent fact that appears absurd from a viewpoint of rationality: the death and resurrection of a person named Jesus. The notion of the absurd also resonates in the world of art. This is the heyday of surrealism, of seeking ecstatic experiences on the border between life and death, driven by the notion that everyday reality obscures yet another reality or deeper layer (as shown by the magic realism and surrealism in painting and poetry). It also left its mark on the philosophical domain, in the theme of contingency and the deeper layers of consciousness. Chance, fate and the deeper layers of human existence become central themes in the hermeneutics of the situation, creating a hermeneutics of the facticity (which would lay the groundwork for the so-called 'existential philosophy'). Heidegger is a key figure in this pursuit, particularly the early Heidegger (1987) from 1919 onwards, and the earlier Heidegger (1962) of *Sein und Zeit* ('Being and Time'). His ambition is to explain the lived situation based on its factual qualities, in the practical dealing with things, preceding objectifying and theoretical knowledge. Heidegger coined the term pre-predicative (as opposed to predicative) to describe what is primarily meaningful and can be done ('Bedeutsam'), before it can be said or predicated (Heidegger 1962, 148–153). He introduced this distinction at his very first public appearance, and it would actually go on to underpin his whole work (Heidegger 1987, 13–121 – the 1919 Kriegsnot semester).

The sphere of meaningfulness refers to the world as a sum of situations as well as their horizon: the world as it is found, from which one lives, which 'exists'. Then again, man is also capable of engaging in a relationship with the world into which he finds himself thrown. He 'must' make something out of his life by designing a life's project from the situation he finds himself in. And he must do it now, else he'll be gone and it's too late. And yet in spite of the predominant presence of contingency and coincidence in the world, it is neither coincidental nor contingent *that* man should find himself in a world. Man finds himself essentially in-the-world, defined by his own unique shapes of space and time, a specific categorical hierarchy and specific orders of being.

Obviously, this view is subject to criticism, which was voiced from early on, taking two distinct forms. The first criticism is that with Heidegger the role of the Other is of secondary importance (without even considering the question that the role of the Other might be a moral one), while the second criticism argues that no space is allowed for the conception of culture, or of the objective mind. On closer inspection it turns out that the two types of criticism are actually closely linked, referring back as they do to Heidegger's tenet of the solitary I or 'solipsism', which relegates the Other to a subordinate position, not leaving any conceptual space for the notion of culture. In Heidegger's view, the world is primarily, in each case mine ('jemeinig') rather than ours. Its emphasis on the isolated individual, left to his own fate, strongly reflects a rejection of dominant ratio-based lines of thought: Kierkegaard versus Hegel. This emphasis also betrays one-sidedness of this approach. And yet the notion of situation itself might open up ways to correct this view. Indeed, being maintained intersubjectively, a situation is defined by inertia. We could say that Gadamer (1900–2002), an autonomous student of Heidegger's, actually anticipated this defect in the 1950s. He pointed to the weight of history and the power of tradition, to which man must submit even before becoming aware of it. More than design an existence, man 'must' conform to the world that exists. Even if a person emigrates, as a next step he must immigrate, integrate into society and live by the customs and habits of his new home land, appropriating its objective mindset. In the process of assuming this new identity, something is inevitably left behind and therefore lost. In the following, whenever reference is made to 'situation', this should be taken as a broad and generalised concept that includes the culture and the Other, even though these themes will merely be touched upon. This will be done within the context of the third type of hermeneutics, that of the signifier.

Hermeneutics of the signifier. This type builds on the hermeneutics of the situation and its emphasis on thrownness. However, the two aspects that it neglects will now become central themes: the others (the Other) and culture (Otherness). In the 1960s and 1970s, the French structuralists were defining forces within this development. Structuralism became a child of its time, as the programme of hermeneutics of the situation (taking the form of existential phenomenology) had lost its momentum, its defects clearly showing. Structuralism could now step in to provide the answers. This development did not come about overnight, as structuralism was the product of a quintessentially French tradition that gives prominence to concept and theory rather than experience. There is every reason to regard Lacan as the linchpin in this effort, being among the first to criticise the phenomenological concept of lived experience ('expérience vécu') as the ultimate source. Moreover, spanning more than three decades, his work can be seen as building on the achievements of Lévi-Strauss, a champion of structuralism (whom he held in great esteem throughout his career), but also as an inspiration to Derrida, whose views of deconstructivism owe more to Lacan than he would have cared to admit, while the reverse is also true (Miller 2005, 232). In Chapter 3, which deals with Lacan, this will be discussed in more detail, but obviously an introduction is needed first. Indeed, Lacan would have denied this affiliation most certainly. From a wider perspective, however, this mood of thought appears to be a fresh offshoot from the ancient tree of hermeneutics, even tracing back to early Romanticism (Frank 1997; Handwerk 1985). Even in the first type of hermeneutics language is relevant as experience needs to be expressed, and each experience will have pass through the language grid. Next, language manifest itself as a component of the situation into which the person has been thrown. Here, with the hermeneutics of the signifier, the emphasis is on the formal structure of language, being a system of differences, with terms ('signifiers') differing among themselves, but also differentiating in what they express and define.

The word 'signifier', a translation of the French 'signifiant', stresses the formal and differential aspect of language. From this perspective, the language is made up of formal and empty terms or signifiers, which carry no intrinsic meaning and will not become meaningful until combined with other, different terms. (The word 'term' would be an effective synonym of 'signifier' in terms of expressing its semantic emptiness, its lack of meaning and the prerequisite of caesura.) Combining them, however, will produce meanings and concepts that allow statuses in the world to be named and articulated: This is red paint, this is a green house, this is mine, that is yours, you have no right to it. Thus, language becomes part of something bigger – culture – that controls the relationships among those who share this culture. Together, language and culture can be referred to as the symbolic order, which is an equivalent of the 'objective mind' concept.

In his approach, Lacan has his own unique way of looking at speech and language. Rather than producing an image of reality, as was suggested by, for example, the early Wittgenstein, language does offer a productive representation of reality, which puts reality itself, the real at a distance and causes its immediate experience to be lost. The distance created by language simultaneously brings the dimension of absence, loss and lack into being. The experience of a lack as a lack, however, will lead to a desire to remedy this lack, which means that 'language' and 'desire' are closely connected. Desire is maintained as well as produced by language. Indeed, a basic desire is expressed through an actual demand, while desire itself (for example the desire for love) remains unfulfilled when it is responded to. This demand therefore leaves a remainder, which in turn kindles desire. Lacan would highlight the significance of this deficit or lack that defines human existence (*manque à être*), considering the relationship of man onto the world as fundamentally broken, for the very reason that language is the mediator of this relationship. At the same time, this fragmented state enables the subject to distance himself from the world, to contemplate and reflect and thus make choices. Besides creating the possibility of desire, language enables reflection (see below).

Language leads to representation, to objectification of the outside world. In this process of shaping the outside world, not only language – the word – but also the image is a contributing factor. The same applies to the shaping of the inner world, the shaping of a stable and distinct I, of a subject. The hapless new-born is completely dependent on its environment, on others who are supposed to provide care and protection. Undoubtedly it will experience feelings of tension or relaxation, but there is no 'self' yet – it is still waiting to be shaped. Initially, this process will take the form of the images or figures that are presented and which the child will identify with. The parent's smile is echoed by the smile of the child, which makes the child feel happy and the parent perhaps even more so. The relationship is mirrored on both sides, and so is the emerging 'self'. The child will also see its reflection in the mirror, in the image it returns: 'That, there, that's me, apparently'. Thus, a first form of identity is being offered, constituting the quintessential experience of the mirror stage. In this regard Lacan builds on the work of Wallon (1949), whilst connecting the body image to the theme of narcissism, as has been done before by Schilder (1935), a neurologist who was close to Freud. Lacan's elaboration, however, proved to be very fruitful.

Driven by images, this type of identification is defined as 'imaginary'. It is quite an apt term, referring as it does to something that it is imaginary, fictitious. It may give the child a sense of bodily unity and control of which it is not capable yet. This type of identification might be described as being defined by alienation, and this thesis will go on to define Lacan's work: any identification represents a type of 'emigration' and therefore also carries an element of alienation. In this case, the alienation is found in the assumption of a narcissistic component, as the child believes itself to be greater and more powerful than it actually is. The imaginary and mirroring type of identification does not end after childhood, but will permeate a person's entire lifetime, which stimulates but also gives rise to conflict: 'you a red cup, me a red cup too' – 'you get promoted, I want to get promoted too'. Which makes a mirroring or dual order essentially instable, because it is also associated with rivalry, envy and aggression. This will become a key theme in the work of the French philosopher René Girard. As opposed to Girard, however, Lacan does not look for a solution in the figure of the scapegoat who is supposed to guarantee social stability – although this figure might temporarily fulfil such a role (Girard 1982). Instead, Lacan sees a more permanent solution in introducing 'the third', an order that includes and supports the imaginary relationship, and attributes right and duties.

Lacan introduces the figure of the third in the form of the (m)Other, who puts the child in front of a mirror and has power over this child. The mirror experience – that, there, that's me – is thus confirmed – 'yes, that's you' (Lacan 2002, 678). This means that the imaginary identification is qualified as well as confirmed, as confirmation takes place from the position of a third, from an outside space. The purely dual relationship is now replaced by a triangular relationship. Instead of – or rather in addition to – the image appears the word: 'That's you, mummy's sweetheart' (or a similar term of endearment).

This will free the child from the alienation brought on by identifying with a (mirror) image, but that is not enough to provide access to the 'realm of freedom'. Rather than disappear, alienation will take on a new form, because any identification will lead to renewed alienation. Just like the child does not coincide with the mirror image, so does it fail to coincide with the way it is referred to. We see a shift in alienation from the imaginary to the symbolic level, or from the imaginary to the symbolic order. Symbolic identification brings its own unique type of alienation: 'That's you, and you need to be that way to be mummy's sweetheart, for mummy to love you'. The dependence of the Other will not disappear either and also shifts – from the vital level to the level of language, the symbolic level. As a result, the child will depend on the terms in which it is referred to in addition to a vital level of care. This means that man, more than being dependent on the Other, who has a hold on him, now becomes dependent on his words, with the Other's language having a hold on him.

In the process, the child is empowered to get a hold on the world itself, which is partly shaped by language. Thus, language renders its own unique contribution to the shaping of a world, as it names the world (subject and objects), which can now be identified an objectified. This means that the scope of the symbolic order is more specifically (though not exclusively) that of the objectification from language: 'There is a chair and look, there is another one, and a stool, and that's a mirror over there'. And next to it, the imaginary quality of the figures perceived by the child appears not to be discursive or predicative in nature, but closely matches the phenomenological concept of the pre-predicative.

1.3 Three Levels of the Human Condition Revisited

It should be clear by now that the three types of hermeneutics distinguished are more intimately connected than one might think, which would strengthen the case for putting them together under the header of hermeneutics. As well as being linked to each of the 'three levels', they are connected individually and dialectically in a 'hierarchy-based unity'. With the types of hermeneutics being defined, this may be good time to revisit the three levels of the human condition. The path followed thus far allows the brief outline of the three levels offered in the foregoing – intentionality, world, language-dependence – to be taken together and explained in some more detail. (See for an application to the field of psychic reality and human action: Mooij 2012, 123–138, 160–170; 2010, 281–298.)

Intentionality. We saw that the addition of the pre-predicative type of intentionality was an important one. The scope of intentionality extends beyond the sphere of judgement, as it also includes the stage preceding judgement before something is known, of being affected before realising it, of what is unwittingly expressed: the sphere of customs and habits, of day-to-day dealings with things that are self-evident, actions that can be performed without thinking. All these events take place pre-consciously, before people will actually become aware of them. This essentially highly complex relationship can be named in different ways, each of them highlighting a particular aspect: passively, without an active I-involvement (Husserl), pre-predicatively (Heidegger), pre-objectively (Merleau-Ponty), or proceeding according to the Gestalt perception of an image (Cassirer, Lacan). Objects will appear not as objects but as invitations, as being fit for a particular purpose, much like a shady trees invites you to lie down under it, or the self-evidence of occupying an empty chair – we may speak of 'affordances'. In this enumeration, it is not the distinguishing terminology that is important (nor the different philosophical backgrounds) – what truly matters is the wide range of aspects they reflect. An opulent summation of this mode of experience, also in relationship to behaviour, is offered by Erwin Straus (1935, 116–311). Jointly, these non-objectifying forms of intentionality find their opposite number in the discursive or objectifying type, which they actually underpin: the objectifying perception, the voluntary, intentional action and discursive thought. These relationships will be discussed in greater detail later in this book.

In addition to the dual mode, intentional phenomena also share a number of characteristics, as had been noted in passing before. They are (1) interpretative, (2) normative, and (3) intersubjective in nature. First and foremost, intentional phenomena are *interpretative*, as was stated before. In the field of perception, for example, to see invariably means to 'see as'. While experiencing a landscape as peaceful, in an objectifying way we could see a strip of asphalt crossing it as a poorly maintained road. Initially, Husserl believed that an interpretation-free core was embedded in perception, but later he rejected this thought. Since then the idea of the interpretative quality of perception has become a cornerstone of phenomenology as well in a variety of related philosophical movements. Their interpretative quality also makes perception and other intentional phenomena as well *normative,* as they are subject to argument: You are right about that, you are doing this wrong, that is not true, this emotion is not sincere. It means they are made subject to a standard (of correctness, of truth, of authenticity). This normative component sets them apart from sheer phenomena of nature (even though that is what they are in part). Or perhaps better said: Intentional phenomena are subject to a dual regime. An action is a physically and physiologically driven movement as well as an intentional phenomenon, guided by rules and therefore normative. The physical event remains a phenomenon of nature while being transformed into a cultural phenomenon: This is done intentionally, that happens by accident. Culture creates rifts. It bisects natural coherence, offering 'moments of truncation'. The same applies to language. A language utterance is a physiological event, but can also be regarded as a meaning-distinguishing entity ('phoneme') which, combined with other, different phonemes, produces meaning-carrying units ('monemes'). The phonetic distinction between 'deaf' and 'dead' is merely gradual, but phonematically they conjure up two different worlds. The science of phonetics (physiology of sounds) deals with the former aspect, phonology with the latter. Both look at regular patterns, but of a different kind. This 'dual regime' therefore points to a fundamental difference between naturally occurring regularities *and* rules, the differences between the regular patterns of low and high tide and the sand ribbons they create on the beach, *and* the rules that apparently need to be followed. It represents a variation on the classical distinction between 'physei on' and 'thesei on', between what grew naturally *and* what culture has brought into being.

The word 'apparently' betrays yet another characteristic of rules. Following a rule does not necessarily mean that the person involved is subjectively or reflectively aware of the rule followed. Most people will speak a language without being aware of the rules they obey speaking it, just as people in their daily dealings will be little aware of the subtle rules of conduct they observe. This will not come to the fore unless a person violates the 'code' and is confronted or may have to suffer the consequences. The rules adhered to in actual speech are also likely to deviate from those written down in grammar textbooks for that particular language. The following of rules commonly happens as a matter of course and effectively applies to all intentional and rule-driven phenomena. Which leads us to the final characteristic of rule-following: intentional phenomena are embedded in a social order.

In regard of the thesis of the *social* nature of intentional phenomena, Wittgenstein's argument of the impossibility of a private language has become something of a classic. (Also worth mentioning is Hegel, the very first to highlight the social dimension of human knowledge.) Although Wittgenstein's argument may be a different one, it sends a strong and clear message. First and foremost, he claims that private-mental events to which the word at large would have no access cannot exist. His criticism can be summed up as follows: Assuming that *only* I am able to know something, *I* cannot really know this, because this would rule out the possibility of verification and therefore of knowledge. For mental events to be understandable and knowable – to the other as well as the person involved – they need to be made subject to a set of public rules. Essentially they need to provide access to the other. This aspect of knowability would include all modifications of intentionality (as well as its derived forms, such as affects, fantasies, etcetera). This is a key argument, considering that the so-called first-person perspective and the third-person perspective are often opposed, with the other essentially being denied access to the inner workings of a person's mind. This argument effectively qualifies the opposition, meaning that the other will always 'look over his shoulder', even from the first-person perspective. Thus, the he-figure becomes incorporated into the I-figure. What I see is also affected by what the other sees. By extension, this also applies to how I see myself, a process in which the other is implicated.

'Knowable' is obviously not the same as 'actually known'. After all, man has only very limited knowledge of the inner workings of other people's minds as well as their own mind. It all comes down to the limited scope of intentional knowledge. A person at work will be aware of the fact that he is working, but may not always be aware of what else he is doing as he works (toeing the line, engaging in passive resistance, having fun, trying to excel, slacking off, etcetera). To actually become aware, reflection is needed, as this will provide insight into the deeper, unconscious layers of unconscious desire (see below). A person may be hard to read by others, but perhaps even more so by himself. One will have to wait and see what a person will do or how he will treat others – even more so because the other often will see more clearly what goes on in a person's mind than the person himself (for the very fact that the latter is directly involved). The other person will see a facial expression and hear the intonation of their voice, something the person himself can interpret only through the other person's reactions. We see the other but not ourselves, and see ourselves through the other: Does he still recognise me? This problem of the other and of social embedding leads us to the second level, that of the world.

World. We already saw that the second level, the level of the world, refers to the sum of objects (taken broadly) or to the 'horizon of understanding' from which they can be understood. The horizon of understanding includes the categories in which these objects are presented. The most fundamental categories are space, time and intersubjectivity. Both space and time can be either external or physical in character – the *physical space and physical time* – as well as being internal or subjective – the *consciousness of space and time*. The time axis (t_1, t_2) of external, physical time is opposed with the ecstasies of present, past and future of internal, subjective time, with the 'now' at its centre. As the metronome, the time-keeper, is ticking the time away (tic, toc, tic, toc), I myself will experience time in terms of 'just now' and 'soon'. This distinction between the two manifestations of time represents a traditional theme in time philosophy. A similar distinction can be made with regard to space: We have an external, physical space defined by three objective coordinates (height, width, depth) as well as a space of experience that is dominated by 'near' and 'far', with 'here' at the centre. And just like the philosophy of time sometimes presupposes the presence of a third form of time that would serve as a mediator between external and internal time (Ricoeur 1985), so will the question pose itself whether mediation might also be at work in respect of space (external space and consciousness of space). What are these mediating forms of time and of space?

Firstly, the third form of time. We could say that the infinite external time and internal time are merged while being transformed into the temporality of the subject which presumes its finiteness – which introduces a third manifestation of time. After all, the young child is faced with the task of reconciling the message received from outside, 'time to go to sleep' ('t_1'), with the indefinable inner experience of 'just now' and 'soon'. It may find that its life is finite and unfolds between birth and death (which may be a thing of a distant future, but is a certainty nonetheless), allowing it to internalise external time (up to a point). In turn, this will produce awareness of a future that is still open – 'later when I grow up' – as well as of a past that may be remembered, but cannot be undone by some act of magic. More than just live 'in time', the child becomes temporal *itself*. The process of transformation from external and internal infinity to finiteness and temporality, therefore brings limitation, or even castration. This will lead to a third manifestation of time, namely a symbolic or dimensional time, which allows a person to live from any of these dimensions: from the past, focused on the future, or predominantly in the 'here and now', respectively. A similar process of limitation will unfold in the spatial dimension, in the constitution of a spatially and corporeally situated object ('corps sujet') living within an world with which it is connected by means of a 'intentional bow'. Just like man *is* temporal, so *is* he spatial in nature. This represents a third manifestation of space – a symbolic, dimensional space that allows man to live from any of the three dimensions: from above – adopting a bird's eye view – with himself at the centre, or living from the margin – outside looking in – respectively. The limitation brought on by finiteness will therefore also impact the intersubjective level: Yes, the other does contribute to shaping and limiting my world. The world is my world, but to the extent that it is my world, it also belongs to others.

Structure. That which is described as an experience and has been interpreted from a situation can become part of a structure, most notably the structure of a language and, from a broader perspective, the structure of a symbolic form or symbolic order, of laws and rules with language at their centre. Becoming part of a structure represents the third level in the experience, situation and structure sequence. This third level is that of the objective mind. The fact that the order of structure, of language and rules, is important is certainly not a recent finding. It makes that intentional phenomena and the life world are pervaded with norms, that they have a normative quality, defined as they are by moral or legal norms or standards as well as by daily life norms. Their significance already became evident in the discussion of intentional phenomena governed by a rule. Indeed, perception passes through the grid of language, which is shared by a language community. From this perspective, the objective mind is seen mostly in its autonomy, in its deeper layers, at the level of immutability. The individual may have some hold on his own situation, but not on the language with which he grows up. This relationship should not be interpreted in terms of an interaction, as this would be a gross overestimation on the part of the subject. Language having a complete hold on the subject, the subject is forced to bend to its rules. This will have implications for the subject's state of existence, as was mentioned briefly with regard to Lacan: the birth of a desire and the possibility of reflection. They will discussed again briefly (as a preamble to a more detailed discussed of Lacan in Chapter 3).

The implications of the subject's dependency on language. First of all, language dependence leads to subjective dividedness, produced by the general quality of linguistic terms. Rather than mirror a predefined reality, language enables us to draw together a variety of phenomena under a single denominator. Language plays an active role in determining 'what is'. For the very fact that terms are general, no term will suffice to capture the unique quality of the subject. The subject cannot identify itself completely with any of the qualifications nor with the sum of qualifications: 'I'm unhappy, I'm a teacher, an uncle, a car owner', etcetera. Thus, the subject will be split up into the subject of what is said *and* that of the speaker who fails to meet any of the qualifications and will therefore remain unsaid. A dichotomy or bisection results – which may be put on a par with the bisection occurring between the conscious and the unconscious (according to Lacan). This dichotomy effectively creates a distinction between (unconscious) desire and (conscious) demand. Desire expresses itself through a demand ('I want chocolate') but will not merge fully with the demand and actually transcends it (for example, in the form of a desire for unconditional love, total independence or utter dependence). Here, the subjective perspective finds both its basis and ultimate contours, with the deeper layers surfacing. The difference between (conscious) demand and (unconscious) desire may seem insignificant, but it is in fact essential. A demand is controllable and strives for control, while the unconscious desire wants more: 'a bit more', 'another one', 'alright, another one' ('encore').

Besides creating the possibility of desire, language enables reflection as well, we might argue: Is this a treat real or am I imagining things? Is it wise to do this or will it lead to excess? And what's wrong with excess anyway, why do I shy away from it? Whichever form it may take, the possibility of distancing oneself, which is the basis of reflection, appears to be given with language. What are we supposed to make of this? For the sake of hypothesis we could offer two reasons. Firstly, language introduces a set of logical modalities, such as denial, possibility, necessity, etcetera, while language being a prerequisite for gaining access to logical space (Sellars 1997, § 31). The introduction of this logical modality set brings a huge widening of the experience horizon. It means that experience itself can be 'modalised'. I am able to imagine that what is can also *not* be. Things may be different than I think they are: 'You do not have to see it that way, there are other possibilities too'. The second reason would be that language by definition refers to other language users, each of them contributing their own unique perspective in a process of linguistic intersubjectivity. Thus, language offers the possibility of changing perspectives: 'I see it like this, but this other person apparently sees it differently'. Within the context of the human condition outlined, the two factors taken together – inter-subjectivity *and* logical modalisation – constitute the basis for reflection or deliberation (obviously without considering biological factors). The intentional insight given with (predicative) intentionality – when I'm at work I know that I'm working – now gives way to reflective insight: 'What else do I do when I'm working, am I obedient, do I really want to be, what are my deeper motives?' Thus, language empowers man to choose what he wants do after deliberation, out of 'free will'. Summing up: Man is a being that interprets itself and the world and is thus capable of self-determination. That is the basic philosophy of hermeneutical anthropology.

The body. So how exactly does the relationship with the body fit in all this? As mentioned before, intentional phenomena follow a dual regime. So how should their relationship be described? To even begin to answer this question – if the question can be answered at all – we would have to engage in a lengthy discussion. Outlining the problem is a challenge in itself, and any outline given will inform the resulting answer. That is why we shall limit ourselves to offering a limited number of keywords. The line of thought presented here seems to have at its heart that natural phenomena and intentional phenomena are categorically different and yet can go together. A perception is not a sensory stimulus, an action is not the same as a movement, as intentional phenomena are always associated with an intrinsic form of 'knowledge'. When I do something, I'll be more or less aware of doing it. Thus, man envisages reality while acting or perceiving, thus representing reality, while being engaged in a variety of intentional attitudes. 'It is so' is replaced by: I believe it to be so, I hope it is so, I'm afraid it is so.

Next to a categorical difference, we *also* see an actual merging of the two heterogeneous entities – of the physical (the body) and the mental representation (the mind). We distinguish two classical doctrines of unification's between the mental and the physical. First of all there is the 'two sides to a coin' doctrine (the Spinoza type), and secondly the doctrine of interaction (attributed to Descartes, maybe wrongly so). Without attempting to engage in debate, a third option could be suggested. The term 'foundation' might more aptly describe the relationship between the biological and the mental (even though this term would be a metaphor only). Thus, the biological substrate can be regarded as the foundation that enables both actions and experiences to take place, whilst eluding a description of actions and experiences in terms of any physical or physiological substrate. It would be possible, however, to look more closely at biological conditions of perception, of actions, of anxiety episodes or mood swings, etcetera. This will unveil correlative relationships that, however, cannot aspire to be more than just 'correlations'. And yet these conditions are the base of mental functions, which are co-determined by factors concerning experience, situation and structure. As a result, biological, biochemical and electrochemical factors become conditional elements of a highly complex and arcane body which is not likely to be fathomed any time soon. The condition of the body and the brain drives psychic functioning and influences experience, making actual signification wholly dependent on biological conditions. In addition, signification relies on the external situation and on the way in which a person see and expresses himself and his situation. In other words: Feelings of rage about experienced injustice are not biochemically determined. Then again, meaning fulfilment or interpretation does have its effects on the body. For example, the person who wears himself out, or allows himself to be worn out (for whatever reason), in the absence of compensating mechanisms will have to face dysregulation of one or more neurotransmitter systems (resulting in burn-out, depression and anxiety) at some point in time.

Aristotle described man as a living body, gifted with ratio and language *as well as* being part of a community. This section discusses man as a 'living body', but it is a small step to community and language. Man, a child, is born as a needy body, after which the other and culture will embrace it, shaping and kneading it – from the very first skin contact with the mother. The body carrying the imprint of this first touch is a 'signified body'. The human body is more than 'embodied cognition' – it is actually a reflection of the primary interaction with others and with the culture of the environment. Thus it also represents an embodiment of culture.

The body is shaped and transformed (passively) by the other, whilst being the (active) carrier of experience, of interpretation and signification (in terms of social and cultural contexts). The metaphor of the relationship between body and mind can therefore not be one of 'interaction', or 'the two sides of a coin', but is defined by circumlocution: Rather than being straightforward, the relationship between body and mind should be conceived as being circular, following the circuitous route of the world. 'Mind' should be taken to mean only initially that the body, the organism, stands in a formative relationship to the world. This may not render the problem less complex, but it does make it more manageable. Here is an example: Biochemistry (neurotransmission) determines the mood of a person (as being depressed), which in turns colours the world (as being depressing), which thus modified enters the mind of this person. Yet other stimuli contribute to this modification: interventions by others ('don't give up'), perspectives from the situation (rivalry) and culture (guilt and shame). This will either increase or diminish tensions, thus worsening or improving the person's mood, which will have its repercussions on the body. Their source lies in input from the world, not in thought or feelings. All spheres – the physical, the intentional, situation and culture – are involved yet retain their autonomy. This becomes evident from experience, as culturally and situatively defined experience is not only reflecting the state of the body, just like the body in its turn often takes its own course.

Now that we have outlined the three levels of the human condition (and of a putative relationship with the biological substrate), addressing the contribution of the three types of hermeneutics, the question of its possible application could now be raised. We already saw the value of phenomenology for psychology and psychiatry, particularly with regard to its descriptive branch, which is psychopathology. It would therefore be justified to consider the value of the model of the three levels of the human condition and of the three types of hermeneutics for this discipline. Needless to say that other scientific disciplines might also be suited to this approach, including the social-cultural sciences and law, but the great advantage of psychopathology is that Lacan's philosophy is partly relying on psychopathology.

1.4 Application in Psychopathology

Essentially, psychopathology is conceived as the description of a mental disorder, of psychic phenomena labelled as abnormal or pathological. The emphasis on description suggests that it is too early to look for an explanation of the disorder – in biological, theoretical, psychodynamic, sociological terms. Nor does it stand in competition with a classifying approach of the DSM-IV/5 type, which brings its own unique sophistication and applicability, but it can contribute to a more in-depth description of phenomena that were defined operationally within its context. This requires the presence of a global system, however. It might be useful to draw on the traditional distinction between the neurotic disorder, the psychotic disorder, and the personality disorder, which takes up an intermediate position between the two first disorders. 'Neurotic disorder' is a term that may have fallen into disuse, but this does not eliminate the domain itself, which is why the term will still be used here.

The *neurosis* is not far removed from normality, as becomes apparent from its symptoms: a strong need for control (such as compulsive phenomena or an overbearing manner), anxiety (e.g., taking the form of phobias), or emotional instability (histrionics). The close relationship with normality becomes apparent from the fact that similar symptoms also appear in normality. Many people have peculiar habits or idiosyncrasies (such as the need for control, anxieties, perversities, mild or severe addictions, group dependence) that remain manageable, however, and indeed have a stabilising effect, allowing them to function more or less normally. This stabilising effect sets these apart from truly neurotic problems, where these symptoms or excesses just have an invalidating effect, causing the subject to suffer and maybe seek help (sometimes encouraged by people around them). Thus, neurotic symptoms are the result of a disruptive process seen in a symptom that originally has a stabilising function but becomes overburdened: A mild tendency towards phobia develops into panic, alcohol use goes out of hand, availability to the other leads to exhaustion and ultimately depression, etcetera. In other cases a person may become upset by his own cruelty or lack of will, which is (wrongly) experienced as being alien to his person. Within the neurotic spectrum, the effect of invalidation are limited, because both in the neurotic person and in normality, the relationship with the world remains intact, which is precisely what causes suffering.

The *psychosis* is found on the opposite side of the spectrum. Here, the relationship with the world is highly fragile or has even been severed, leading to a failed reality-testing, as may become apparent from symptoms such as hallucinations ('object-less perceptions') and delusions ('incorrigible aberrations'). The psychotic person lacks insight into his own condition – depending on the extent of psychosis – and 'believes in his own symptoms' rather than considering himself ill. He truly believes he is being conspired against, in the case of a delusional disorder, sees himself as a worthless person, in the case of melancholic disorder, or feels utterly exposed in the case of schizophrenia – and this belief is unshakeable.

Finally, the *personality disorder* (its most serious forms) takes up an intermediary position. It is found halfway between psychosis and neurosis, in the sense that reality-testing (unlike with a psychosis) is not cancelled out but is impaired or split, resulting in the juxtaposition of two opposite worlds of experience, without the person involved actually suffering from the disorder (unlike in the case of a neurosis). In the case of the personality disorder, the other – the partner, society, a victim – will be the first to suffer. Society will bear the brunt of the extreme narcissism of the narcissistic personality (the psychopathic manager), while the partner of a person with a borderline personality disorder will suffer from his need for both fusion and rejection. Or, he will leave colleagues drained by leading a life that to all intents and purposes 'appears' to be completely normal, while inside this person there is only emptiness and chaos (the 'As-if' personality).

Following on from this summary of the psychopathological field we will turn our thoughts to the question whether the three types of hermeneutics might render some form of contribution to the psychopathology outlined. A brief discussion of the three levels of the human condition will also be included. In fact, the history of psychopathology is characterised by a significant hermeneutical tradition, with Jaspers (1997), Binswanger (1957) and Lacan (2002) as key figures with their key publications: *Allgemeine Psychopathologie* ('General Psychopathology') in 1913, *Schizophrenie* ('Schizophrenia') in 1957 and *Écrits* in 1966. Rather than describing its historical contribution, we need to look at its significance today. The three types of hermeneutics will be addressed based on the 'three levels'.

Hermeneutics of the signification. Here, phenomenology comes to the fore, a discipline that focuses on the description of psychic phenomena, which obviously represents a key field of research in psychopathology. The focus is on the first level, the level of intentionality. It may offer a contribution to the description of anxiety, compulsion, dependency, hallucinations and delusions, but in practice this turns out to be no easy matter. A person without first-hand experience of hallucinations will be hard put to describe the phenomena of 'hearing voices'. Here, phenomenology may add value by disproving the traditional definition of this phenomenon, which is 'perception without object'. An object *is* in fact present – the voice heard by the person involved – but there is *no* perception – with the subject involvement taking place at quite a different level than with perception itself, as the object (for example, 'the voices') will have a hold on the subject from which it cannot extricate itself. Lacan repeatedly emphasised this point. Offering a description is not just challenging when it comes to describing types of experience that are a far cry from general human experiences, but also in regard of more accessible phenomena. For example, anxiety is an emotion experienced by most people, but offering an apt description of its unbearable quality turns out to be quite a daunting task. And yet it remains the task of phenomenology to offer as objective a description as possible of psychic phenomena and their mutual delimitations. So what exactly is the difference between a compulsive action a person must perform, *and* an urge that a person finds irresistible (through lack of will power or through addiction) *or* an impulsive action that feels as though it is happening to this person? The actions may look more or less identical from the outside, but most likely the interior experience is fundamentally different. For one thing, there is a phenomenological difference, namely the difference between 'I must do this, else I'll become very frightened' (in the case of compulsion), 'I wanted to do it, but then again I didn't' (in the case of lack of will power) and 'I did it, even though I didn't want to' (in the case of impulsive actions, with the subject losing control but 'doing' it just the same). These examples share one characteristic, and that is that they invariably refer to conscious, predicative phenomena, which makes them even more poignant: A person who feels compelled to check four times if he actually turned off the gas, will be very much aware of the fact he is doing this; a person consuming yet another alcoholic drink will know perfectly well he is doing the wrong thing, etcetera. They belong to the domain where phenomenology was first practised: the analysis of the intentional, of the active, conscious I-involvement: 'I' did like this or 'I' did it like that.

Not just the predicative, conscious sphere is relevant, but so is the pre-predicative, pre-conscious sphere. This pre-conscious element is of key importance to psychopathology as well as phenomenology. In the case of a mental disorder, it may be 'deteriorating', a case in point being the 'latent' type of schizophrenia, without hallucinations or other alarming symptoms. Its onset often goes unnoticed and is not associated with tell-tale symptoms such as hallucinations or delusions. Instead, it is characterised by a gradual decay of social and emotional competencies. What in most people happens automatically, is self-evident – how to behave in the presence of friends, how to buy groceries and smile at the right moment – no longer happens by itself and requires active thinking. Or, to phrase it differently: Capabilities governed by the pre-predicative type of intentionality (habitual functioning, social competencies) are no longer driven pre-consciously and need to be triggered consciously or even overconsciously. From a phenomenological perspective, we could speak of 'a loss of natural self-evidence', of primary *Bedeutsamkeit* (Blankenburg 1971). The balance between the pre-conscious 'I' and the conscious 'I' is lost. This would qualify it as an 'I-disorder' or 'ipseity-disorder', where the loss of a primary and pre-conscious type of communication with the world is compensated for by reflection, leading to a hyper-reflected type of being-in-the-world. This person is constantly 'scanning' his inner world, with the outside world lacking the quality of reality (Gallagher 2005, 183–184).

Hermeneutics of the situation. This also marks the transition to applying the second type of hermeneutics – that of the situation – which refers to the second level, that of the world. Rather than describing intentional phenomena, it focuses on the way in which these phenomena are embedded in a person's world. A person with a compulsive disorder will suffer from compulsive phenomena, while his entire world is commonly structured in a highly typical manner. His world is dominated by order as well as by chaotic hiatuses. This would enable us, in the field of psychosis, to describe the specific world of melancholy, of delusional disorders and of the range of worlds that is associated with schizophrenia. Belonging to the hermeneutics of the situation, this type of description is more interpretative and less focused on unequivocality than phenomenology (which is part of the hermeneutics of the signification), but is equally legitimate. This type of analysis is practised mostly in the field of anthropological psychopathology, which often contributes enlightening views. Melancholia – the serious, psychotic type of depression associated with delusions (including the delusion of the irreparable debt) – can thus be 'reduced' to a typical disorder of time order. Indeed, 'suffering from time' is a key component of this disorder (Theunissen 1991). The subject experiences the present as being infinite, with time passing at a snail's pace, rendering the future hopeless – in fact, there is no future ('it's a catastrophe'), while the subject keeps returning to the past ('if only I had done this or that'). This constellation suggests the presence of a serious disruption of time consciousness, with a 'reversal' of normal relationships. The future has taken on the (immutable) qualities of the past, while the past (to which the subject keeps returning) in its turn has acquired the quality of a future that is yet open (Binswanger 1960). And just like the melancholy state may be interpreted as a disrupted time perspective, so can the delusional disorder, or paranoia – the delusional state of persecution that makes the person feels treated unfairly – be understood from a disrupted relationship with the Other, who has now become the persecutor. This means that schizophrenia, as the third type of psychosis – characterised by the limits between inside and outside falling away – might be explained as a disrupted relationship with the body (and its attendant experiences). Which leads us to the third type of hermeneutics.

Hermeneutics of the signifier. Here the central theme is that of delimitation, which concerns the third level, of language and structure. According to Lacan's line of thought, 'language' produces reality by naming it and symbolising it by putting brutal reality, the real on a distance, where language introduces a lack, with desire hovering around it. This lack may have been established effectively, partly effective or, as a third possibility, may not have been established at all, with each of these modalities having psychopathological significance. In the case of a neurosis and normality, the lack is addressed effectively, enabling a life-defined-by-desire, with all its ambitions and disappointments, while obviously also carrying the risk of experiencing self-loss or excessive behaviour (such as extreme aggression). In a person with a personality disorder, its function is impaired, meaning that a rift is seen between two mutually unconnected worlds of experience, with excess being part of the life style (which can be harmful socially but, in the right context, may also produce aesthetical value). In the case of the psychosis, the distance or lack is too small and may even be absent, which means that the person involved will be overwhelmed by brutal reality, by excessive experience, as in the case of a manifest psychosis. This does not take away the fact that such a condition might be compensated for by some device that offers protection against manifest psychosis – for example by choosing a particular profession, by working very hard, by living in isolation or by writing books. Besides, the occurrence of a psychotic state does not necessarily point to the presence of such a specific and fragile structure, as each man has his own unique fragilities which may be decompensated (should compensation fail). And yet normality, including neurosis, does offer some level of protection, having instituted a life-by-desire, with its forms of partial satisfaction and bearable unfulfilled desires. As a result, neurotic desire may be described depending on the way this unfulfilled quality is dealt with – for example by 'control and restraint' in the case of the compulsive neurosis, or by 'this is not going to happen for me anyway' in the phobic-avoiding person. These neurotic manoeuvres produce a curtailing of desire while leaving desire as such intact.

The subdivision into neurosis, psychosis and personality disorder may be a traditional one, but a normative element will also be at work, which is true for the conception of a mental disorder per se. At the very least it has social, psychological and biological components – which obviously complicates the problem. At an even more fundamental level, this norm has an anthropological quality, to the extent that a mental disorder can be seen as a disruption of the process of establishing desire, of the relationship towards one's own body, to time, etcetera.

1.5 An Inquiry into Possibility: The Capacity to Symbolise

The three levels of the human condition worked out by the corresponding three forms of hermeneutics, constitute a basic framework for man that offers the possibility of substantiation in the psychopathological domain. The question of its foundation still needs to be addressed. Rather than attempt to analyse actual relationships we need to look at its possibility or context. How exactly can intentionality, being-in-the-world and language provide access to reality (always in a specific way)? Can they actually do what they are supposed to do? The answer may seem obvious enough, but it is not.

Does language provide an authentic form of access to reality, or does it effectively obscure and obfuscate reality, as was argued by language sceptics? Does perception allow us to glimpse the truth or is it 'Falschnehmung'? Can the life world, with its freedom of will, survive as a legitimate gateway to reality or will the results of modern science prevail? Instead of addressing factual issues such as the structure of the life world – the *quaestio facti* – the question should focus on the validity of pretended knowledge – the *quaestio juris*. This would refer to its legitimate basis or condition of possibility, not its factual nature of a particular way of understanding. Reflecting a shift in emphasis from reality to knowability, Kant labelled this type of inquiry as 'transcendental'.

This question can be approached from each of the 'three levels'. Taking the level of intentionality as a starting point, we arrive at an original meaning-giving consciousness as a structuring principle (as with pure, transcendental phenomenology). At the level of the situation the focus will be on human existence, while the level of language will put the symbolic function, the capacity to symbolise, centre stage. In the following, the third option is taken as a starting point. The hypothesis to be tested is whether the three levels of the human condition can be made possible or supported by the capacity to symbolise. Throughout this explanation, reference is made – either explicitly or indirectly – to the two other options (the transcendental phenomenology and Heidegger's earlier philosophy), but this is mostly done in support of the choice for the issues of symbolisation as being the most fundamental field.

The symbol concept is taken rather broadly here. At one end of the spectrum we find the symbol concept in the soft sense of the word – a rose as a token or symbol representing love. At the other end we find the formal or hard symbol concept of modern science. In between lies the broad field of experience, of the life world, of language and culture, each of which also have a symbolic quality: the symbolism of social life, for example of an official symbolising authority, of presenting gifts that symbolise a social connection, etcetera. According to this hypothesis, a common trait would be that they all go back to the process of symbolisation, where something is not 'itself' – the official – and only acquires meaning by representing something else – authority. Something does not become recognisable and knowable until it represents something else. Something 'is' only if it is token *as* something else as well. Most likely, symbolisation is connected with this *as* at every level. At least two levels are relevant. The act of symbolisation *within* a world (official/authority) should be distinguished from a type of symbolisation of brutal reality *into* a world – a fundamental, radical type of symbolisation that will of course play out in any factual symbolisation. This may sound more metaphysical than it actually is, because this world always represents a multitude of worlds: the life world, the world of science, the world of the young child. And if a metaphysical question arises – 'why would there be something rather than nothing?' – it will flesh out to take on a functional form.

Guided by Cassirer and Lacan, the issues of symbolisation and representation will be discussed in depth later in this book. The choice for Cassirer (1874–1945) is an obvious one, seeing that he was the first philosopher to address the issue of symbolisation in a consistent way. He put the problem on the philosophical agenda and outlined its contours. Following in Kant's footsteps, he adopted an approach that fits in nicely with the question at hand, as he made a study of the legitimate basis or validity of knowledge pretence. He also broadened Kant's philosophy into a theory of culture. And yet, for a number of reasons, his philosophy has never earned the place in history it should rightfully be assigned. This is not the case with Lacan, although his philosophy is not particularly well known either. Then again, he did manage to put the theme of symbolisation on the map through his concept of the symbolic order. Most notably, he looked at the *impact* of the process of symbolisation on man's specific mode of existence. Yet another difference can be identified, not so much in practical elaboration as in theoretical point of departure. Cassirer embraces the primacy of signification in his discussion of the question of symbolisation, a choice that is called into question by Lacan, while embracing the primacy of the signifier. It leads to significant differences as well as mutual correction, in cases where similar points are addressed. The conclusions thus drawn will be applied to the outline given of the human condition and its 'three levels' – in Chapter 4. In the Chapters 2 and 3 on Cassirer and Lacan respectively an attempt will be made to describe the basic structure of their philosophies without any bias towards the view of man outlined here. The idea is to make a fresh start.

CHAPTER 2

Cassirer

The first to provide an in-depth and comprehensive discussion of the issue of symbolisation from an historical and systematic perspective, was Ernst Cassirer (1874–1945), in his *Philosophie der symbolischen Formen* ('The Philosophy of Symbolic Forms'), which was published in three volumes between 1923 and 1929. Partly as a result of what he referred to as the 'the misfortune of times' this project never got the attention it merited. Acting on a strong sense of foreboding, the Jew Cassirer was among the first to leave Germany after Hitler had come to power. Cassirer came from a wealthy family with many connections in the scientific and artistic world in Berlin. He left the city in 1919, when he was appointed professor at the newly founded University of Hamburg. As a student, he developed a fascination for Kant's philosophy, particularly the interpretation and actualisation of Kant's views offered by Hermann Cohen (1842–1918), the charismatic champion of Neo-Kantianism. Being encouraged by his teacher George Simmel, he moved from Berlin to Marburg, where Cohen held a chair for philosophy. Whilst remaining faithful to Cohen's approach, Cassirer would eventually develop his own philosophy of culture. Deeply conversant with all domains of philosophy as well as the natural sciences and humanities, he was well equipped for carrying out such a huge task. While being engaged in debate with the likes of Albert Einstein, he was also a great authority on Goethe – indeed, he would put Goethe on a par with Kant as foremost philosophers, which explains why his project strongly resonated with Goethe's views. For one thing, he was a 'homo universalis', a universal scholar equipped with a phenomenal memory, capable of memorising just about anything he read. His doctoral thesis was on Leibniz, and later on he produced a broad history of modern philosophy, focusing on epistemology (with Kantian overtones). In his first systematic principal work *Substanzbegriff und Funktionsbegriff* ('Substance and Function') published in 1910, Cassirer (GW 6/2000a/2015) laid the groundwork for his own concept of philosophy, albeit it still wholly in line with the basic tenets of Cohen's Neo-Kantianism. His fundamental assumption was that knowledge is not about an autonomous entity existing outside us ('substance') that merely needs to be read, but that knowledge depends on man's functions of knowledge. This would remain a fundamental principle throughout his work.

This chapter will start with an outline of Cassirer's effort and its roots in the 'back to Kant' movement, followed by a brief discussion of his relationship

 | DOI:10.1163/9789004373662_004

with Heidegger (with whom he engaged in a debate that has become famous). Next, Cassirer's 'toned-down idealism' will be discussed and illustrated based on the well-known example of the 'simple line' (*Linienzug*): the fact that even a simple thing as a line carries a set of intrinsic meanings. His toned-down idealism can be summed up as man being able to frame, shape or symbolise reality or being in a number of ways, which process of framing or symbolising must take place within a set of frameworks or orders. The various modes of symbolisation and the range of frameworks that accommodate them he refers to as 'symbolic forms', which he goes on to distinguish into, e.g., myth and religion, language, and modern science. Each of these three symbolic forms is dominated by a specific type of symbolisation or representation. These symbolic forms will be discussed individually, to be followed by the question whether we are potentially witnessing the birth of a whole new symbolic form: the world of virtuality. As a result, the subject matter of this chapter will be limited to Cassirer's contribution to the issue of symbolisation. His comprehensive body of work includes numerous historical studies (on the Renaissance and the Age of Enlightenment), on philosophers among which Descartes, Leibniz, Kant and essays on literature, as well as works on the principles of mathematics and of modern physics, his discussions with Einstein, and political studies where he makes a case for the rule of the law, etcetera, all of which fall outside the scope of this chapter.

Cassirer has remained a relative unknown, which can be explained by Cassirer's personal fate as well as by the nature of his work. For one thing, he was not the charismatic leader type that starts a school of thought and rallies students around him. Never out to force his views upon people, Cassirer was a gentle soul avoiding conflict and looking for reconciliation, whilst being also somewhat vain. Contemporary descriptions speak of a somewhat bookish but amiable and highly sophisticated person, who preferred a life of tranquillity. After his Berlin period, however, his tenure as a professor in Hamburg forced him to lead a more public life. He married Tony Bondy, a distant cousin, and the couple had three children whom he treated with much kindness. One of them would become a philosopher, another a photographer. His lack of official ambition in official domain was striking. For example, he turned down an invitation to come to Harvard and work as a lecturer for one academic year. Notwithstanding, he would go on to rank among the then foremost academics of his time. 1929 was the year of the now famous debate in Davos with Heidegger, then the 'coming man' (Gordon 2010). The change of power that took place in Germany a few years later did not come as a surprise to Cassirer who, as the first-ever Jewish rector of a German university, had witnessed anti-Semitic sentiments at close quarters. Hardly a new development in 1930s Europe, anti-Semitism was actually deeply embedded in its culture, and the fact that Cohen was the first ever Jew to be appointed professor of philosophy in Germany is telling in itself. His hasty emigration was frowned upon by many of his academic peers, and it certainly contributed to his name virtually being relegated to oblivion in Germany. After moving to Britain, where he remained only briefly, he went to Sweden and would spend the final years of his life in the United States. His comparatively early demise in 1945, in New York, kept him from fulfilling a role in philosophy after the war. Shortly before he died, he published a summary of his philosophy, focusing on its anthropological aspects – *An Essay on Man*. After his death, a volume of the prestigious 'Library of Living Philosophers' was published that was entirely devoted to Cassirer's philosophy – which was quite exceptional, considering that the scope of the series was essentially limited to living philosophers (Schilpp 1949, 1966). His brief stint in the United States earned him something of a reputation there. Of significant importance was the publishing of an English translation of his principal work in the 1950s (Cassirer 1955a, 1955b, 1957). It would lead to a number of American philosophy departments including studies of his work, which subsequently influenced several American philosophers (including Suzanne Langer, Wilfrid Sellars, and Nelson Goodman) as well as the late 20th-century American pragmatist movement (Renz 2011). In Europe, Cassirer had a major influence on Merleau-Ponty, who was indebted much to his work (Bernet 1994; Feron 2009; Van Vliet 2013). There are also ties with the French structuralist movement championed by Lévi-Strauss (Van Vliet 2013). No specific influences can be pinpointed, but there have been a number of personal contacts – for instance, the structural linguist Roman Jakobson and Cassirer had met during a hazardous sea voyage between Sweden and the United States, both being on the very last ship to make the crossing (T. Cassirer 1981). Also, Jakobson and Lacan were close friends (Lacan 1975, 19).

Cassirer was fairly well-known in France, and the 1970s saw the a full translation of his chief works in three volumes (Cassirer 1972), later to be followed by a publication of his *Oeuvres* ('Works') on a very large scale (Cassirer 1988-). This is quite exceptional, certainly by French standards. *Scilicet* magazine, of which Lacan was editor-in-chief, published a detailed study on Cassirer (Anonymus 1976). As international attention grew, a serious Cassirer undertaking got underway in France (Capeillères 2003; Seidengart 2013), in Italy (Ferrari 2003) and Germany (Krois 1987; Braun 1988; Paetzold 1994; Schwemmer 1997a; Orth 2004, 2008) particularly since the 1980s, with renewed interest in the United States (Verene 2011). Add to this a major investment in a large-scale critical edition of his collected works, *Gesammelte Werke,* (*GW*) in 25 volumes (Cassirer 1998–2008) and of his literary legacy, *Nachgelassene Manuskripte und Texte* (*ECN*) in 18 volumes (Cassirer 1995–2017). It adds up to 43 volumes.[1]

Nonetheless, the resonance of his work has remained limited (Recki 2013), and the fragmented course of his life was certainly a contributing factor. Many major Weimar philosophers would share his fate, but not Cassirer, whose moving to the USA earned him lasting repute in the Anglo-Saxon world. And yet it is not the external factors alone that account for this limited resonance – his personality and the nature of his philosophy play a part as well. Cassirer was not a man with a complex character, as far as we are able to tell (Cassirer, T. 2003; Meyer 2006). His publications were not particularly intriguing or profound, written as they were in a rather dry style, but he used clearly understandable language, explaining complicated matters in a simple way, which might suggest that his message was also simple. Instead of using the words of a master-thinker out to captivate his students, he is the teacher who is deluging his listeners with information, causing their attention to stray. His tone is conciliatory, which results in a somewhat bland language that lacks truly provocative statements. In terms of the content of his work, he was often seen as one of the last great philosophers of culture (Skidelski 2008). Reputation-wise, if justified, this would present in our post-modern age a lethal blow, as it would relegate him to the mausoleum of history. However, this does not him justice, because rather than concerning himself only with culture in a narrowed-down sense ('European culture'), his final focus is on culture per se, on man's cultural or symbolic mode of existence: the broad concept of culture embraced by Lévi-Strauss as well as Freud in his 'Civilization and its discontents' ('Das Unbehagen in der Kultur'). However, such a qualification is to a certain extent not untrue either. Indeed, he was a staunch advocate of the Enlightenment, considering modernity to be the irreversible outcome of European culture: He saw history of man as the history of self-liberation. Still, Cassirer's importance does not rely on his being a champion of the Enlightenment, but rather on having put symbolisation and the symbolic mode of existence of man, in its full scope and with all its ramifications, on the philosophical agenda. To build on this concept, Cassirer drew on a wide range of sources: ethnology, linguistics, modern mathematics and topology, modern natural sciences, Gestalt psychology and neurology. His scholarly talents certainly helped this effort but also

1 Titles of Cassirer's work cited in the text and notes are referred to the GW and the ECN editions, to be followed (/) by a reference to the English translation, if available. *Sigla* (PsF, I, II, III) are only used in case of reference to the *Philosophie der symbolischen Formen* (GW edition) to be followed (/) by reference to the corresponding page of the English translation (e.g. Cassirer 1955a, 1955b, 1957).

had a downside, for where to find someone knowledgeable enough to discuss these matters with? Also, in the multitude of subject matter discussed the point he tried to make would often get lost. A final problem was his conceptual framework. Indeed, Cassirer had developed his philosophy of culture from a Neo-Kantian perspective (which seems to be outdated, to all intents and purposes, and which he never abandoned).

However, today the scene has changed once again, as philosophy is now under renewed pressure to develop a scientific focus. Many master-thinkers failed to stand the test of time, and the history of Neo-Kantianism is an intriguing one in this respect. Historical Neo-Kantianism, which also produced thinkers such as Cassirer, managed to survive at an underground level (Makkreel and Luft 2010). According to this line of thought, comparative studies have been undertaken concerning the relationship, if any, between Cassirer and, for instance, Husserl's phenomenology (Luft 2011; Möckel 2014), American pragmatism (Renz 2011) and Lévi-Strauss' structuralism (Van Vliet 2013; Möckel 2013; Luft 2015b). Along the same lines, the present book on Cassirer and Lacan, another representative of French structuralism, has been conceived. Moreover, in a more general sense, Neo-Kantianism never lost his relevance as far as the focus is on protecting Kant's phrasing of the problem, while matching its answer to whatever demands may be imposed by what is topical today. For us, its relevance essentially is for today's situation rather for one in the past. Cassirer repeatedly stressed the fact that what matters is not the answer itself but the orientation of the question asked, which means that rather than focusing exclusively on historical Neo-Kantianism of the late 19th and early 20th centuries, we should ask ourselves what exactly Cassirer might contribute to the understanding of the present (Schwemmer 1997b; Barash 2008; Kreis 2010; Friedman and Luft 2015; Endres et al. 2016). His fundamental contribution could simply be summarized by postulating that man's cultural mode of existence means that his access to reality relies on symbolic systems representing reality, by definition rendering direct access impossible. Reality is not 'sold individually' – an idea that hasn't lost anything of its topicality today. Obviously, this notion dates back to Kant, with Neo-Kantianism adding its own elaboration on which Cassirer built to develop his unique theory of representation. In this context, it may be expedient to examine the core of historical Neo-Kantianism on which he built and which in its turn refers back to Kant.

2.1 A Return to Kant

Indeed, the question of access to reality was the same question raised by Kant in the 18th century, who was arguably the first to phrase it in such a way. Rather than inquire into the essence of reality, his ambition was to get to the heart of how reality can be known. The answer will lead to a theory of knowledge rather than any specific knowledge. This type of knowledge does not focus on reality per se but on what is enclosed in each valid form of knowledge of reality; rather than referring to the state of being of things, the focus is on knowledge. Since Kant, this type of research into the fundamentals and limitations of knowledge, has become known as 'transcendental'. Initially (but not exclusively), a Kantian brand of philosophy would therefore be a theory of knowledge, an epistemology. Cassirer likes to explain this by referring to the following quote in Kant (1965, B 303): 'the proud name of an Ontology that presumptuously claims to supply, in systematic doctrinal form, synthetic *a priori* knowledge of things in general (for instance the principle of causality) must, therefore, give place to the modest title of a mere Analytic of pure understanding'. The brand of ontology that pretends to have a priori knowledge of reality must yield to an analysis of the functions of understanding. Cassirer rules out as a true follower of Kant, any pre-critical reference to reality or substance without any reflection on knowledge process itself. This Kantian perspective brings a specific notion of the role of the subject. Not merely supposed to passively observe reality as it is, the subject is assigned an active role in the knowledge process. The – human – subject provides the framework in which things find their order and reality can present itself. This view is reflected in the ethical domain as well, which now regards man as the owner of freedom and being capable of self-determination. This shift in thought is commonly known as the Copernican Turn, as it defines man as the initiator within the domains of action and knowledge. Indeed, the fact that man is able to perceive in space and time and to think in terms of causality and reciprocity does not necessarily imply that reality is spatially, temporally or causally determined in itself, but merely that it manifests itself within these forms. According to Kant, this finding does not detract in any way from the universal validity of knowledge. Quite the contrary in fact – the finding that knowledge invariably depends on forms of intuition in space and time as well as on causality and other fundamental categories of thought actually underpins the universal validity and certainty of knowledge thus obtained.

After Kant, the cultural scene had irreversibly changed, with Hegel entering the fray, who pointed out that any form of knowledge and morals is to be socially embedded. Later on, a host of new and ground-breaking discoveries within the realm of natural sciences (physics, chemistry and medicine) came into being and would ultimately lead to the birth of a materialistic world image that still holds sway today ('no thoughts without phosphorus'). Also, the advent of non-Euclidian geometry would rock the world of geometry to its foundations, putting paid to an unchallenged 2,000-year-old tradition of Euclidian geometric principles. Contrary to what Kant still believed, Euclidian laws of geometry proved not to be universally valid, being reduced to a limited instance of, or transformation within a far more comprehensive system. Also, mathematics had explored new territory that eluded observation (topology), whereas Kant believed the connection between mathematics and intuition to be essential. Also in the field of natural sciences, thermodynamics for example, new developments turned out not to match the traditional physical laws formulated by Newton. Moreover, the humanities had claimed their rightful place in the scientific world, which Kant had not anticipated, as his views relied strongly on the natural-scientific experience. Thus, the late 19th century saw the rise of a broad debate on how the humanities as well as recent developments in natural sciences should be incorporated within the overall context of 'science'.

In these debates, Kant's work presented an obvious frame of reference, offering as he did a framework that on the one hand fully acknowledged modern science while refuting a natural-scientific reductionist approach (of the 'man is his brain' type). This return to Kant would herald the birth of Neo-Kantianism, in fact a broad movement that would go on to include two distinct schools of thought. A focus on the humanities resulted in the re-interpretation of Kant's work towards a theory of values, the so-called Baden School, with Wilhelm Windelband (1904) and Heinrich Rickert (1921) as its key protagonists. Developments in the field of mathematics and natural sciences would lead to the so-called Marburg orientation, championed by Hermann Cohen and Paul Natorp with Cassirer as a student of both. After having published his seminal 1871 book on Kant's theory of experience Cohen (1987) became founder of the Marburg school. He was a charismatic and generous person, while Natorp was an introverted but highly discerning and influential scholar. Both schools found a broad following, although the Marburg school was better and more tightly organised. Here we shall discuss the Marburg orientation, because this is where Cassirer came from (mutual differences between both schools will remain largely undiscussed).

The idea was to modify Kant's views in order to align it with the above-mentioned new developments and discoveries. This modification or revision of Kant's schemata manifested itself on at least three levels. *Firstly*: The construction plan itself was redesigned, which effectively put paid to the dichotomy introduced by Kant between sensibility and understanding, or the distinction between forms of intuition (of space and time) and the forms of thought (including causality). Instead, space, time and causality are addressed at an equal level, representing forms in which the object is established. *Secondly*:

The role fulfilled by the various forms changed, whilst leaving the concept of an a priori moment itself intact. Knowledge includes an a priori component that is not part of the experience itself but does contribute to the constitution of this experience, comparable to causality being a concept of understanding that enables the formulation of actual causal relationships. The universal ambition was abandoned, however, as Newton's law of physics, on which Kant had fashioned his conceptual schema, turned out to be one out of many options rather than being universally valid (as Kant believed). What seemed universal, proved to be nothing more than 'a fact', 'the fact of science'. As a result, the focus was shifted to the factuality of science. Any inquiry into the logic of validity of science should have its point of departure in its factuality (*Geltungslogik*). However, factuality is not synonymous with contingency. The historical and cultural conditions of science will not dilute its validity. Whilst being a fact of culture, science is a fact of reason as well.

Then it turns out that scientific statements should always be framed within a theoretical context, e.g. a particular order of thought. Consequently, they can never be verified in isolation without reference to a comprehensive theory – in line with the Quine-Duhem thesis – while another implication would be that the process of thought produces ('erzeugt') theory-loaded objects. The a priori – the leading principles of experience – can therefore only be established a posteriori, based on experience. It led to what they referred to as the 'transcendental method', which was attributed to Kant, but worked out differently: namely as a description of the fundamental operations of knowledge that can claim their rightful place within a particular field of knowledge (Cohen 1917, iv). And these operations are not given as such but need to be reconstructed, departing from the factual state of science, as being its logical conditions of possibility. The reconstructive method of Kant was adopted, but has been given a plural elaboration. Indeed, there is a fundamental difference between an a priori concept serving, on the one hand, as a constitutive component of experience per se as proposed by Kant and, on the other, as a logical precondition for a historically given body of factual or scientific knowledge. The ambition is significantly more modest and might be compared to the project of a descriptive metaphysics – the conceptual infrastructure of experience – developed by the British philosopher P.F. Strawson (1959), also more or less in line with Kant. The prerequisite of an ultimate justification ('Letztbegründung') that Kant had been seeking, was abandoned by the Neo-Kantians. This step follows logically from taking 'the' actual status quo in science – which invariably represents 'a' particular actual status quo – as a starting point. *Thirdly*: Contrary to Kant, particularly in his early work, no heed was paid to the subjective sources of knowledge of man (Kant 1965, A 96–116). Which is perfectly understandable, the focus being on the objective validity of knowledge rather than the process of its acquisition: on the 'context of justification' rather than the 'context of discovery'. Initially, Cohen limited his scope to the scientific realm but later on, in line with Kant, he went on to broaden this concept by introducing into the system ethics in the sense of morality, and aesthetics in the sense of an aesthetic experience. The system was thus expanded, while the approach itself remained unchanged, with ethics being underpinned by a factum as well, e.g. the fact of law (Philonenko 1989, 68–71).

This system, however, had more or less run its course. As an initial step away from its doctrine, Natorp (2013) started to focus on the subject side of the process of knowledge acquisition and the role of psychological consciousness, drawing on Husserl's emerging phenomenological approach, while later on Natorp's ideas would in turn influence Husserl (1966) concerning the analysis of the so-called passive (pre-predicative) mental events (which ar not given directly, also in Husserl's view). In Natorp's view, however, no subjective consciousness in any form whatsoever, is given directly, subjectively, by introspection. Only by means of an analysis of factual, objective knowledge can we attain knowledge of the subjective forces of consciousness that have generated these (Cassirer 1996, 150–151). And in doing so, Natorp remains faithful to the basic tenets of Marburg Neo-Kantianims. In his specific interpretation, subjective consciousness is structured as representation: When I see a tree, it means I conceive an object *as* a tree, and this conceiving has a relational character rather than being a psychical act in Husserl's sense. Consciousness does not 'animate' sensory impression with meaning, as Husserl would say, but an impression is invariably already related to something else (an earlier impression, an image or concept) and it is this relationship, and not an psychical act, that bestows meaning. Thus, consciousness has a relational as well as a representational structure. Indeed, consciousness cannot be explored by introspectively considering psychic acts but has to be reconstructed based on that which it creates. And what it creates is a world.

2.2 Cassirer's Ambition

Cassirer builds on this idea, broadening it in two ways. First of all, he argues that rather than one level there are actually three distinct levels of representation. Next to the objectifying form ('that is a house') we distinguish a pre-objectifying form ('this place feels uncomfortable') and a formal form ('is there carbon monoxide, or CO, in the air?'). Cassirer applies this distinction to the individual *psychological consciousness* or subjective mind, following in the footsteps of Natorp in terms of the attention devoted to psychological consciousness. As a result, he offers an extension by introducing stratification, proposing three levels of representation: pre-objective, objective and formal. Traditional Neo-Kantianism as championed by Cohen, however, was not concerned with psychological consciousness, but assumed the presence of a general consciousness underlying science as a cultural domain. Which leads us to the second type of broadening. Cassirer introduces a similar stratification within this *general consciousness* to add diversification. No longer bound by the type of consciousness underlying and informing science, it now also included forms of consciousness that found their expression in myth, religion, daily experience, technology, etcetera. Also in these worlds (of myth, religion, etcetera), the various modes of representation, or combinations of these modes, can be recognised (PsF III, 518–525/447–453). Consequently, the recognition of *stratification* within psychological consciousness returns in general consciousness, which leads to a significant *broadening* of the scope of claims of its validity and meaningfulness (which now also include the cultural domains of myth, religion, and art). It should be borne in mind, however, that a psychological consciousness (of a single person) will always be part of a community and consequently of a general consciousness as well as the culture of which this person forms part. And each form of consciousness will constitute a world. Crucially, instead of referring to 'a forming of the world' he speaks of 'making for the world' – *Gestaltung zur Welt* (PsF I, 9/80). And where he (GW 9/2002d, 136, 304) initially spoke of 'world understanding', this should not be interpreted as an effort to understand the world that already exists, but in terms of conceiving reality *as* a world. Reality, if disclosed, will appear as a world – a world in a plural sense.

Invariably, the 'making for the world' will be driven by various types of representation. As mentioned before, we may distinguish three types: the pre-objectifying (from primary perception), objectifying (from language) and formalising (from science) types. Water can be refreshing, a threat, a means of irrigation, or H_2O, as the case may be. In all cases, however, anything will not *be* something unless it has become part of a referential structure. 'What is', is preceded by a formula, a concept, an image or atmosphere – by 'a meaning'. Being can only be conceived from a perspective of meaning, reality per se can only be given from and be part of a perspective of meaning, which sums up Cassirer's main thesis: 'no being is tangible or accessible except through meaning' (PsF III, 345/299). We are unable to inquire beyond this level of meaning. In fact, rather than one single perspective of meaning there are many perspectives, reflecting a plurality of perspectives and meaning and, consequently, of worlds. The world of a child is a far cry from an adult's world, the mythical world is nothing like the world of modern science. This plurality betrays the influence of Goethe, next to that of Kant and the Neo-Kantians. Indeed, in his now famous critique of Newton's natural sciences, Goethe responded with his alternative theory of the light – a phenomenologically tinged theory, as it might be described in retrospect. Cassirer considered both conceptions of nature, Newton's as well Goethe's, to be valid in their own right, each representing their own unique scope. As a matter of fact, the first indication of the concept of the symbolic forms can be found in Cassirer's article on Goethe and mathematical physics (GW 9/2002d, 268–315).

With respect to Neo-Kantianism (with Kant in the background) we can identify two novel aspects. New is the role attributed to language, not only vis-à-vis Kant himself but also within modern philosophy as a whole. Well before the Post-World War II period, when this theme would dominate philosophy, he put it on the agenda, offering a comprehensive elaboration. Another new element is the recognition of the role of the pre-objective experience as being essential – experience of expression' (*Ausdruck*). This basic layer of experience is to be on a par with the pre-predicative sphere of perception and movement, of what is self-evident in perception and actions. Hardly a new theme, it had more or less simultaneously been introduced by both Husserl (1966) and Heidegger (1962) in the 1920s, while Litt (1926) and Straus (1935) offered a profuse, empirical description. Yet Cassirer chose to make it the second major anchor point of his philosophy: the non-propositional experience, with myth as its prototype. This represented a major departure from Kant and traditional Neo-Kantianism. According to the Neo-Kantians there was only one valid world, the world of modern science, on which the life world should be fashioned. Cassirer breaks with this view, arguing that next to the world of modern science there is the life world, the world of myth and religion, and of art. Each world offers its own unique form of 'knowledge', each of them being indispensable, with mythical elements being present even in modern science. Cassirer spoke of mythical knowledge, of art as knowledge, of scientific knowledge, offering an juxtaposition that would have been anathema the Neo-Kantians. Indeed, thus phrased Cassirer's views are much more in line with the French tradition of comparative epistemology adopted by the early Foucault and Bachelard (Janz 2001). Moreover, the concept of distinguishing various degrees of knowledge, of consciousness is hardly new, as we find in Kant and in Hegel a three-partition as well: a distinction between, for example, primary perception, intuitive perception and understanding. New, however, is the attribution of validity even to the most basic level, being rephrased as mythical consciousness, within the context of modernity with Neo-Kantianism as its most radical exponent. Of course, this qualification did not keep Cassirer from appreciating the formal level of modern science as presenting the highest achievement of mankind: He remains a champion of the Enlightenment and a true follower of Kant, following in the footsteps of Neo-Kantianism.

Moreover, Cassirer adopts the Neo-Kantian transcendental approach of reconstruction, inquiring into the conditions of possibility of validity of different forms of consciousness. Where Neo-Kantianists played out this method in the realm of science (and that of ethics and aesthetics), Cassirer chose to broaden its field of application. This allowed mythical consciousness to be reconstructed based on the mythical world constituted by images, while language would be the tool needed to reconstruct the consciousness underlying the factual life world. Only by starting with the actual result, the actual culture as a product (*Ergebnis*), can the underlying functions be identified: 'The content of the mind is disclosed only in its manifestations; the ideal form is known only by and in the aggregate of sensible signs which its uses for its expression' (PsF I, 16/86). This exemplifies the Neo-Kantian transcendental analysis, a method that Cassirer (1996, 165) never truly abandoned: taking factual culture (*Ergebnis*) as a starting point, in order to identify and reconstruct the form of consciousness it expresses. The making for the world thus reveals reality, but this revealing will always be plural and essentially partial by definition. Thus, according to Cassirer (PsF III, 1/1), reality (*Wirklichkeit*) is revealed (*offenbart*), while being simultaneously concealed (*verhüllt*). Here Cassirer utilises, albeit not unintentionally, Heidegger's (1978, 31) vocabulary, which betrays a hidden convergence of – or even a similarity between – both projects: Reality can be disclosed, while being concealed as well. To which Cassirer adds that any ambition to lay bare a primal stratum of reality, without any concealment, in which reality itself may be apprehended free from all symbolic interpretation, cannot be fulfilled (PsF III, 3/2).

Notwithstanding, the mind of man does rely on sensory impressions, in line with the role of receptiveness that Kant attributes to the sensory system, as a counterpoint to activity, to the spontaneity of the understanding. Kant keeps the two domains strictly separate, devoting a substantial part of the *Kritik der reinen Vernunft* ('Critique of Pure Reason') to addressing precisely this disparity. However, both the Neo-Kantians and Cassirer no longer hold this dichotomy to be valid. Matter and form have become inseparable, which eliminates any condition that would precede it – a bare primal stratum of reality – from the start. Being cast in a mould from day one, reality, including the reality of inner experience, never presents itself in an unformed state. By the same token, this mould is not a given as such either, but needs to be reconstructed from concretely formed material found in the world, in variety of cultures. All this goes back to Kant's critical question, but gives it a broader context. Kant's tenet is still part of this view, but has undergone a multiple, plural elaboration. Thus, moving from Kant to Cassirer seems to be only a small step. Yet, it expands the world of the potentially valid experience – the world of culture – in a way that Kant himself would have shirked from. This expansion is finite, however, as it simultaneously offers a criterion for delimitation: A valid experience is possible only by virtue of delimitation, by being cut off from the immediate experience. Which makes the step from Kant to Cassirer *not* similar to a step from Kant to Hegel. Immediacy (*Unmittelbarkeit*) is a central theme with Hegel as well, but only as a moment to be eliminated in universal mediation rather than in the form of something that is closed off, excluded. Cassirer, by contrast, stresses the moment of exclusion, repeatedly formulating it like this: the paradise of pure immediacy is closed off – *das Paradies der reinen Unmittelbarkeit ist verschlossen* (PsF I, 49/113; PsF III, 46/40). This phrase is a quotation from the Romantic author Heinrich von Kleist, that Cassirer uses quite often, thus clearly revealing his ambition. Without any doubt this represents a Kantian motif. But it reflects an (early) Romantic motif as well, as can be seen in the quotation borrowed from Von Kleist. Indeed, (early) Romanticism takes up an intermediate position between Kant and Hegel (Frank 2010). According to Romanticist views, man may enter the world, whilst being separated from reality as such as well, a full merging of the two being out of reach. Culture can come into being only if embedded in this caesura, manifesting itself through the process of separation, of the severing of this bond.

And how does Cassirer fit in all this historically? Cassirer stood firmly in the tradition of Marburg Neo-Kantianism, which he broadened in a significant way, whilst building on the method associated with this tradition ('method' should be interpreted rather loosely here). Whether he still was a Neo-Kantian or no longer one, is a question that is difficult to answer, as opinions differ widely. In the final reckoning it may not be all that relevant, if only in light of the sweeping and essentially open nature of Neo-Kantianism, basing itself as it does on the fact of the present, the 'topicality of the here and now', without being tied in any way to the 'topicality of before'. Be that as it may, Cassirer was definitely not a major autonomous thinker or intriguing philosopher comparable to the likes of Husserl or Heidegger, each of whom brought a speculative force that pervaded both their personality and writings. Cassirer simply lacked those qualities – which does not necessarily detract from the value and significance of the work itself, however. Its strength lies in the order of the fortunate choice rather than in the magnitude of the design. By means of a small modification he manages to produce a mutation of the Kantian project into a theory of culture, by making a true case for it, by highlighting the significance of the *caesura* effectuated through culture. Yet, the emphasis on the *caesura* causes this theory to be indebted to early Romanticism as well: the paradise of pure immediacy is closed off. Thus the project finds a new potential, opening itself up to a whole gamut of modes of experience. It is this very theme that is played out in the background of Cassirer and Heidegger's key debate.

2.3 Cassirer and Heidegger

Heidegger and Cassirer locked horns in their famous debate of 1929 (Heidegger 1973; Friedman 2000; Gordon 2010; ECN 17/2014). Ever the seducer, Heidegger won the day at the expense of the conciliatory Cassirer in this epic academic combat. Heidegger cleverly played the card of young age, whereas Cassirer represented the cultural elite to the students of the late 1920s. They never treated each other less than courteously, however. As was to be expected, any themes where they might find common ground were hardly addressed. And yet these themes do exist. Fundamentally, Heidegger would likely not have disagreed with Cassirer's basic thesis which states that being can be conceived based on meaning alone. This thesis provides solid common ground. Yet what Heidegger did was inquire into the *Sinn von Sein*, the meaning of being: what does it mean, 'being' anyway? By way of preparation, he set out to examine the 'meaning of being' of human existence, by capturing the fundamental quality of human being, of human existence (*das Dasein im Menschen*).

It turns out that a significant parallel could be identified, which was particularly evident in the early years of Heidegger's (1987) philosophical career the years before *Sein und Zeit* ('Being and Time') in 1927 has been published. Heidegger strove to establish how and where meaning and signification come to the fore in the world, how and where the world may appear as being meaningful (*Bedeutsamkeit*). Heidegger situates this place and time in man's practical dealings with things, in objects being 'ready-to-hand', with 'the hammer' as a key example. Hammering reveals the experience of meaning, which even precedes more material questions such as 'Am I doing this right?' or 'Why am I doing this in the first place?' He may well have been inspired by his own experience as a child of a cooper, thus relying on his own source of meaning (Zimmerman 2005, 12). Unlike the spheres of objectification and of theory, the pre-objective sphere lays the foundations for the fullness of meaning. From his unique perspective, Cassirer asks a similar question: How can I, at the most basic level, engage in a meaningful relationship with that which exists? The answer he provides is of a similar nature. Rather than pointing to the field of labour and action (*poièsis*), he highlights the field of perception (*aisthèsis*), more specifically the Gestalt experience: the menacing quality of the dark, the sense of abandonment one may experience in a forest. This is where the primary sense of being, of becoming aware that 'there *is* something' manifests itself. The parallel between question and answer is unmistakable, however. The readiness-to-hand in our every day dealings in Heidegger's sense and Cassirer's Gestalt perception are both part of the same sphere, which is the pre-objective experience. This parallel had actually been identified by Cassirer (PsF III, 167n/149n, 184n/163n). And it is hardly surprising that Heidegger (1928), in a critical but considerate book review, should have paid attention to Cassirer's discussion of this topic as well.

Despite their common roots, the projects are obviously quite different. Heidegger conceives human existence as being determined situatively as well as being open to possibilities. Man is defined as a 'thrown project', who is forced to design his existence from the situation in which he finds himself, in which he has been thrown. This situation turns out to be finite, as is human existence itself. Cassirer is not likely to challenge this conclusion as a temporary outcome, for the simple fact that it is in keeping with Cassirer's basic tenet which holds that 'being' can only be understood from 'meaning', in this case a 'given meaning', meaning given in a situation. And of course man is finite and mortal, a fact that had been made poignantly clear by the Great War, which was still fresh in their minds and had cut short countless human lives. It is patently clear that the problem for Cassirer lies not in the idea as such but in its elaboration.

The first criticism refers to the absolutization of this point of view, which in Chapter 1 was described as the 'situative' perspective. This criticism refers to the statute of man. Assuming that all things are determined situatively, this would eliminate the possibility of some higher-level truth. Cassirer would argue that man is obviously mortal and finite, while maintaining that a person's life and commitment are non-finite in a different sense. In his discussions and dealings, man will not be guided by situative considerations alone but sometimes also by principles that are not opportune nor situatively determined or merely coincidental, but that do have universal validity. Cassirer (1996, 201–202) adds yet another criticism, namely that Heidegger's philosophy, absolutising as it does 'the situation', leaves no space for the concept of the objective spirit, of culture – which in Chapter 1 was referred to as the structural perspective. Heidegger chooses to neglect the fact that man is part of a culture, of the objective mind. The fact that he raised these criticisms makes perfect sense – the first criticism goes back to Kant, the second one is a product of a Neo-Kantian line of thought.

Regarding Cassirer's twofold criticism, Heidegger (1928) came back with the repartee that Cassirer might be overburdening Kant's central issue: Is it justified to transform the 'critique of reason' into a 'critique of culture?' – *Kann man die Kritik der reinen Vernunft erweitern zu einer Kritik der Kultur*? Cassirer might have chosen to ignore the question, considering that the Neo-Kantians had already added this orientation to Kant's question by highlighting the factual entity of science. After all, the Neo-Kantians regarded science as little more than an element of culture, of the objective spirit. As mentioned before, Cassirer takes a major step beyond classical Neo-Kantianism by conceiving culture more broadly as well as including its history in its variety. In every culture, an a priori is at work that is historically defined but actually determines what can be said or seen in a particular period. Through this qualification and historisation of the a priori, Cassirer anticipates the project of structural history, which would later become Foucault's key theme. Indeed, Foucault (1966) points explicitly, in a brief discussion of the French translation of Cassirer's 'Philosophy of the Enlightenment', to the similarity between Cassirer's project and his own project, which does bear at that time (1970) a Neo-Kantian mark, as he observes himself. Heidegger fails to appreciate its dynamic potential, however.

Heidegger also comments on the statute of man, arguing that Cassirer may have offered a well-defined concept of culture, but that he failed to supply a corresponding definition of the human, subjective mind – and that Cassirer to this end should draw on the concept of man as laid down in his 'Interpretation of Dasein', which describes man as being a prisoner of a situation as well as being finite. This comment fails to hit the mark, however, in view of the fact that, according to Cassirer's description of culture as an end point (*terminus ad quem*) and the human mind as a starting point (*terminus a quo*), both should be interpreted as purely correlative concepts. The human mind is the sum of all formative activities of man, and the culture is its product. He writes (GW 24, 2007c, 313): 'We should use it (sc. the term "Geist") in a functional sense as a comprehensive name for all these functions which constitute and build up the world of human culture'. In other words: the human mind is the functional, effective infrastructure of what culture represents as an actual entity. It turns out that the human mind as such is diverse, whilst providing also a functional and universal unity, which may aspire to a universal truth and validity that – even essentially – includes the ethical domain. Cassirer regards man as an actively shaping, meaning-giving and symbolising being, which in addition to shaping his environment also shapes himself and is thus able to accept responsibility and accountability. Heidegger is likely to agree up to a point. Heidegger holds that rather than lose heart, man should be determined to make something out of life ('but what exactly' is parenthesised). But even if man were to design his life based on future prospects, he would still be tied to the actual situation. He may live from the future, but this future is finite. Man does not live from 'a higher level', from timeless principles. Whilst not denying the situative condition of man, Cassirer (1996, 205–209) argues, on the contrary, that man is also guided by universal principles, including moral principles – whose validity is more than just contingent or coincidental. At the time of Davos, this was in fact a topical debate, and it has remained so to this very day. Apart from that, Cassirer would be able to confirm what Luther had said about finite man being capable of infinity ('finitum capax infiniti') – man is in fact capable of conceiving infinity.

And yet Heidegger does have a point when referring to his 'Interpretation of Dasein' (*Analytik des Daseins*), which included the themes of finiteness, thrownness, and anxiety as the basic state of mind of finite *Dasein*. Its common denominator is 'passiveness', a theme that would come to the fore more prominently in Heidegger's later philosophy. Man is a mere pawn played by fate, caught up in history and the 'history of being'. This notion may have a disculpating effect – with man being a 'victim' in all that he does – but it does hold a significant element of truth, with the life and fortunes of Cassirer as a case in point. Still, the theme of passiveness is hardly touched upon by Cassirer. For example, Cassirer likes to contrast the 'activity of the human mind' with the 'culture as its product', but the primacy lies with activity. Although not neglecting the autonomy or objectivity of culture – of culture as a fact, as *ergon* – he fails to address its retrograde effects on the individual, which in his individuality is stamped from the outside by symbolic forms (as *ergon*), by the symbolic order. It simply lies beyond his field of vision. He is unable to see the introduction into culture as entering a world that is alien, and which therefore brings alienation. Indeed, he writes (PsF III 44/39): 'The entering of the ego as a "spiritual subject" into the medium of the objective spirit constitutes not an act of alienation but an act of finding and determining itself'. Cassirer did allow for the possibility of some degree of an alienation occurring in society, or being produced by modern techniques (GW 15/2004a, 168–177), but rejected the concept of an essential alienation arising from the subject's entering the symbolic space as such (GW 15/2004a, 168–177). Cassirer (1996, 141) would still in his later years caution against any tendency to present the concepts of alienation and 'otherness' in a negative sense (as is done in Romanticism). Still, the experience of culture as something coming from the outside and as truly alienating as well, with all its associated conflicts and strife, would go on to become a key theme in the works of Lacan and other structuralist thinkers. And although Cassirer does allow for conflicts arising between man and culture in its diversity, Cassirer's ultimately conciliatory vision of relationship between man and culture did not match this effort. Cassirer's restraint in these matters should be attributed to his specific elaboration of this theme rather than the notion itself – man as a symbolising being. His philosophical idealism was simply out of step with the mind-set of the post-war age. This was not to change until the closing years of the 20th century.

2.4 The Mind and Critical Idealism

Cassirer's philosophical idealism is actually quite subtle. Its concept of mind is unmistakably driven by idealism. Indeed, knowledge does not reflect a pre-existing reality – as would be argued from a truly realistic epistemological viewpoint – but contributes its own forms. Consequently, rather than revealing itself in a naked form, reality takes a specific and limited form. This is what might be termed the 'idealistic motif'. This does not alter the fact that it is always reality that is disclosed, and that 'meaning' (symbolic ideation, thought) is thus bound to rely on what is offered by the senses. Cassirer considers the role of material reality in the process of world formation to be essential, which represents a realistic motif – and even a materialistic motif (in a broad Aristotelian sense). Consequently, the idealistic and realistic motives represent two sides of the same coin. An epistemological idealism goes hand in hand with an ontological realism, but the epistemology itself is essentially not realistic: The notion that knowledge would be a truthful reflection of reality (a 'mirror of nature') is rejected throughout. Reality requires the presence of the spirit, the mind to show itself, while the spirit or mind needs matter to substantiate itself, expressing itself through the structuring of sensory material (here we must take 'express' in its broadest sense) – without being an entity, a substance itself. Mind does not exist in itself, but has to express, to realize himself in matter, is bound to material expression. The fact that the mind relies on matter, on material expression, may thus be considered to be part of, or derived from, Cassirer's main thesis: being and meaning are mutually connected. As a result the term 'mind' (or 'spirit') would not only refer to the individual human mind, the subjective mind but also to the surrounding culture, which is now called objective mind. To match the two forms of mind (or spirit) he also speaks of two forms of symbolism. Firstly, we have 'the natural symbolism' of the meaning-bestowing consciousness (*natürliche Symbolik*) which as an original spiritual process is contained in every single moment and fragment of consciousness. This natural symbolism constitutes the very essence of consciousness. There upon a second form of symbolism is built: the 'artificial symbolism' (*künstliche Symbolik*) of meaning-carrying and meaning-mediating systems, or symbolic forms (language, science, etcetera). Cassirer argues that artificial symbolism (meaning systems such as language) may have a distinctly autonomous character, yet presuppose the presence of a meaning-giving activity of natural symbolism (consciousness as such), from which they emerge and in which they are rooted. Then again, the symbolic systems have a profound effect on the workings of natural symbolism, and actually nothing falls outside their scope.

Natural symbolism. Natural symbolism manifests itself in consciousness, as its fundamental layer (PsF I, 25–40/93–106). Consciousness works in such a way that a particular element of consciousness acquires a representing function. This may even occur at a pre-lingual level, for instance as a result of the beginnings of segmentation occurring within the flow of consciousness itself, when consciousness itself produces – Cassirer uses rather graphic terms – 'vortices', 'eddies' and 'incisions' (PsF III, 101, 129/89, 116). New impressions thus acquire an initial general charge, acquiring the status of 'first universals', sucked down as they are into a specific field of meaning – lustful, frightening. One might imagine that some form of initial structuring of the pre-lingual consciousness will take place in the very young child. Thereupon, this first segmentation will be differentiated further while acquiring a lingual confirmation and articulation. so that a whole field of perception may be constituted. One side of an object may refer to the object as a whole, a particular shade of colour to the general colour 'red', a point may refer to a spatial structure, a sequence to time and/or causality. One of Cassirer's (PsF III, 231/203) favourite sayings is that of 'the true pulse of consciousness whose secret is precisely that every beat strikes a thousand connections'. All this results in a sensory experience acquiring a meaning (of form, concept, category, categorical system). Apparently, consciousness is structured as a whole, as a closed system, with each element referring to the other. Consciousness contents (representations) refer to other consciousness contents (representations), which in turn refer to what is represented (meaning). It is this highly complex structure that defines the symbolic, representing quality of consciousness, just as Natorp (2013, 54) refers to representation as being at the heart of consciousness: 'das heisst aber (dass): *nicht die Präsentation sondern Repräsentation das Ursprüngliche,* ist'. ('this would mean, however, that representation rather than presentation would be the origin'). Cassirer endorsed this thesis literarily (PsF III, 232nt/203nt).

How then should we define the relationship between consciousness and the thing observed? Cassirer's point of view does not deviate in essence from traditional phenomenology: The states, the contents of consciousness represent or symbolise the object. In his view, there is no causal relationship ('Kausalschluss') between the supposed thing outside and the thing inside consciousness – instead what we see is a symbolic relationship. Rather than regarding the thing perceived as causing a state of consciousness, he identifies a relationship of representation between the perceived thing and the contents of consciousness. A variety of contents of consciousness represents an object, when a relationship is established between this variety of content of consciousness on the one hand and space, time and causality on the other hand. This insertion produces objectivity: The thing is there in that specific surrounding, it is not just a dreamlike state. Because of the relational character of consciousness a content of consciousness is able to 'represent' a thing ('einen Gegenstand *darstellen*') (PsF III, 227/197). Again it should be borne in mind that consciousness is also receptive, relying on the sensory stimuli offered by the senses. What they fail to offer, however, is the concept of a thing, the concept of time (after-each other), of space (next-to each other), or causality (by-each other). Concepts and meanings are thus part of the contribution of the 'mind', which impregnates the sensory with 'meaning', with ideality (concepts, categories). This is indeed more or less in line with Husserl's phenomenological approach, who speaks of 'meaning intention' that goes on to acquire 'meaning fulfilling' in perception: the empty meaning (intention) of 'house' *and* the filling of this void through the actual process of seeing a house, in a corporeal presence (*leibhafte Gegenwart*) – a term being accepted by Cassirer (PsF III, 141/127, 277/240). Indeed, where Cassirer speaks of a relationship of representation between the content of perception and the object perceived, phenomenology refers to an intentional relationship between the content of consciousness and the intentional object, or the intended object. The difference is that phenomenology refers to acts of consciousness that would animate the primitive impression. Cassirer considers this to be a mythology of activities, proposing that meaning is added merely by the relational quality of consciousness itself. And the impregnation with meaning is played out even at the most fundamental level of perception. There is no such thing as a simple content of perception ('sense datum'), which in a next step would be endowed with meaning as was Husserl's view initially (Husserl 1983, § 85; PsF III, 226–227/199–200; see also: Bernet 1992, 139–162; Luft 2011, 235–294; Möckel 2014).

Cassirer introduced the concept of symbolic pregnance (*symbolische Prägnanz*) to describe this primitive interconnection (PsF III, 218–233/191–204). Most likely this concept was partially taken from Leibniz, partially from the Gestalt psychology. This concept holds at least two meanings. First of all, the symbolic put its mark on perception from the start, whilst impregnating it, and secondly, perception is already pregnant with the symbolic (similar to Leibniz referring to the present being pregnant from the future – *pregnans futuri*). This might be illustrated by the classic example of the 'simple line' (*Linienzug*), an undulating line that can be interpreted in a variety of ways (PsF III, 228–229/200–202; GW 22/2006a, 120–121). Which raises the question why Cassirer should have chosen 'a line' to illustrate the concept of primitive symbolisation.

It may be a coincidence, but then maybe it is not (he fails to comment on this). And yet this example is highly apposite, considering that 'the line' is the most primitive 'form of a form'. It evokes the origin of the form itself, the most primitive core of symbolisation. As a result, any given line could be interpreted as a primitive element of art (of drawing), of geometry (measuring), etcetera; and by extension, it could be conceived aesthetically as beautiful, or mathematically as formally correct, and so forth – as in the example of the *Linienzug*. We take it *as* a mathematical structure, or *as* animated totality, *as* a mythical symbol, or *as* an aesthetic ornament. At the heart of the argument – a point that Cassirer keeps highlighting – lies the notion that we are not dealing with a basic entity of perception, namely a line, that is later conceived in a number of ways. Instead, the line has 'always' been conceived in a particular way. We may want to compare this to Wittgenstein's example of the rabbit-or-duck Gestalt switch. (It is by no means coincidental that both thinkers should have derived their respective examples from the Gestalt psychology, the psychology of forms.) The beholder sees either a rabbit *or* a duck. Cassirer would definitely have endorsed Wittgenstein's (1963, Part II, § xi) comment: 'So we interpret it, and *see* it as we *interpret* it'. There is no sequence of first seeing and then interpreting – we see based on meaning, on interpretation: we see *as* we interpret. Moreover, Cassirer would have endorsed Heidegger's concept of understanding as well, yet only to a certain extent. Indeed, Heidegger's (1962, 149) core message is that meaningful appearance of beings invariably involves an event in which an entity is taken *as* being that entity: 'that which is explicitly understood – has the structure of *something as something* [...]'. And he adds (1962, 151): 'Anything interpreted, as something interpreted, has the *as* structure of its own'. Indeed, the importance accorded to the *as* structure conceived as the key figure of human experience connects them both. However, this finding is less surprising than it may appear at first glance, because both ideas emerge from an insight going back to Aristotle: an entity can only be an entity if it is apprehended *as* being an entity (*ens qua ens*). Cassirer, however, *also* qualifies this thesis. According to him, there is not just one 'structure of explicitness of its own' of a phenomenon, but actually a multitude of them. Consequently, anything will be conceived *as* being something *else* as well. Cassirer (PsF I, 33/100) points out very clearly: 'every [...] element of consciousness is represented in and through another'. *That* is Cassirer's core message. Take the example of the simple line, with the line being perceived in totally different ways (scientific, mythical, aesthetic, and so on). This leads us to the next point, at which Cassirer and Heidegger's paths diverge: the importance attributed to the objective mind, of culture in this process, with Cassirer acknowledging and Heidegger denying an intrinsic relationship (at the time at least). It is here that the projects of both Cassirer and Heidegger each start to take their own specific shape, as was mentioned above.

Artificial symbolism. Indeed, 'seeing as we interpret' means we have already moved from the level of subjective consciousness (which is to a limited extent pre-lingual) to language as a symbolic system (PsF I, 39–41/105–107). That lies in the 'we', referring to a community of language users. There is, in a sense, a fundamental difference between natural symbolism (of the subjective mind) and artificial symbolism of the cultural systems (of the objective mind). The difference lies in the dynamic nature of subjective consciousness – the heart throb of consciousness that simultaneously establishes thousands (visual, conceptual and categorical) connections (PsF III 232/203) – whereas factual, existing symbolic systems are based on connections existing within the symbolic system between on the one hand a sensory sign (in modern language: signifier) and meaning (in modern language: the signified) on the other. Then again, in line with Cassirer's suggestion, the artificial symbolism (of language and culture) has an immediate effect on natural symbolism, with the 'contribution' of language adding momentum to pre-lingual symbolisation: 'The "first universal" is only guaranteed by the fact that it finds a hold and a firm precipitate in language' (PsF III, 129/116). Language does not name what is ready to be named, as even something preformed in experience will need language to take its final form: Language is a determining ('bestimmende') force (Göller 1988). Language adds structure to the entity of perception, thus endowing it with form and identity (GW 16/2003c, 241, 260, 280/1946, 17, 37, 61). Cassirer (GW 16/2003b, 80) likes quoting Wilhelm von Humboldt, to whom he owes so much: 'The same action of the mind that enables man to weave a web of language results in man being caught in the very web he waves. This means that ultimately it will be the medium of language, and nothing else, that tells him how to relate to visible objects and how to live'. That is why natural symbolism and artificial symbolism, subjective mind and objective mind, are intertwined. The sensory input of the subjective mind is until its most basic layers stamped by language and the external culture, by the objective mind, not only by its objective factual structure (the vocabulary), but also by its underlying conceptual principle, the way it structures the world: i.e. the shaping form, the 'inward form' in the parlance of Von Humboldt (*forma formans*), and the shaped form, the actual result (*forma formata*). The rationale for combining the objective mind and the subjective mind, under a single denominator is the fact that the two share a common function, namely that of representation (PsF I, 39–40/105–106). Representation is what is presupposed exclusively by consciousness in whatever empirical form – it is the deciding *a priori*. This consciousness builds, by representing reality, a world and culture, while excluding an unmediated presence to reality, as was shown before. Man will have to eliminate presence in order to arrive at representation: 'The concept must sublate ["aufheben"] "presence" in order to arrive at "representation"' (PsF III, 353/307). The immediate presence has to be erased, sublated. There is *no* access to reality unless through images, concepts, formula's (Kreis 2010, 100).

Theory of the concept. Cassirer's 'concept of concept' is in a sense his most basic concept. In his view, a concept is not the outcome of a process of abstraction that eliminates a list of aspects in sequence to leave only the core itself. Whilst defining for instance 'animal', we do not scrutinise everything that is alive, abstracting properties to look for common traits, if any. Indeed, such a procedure would already presuppose the concept being looked for. Instead, the concept, for example, of animal takes precedence. Indeed, any abstraction process presupposes the presence of what should be its outcome: the concept itself. A concept is not the outcome of a process of abstraction, but a 'proposal' to structure the world, actively stamping, determining the world of perception. The concept has primacy and it posits one particular characteristic as being characteristic, 'as being representative' of something (it *setzt*). As a result, it is not of the same order as that which is subordinated to it (that which is understood), but rather precedes it, as ι (ε_1, ε_2, ε_n). The content of the meaning, the intension or ι, precedes the set of elements (ε_1, ε_2, ε_n) subordinated to it. Here, Cassirer refers to Russell's concept of propositional function φ (x) – to which he adds his own meaning (PsF III, 340/295). He speaks of *Satzfunktion*, or propositional function: 'A propositional function in fact is an expression containing one or more undetermined constituents, such that, when values are assigned to these constituents, the expression becomes a proposition'. What does this mean? A propositional function is not an actual proposition or statement – it is an empty proposition, one that needs to be fulfilled to become a real proposition. An example of a propositional function would be: x is an animal. This is not a proposition that may or not be true, because it is empty. Substituting 'a horse' for x turns it into a proposition (which may or may not be true, and in this case it is true). A propositional function thus controls the truth value of factual propositions, while not being a proposition in itself.

What the argument boils down to is that the content (the intension) of a concept, ι, determines its scope (the extension), and thus gives rise to a purely intensional definition of class. The concept has primacy and defines the boundaries of its subordinated class of phenomena. But the intension, the concept is not an entity to be found somewhere but is fundamentally a function. That means that the concept itself is *not* part of the extension, is excluded from it: ι (ε_1, ε_n). Indeed, due to the fact that a concept, a conceptual meaning, is not an entity in itself but functions as a rule, it does not exist in itself outside its functioning. For example, in the sequence of the natural numbers, the unit itself does not exist independently of the series. Just like every addition presupposes the unit to be added in the sequence of natural numbers, so will the unit itself not appear as such, but instead it becomes productive by repeating itself: 1, 2, 3. And by using natural numbers and introducing a numerical order, we are able to count: 'there it is', 'there it is again', 'and again'. Indeed, crucial here is the priority of the conceptual or formal in respect of what is offered by the senses. Or, to phrase it differently: The empirical or sensory is informed by the ideal, the formal – the spiritual. As a result, the theory of concept allows for a broad application, whilst being applicable to the broad field of meaning as well. Meaning always implies its primacy: First the content of meaning is identified, and only as a next step will be determined what this might include. But the primacy is a *functional*, not an ontological one.

This means that Cassirer's theory of meaning takes on a specific quality, setting it apart from other theories. We will not discuss this in detail, but perhaps mentioning a few keywords will suffice. First and most fundamentally, it differs from the naturalistically flavoured semantics proposed by Dretske (1995) and Millikan. Here, dealing with meanings and intentions ultimately comes down to following natural patterns and natural regularities: the project of naturalizing the mind. Secondly, it differs from the pragmatic semantics as advocated by Dewey, the later Wittgenstein, Dummett and many others: 'meaning is use' (which does not quite do justice to Wittgenstein). But once again, the conceptual, in the sense of propositional knowing, is not given due attention. Thirdly, it is different from an empiricist type of semantics, where meaning goes back to sensory impressions ('sense datum'), with sensory impressions representing reality situated outside, duplicating or mirroring it. Finally, it differs from an idealistic type of semantics as proposed by Frege and Husserl for some time, with meanings leading a Platonic existence in the form of ideal images (for example in the sense that numbers would exist autonomously, independently of being thought). Cassirer could be ranked with the latter, idealistic group, bearing in mind that he rejects direct reference to pre-existing ideal objects. Reference in whichever form is never direct but is, in his view, always indirect and mediated by an inferential system with all the elements primarily inferring from each other. Contents of consciousness refer to other contents of consciousness and thus become endowed with meaning in the context of other meanings, fundamentally provided by language, in its objectivity. In the following, whenever mention will be made of the semantic theory of Cassirer, what is meant is this functional definition of meaning, which reflects the core of his philosophy.

In the final analysis, the 'mind' ('Spirit') becomes the all-embracing concept that includes both the subjective mind and the objective, trans-subjective mind. This means that at a subjective level consciousness adds meaning to all that is given, while reality is to be revealed from a variety of systems of meaning, symbolic forms on the objective level. Summarising Cassirer's views on idealism, the Spirit (the subjective and objective mind in their interrelatedness), can be equalled to the primacy of meaning – no more than that, but at least that. The Spirit is a meaning-generating instance, while what is generated by the various forms of the objective mind are objective meanings.

A moral motif. Idealism also comes with a moral motif. This was certainly true for the Neo-Kantianists, in their bid to counter the then prevailing scientific materialism and determinism. It creates the possibility to think of man as being removed from the causality of natural laws in order to safeguard freedom and responsibility. Highlighting the mind as an idealistic motif is also supposed to counter 'naturalisation of consciousness'. This was equally relevant in the case of Cassirer (PsF III, 353/307) in his fight against the 'brain metaphysics' of the time, whose arguments most likely differed little, if at all, from current 21st-century views. It is true that the mind is dependent on the senses and the material system to which the mind is tied, but it also expresses itself through them, thus shaping itself actively – as was shown repeatedly before. This has certain implications for the ethical domain that cannot easily be dismissed. Man is a determining and structuring being that transforms reality but shapes itself in the process as well, thus being capable of self-determination. As a result, man acquires freedom and responsibility, as opposed to the naturalistic and deterministic conception of man (Schwemmer 1997a, 127–195). In line with Cassirer's philosophy, a deterministic brand of the natural sciences would afford only one out of multiple perspectives on reality rather than reveal one single and ultimate reality. Regardless of any further elaboration, this would turn the debate on determinism into a moot point. Man is an *animal symbolicum* that does not coincide with its brain (GW 24/2006b, 31).

Objective mind. Ultimately, this primacy of symbolisation, of the mind, leads to an even more drastic qualification of nature. Instead of offering a fundamental explanation in itself, nature is the outcome of a particular type of symbolisation and thus becomes part of culture. This may seem like a big leap, but it is in keeping with the argumentation. Culture is not only something that is opposed to nature, and nature (of the life world as well as of natural sciences) in fact becomes part of culture and, consequently, of the objective mind. Qualifying Cassirer's philosophy as a philosophy of culture would therefore be misleading, and can easily led us astray if the concept of culture is understood in its limited sense, as is commonly the case. Indeed, Cassirer offers us also a philosophy of nature, namely a philosophy of the nature in the life world as well as the nature of the natural sciences. Then again it should be borne in mind that nature, either interpreted as the nature of the natural sciences or that of the life world, is not a nature *an sich* but is charged with meaning – for example as being overwhelming, as taking its own course, as being mathematically definable, as being unfathomable, etcetera. Nature *is* also culture. A more apposite qualification than 'philosophy of culture' would therefore be 'philosophy of the objective mind', of the symbolic forms (Kreis, 2010, 307–328). This may prevent misinterpretation and is more adequate. Indeed, the objective mind is not a metaphysical actor, an entity creating culture, but is the inner and outer form that culture takes.

2.5 The Concept of a Symbolic Form

The pluriform landscape of cultural domains and the variety of forms of access to reality prompt Cassirer to use the plural (symbolic forms). This multiple quality is essential, seeing that reality is inexhaustible – any attempt at symbolisation falls short by definition, leaving a reminder for other forms of symbolisation, or other symbolic forms. The inadequacy of any symbolic form explains the title of his chef d'oeuvre: *Philosophie der symbolischen Formen* ('The Philosophy of Symbolic Forms'). It was published in three volumes, which appeared in 1923, 1925 and 1929, respectively. In these works, he discusses language (Volume 1), myth and religion (Volume 2), and the epistemology of science (Volume 3), with the third volume also offering an overview of the systematics – which he had not yet developed in 1923. At a later time, a final volume (Volume 4) was edited, containing articles and notes from his literary legacy, which dealt with the subject of symbolisation (Cassirer 1996). Although there may be some difference in the phrasing and approach to the theme over a twenty-year period, there is no substantial break to be assumed (Truwant 2015).

He refers to this research using the term 'phenomenology' – phenomenology of language, of knowledge. In this context, 'phenomenology' refers undoubtedly to Hegel, not to Husserl – although Cassirer in his actual analyses is closely related to Husserl's phenomenology (Möckel 2014). However, Cassirer's description of the various types of meaning (*Sinn*) from both a systematic and a historical perspective reflects also a Hegelian motif. The *Philosophie der symbolischen Formen* was actually conceived as a counterpoint to Hegel's *Phänomenologie des Geistes*, be it set in a different age, using different means and based on a different ambition (Capeillères 2003; Möckel 2004a, 126; 2004b;

Verene 2011). He even considered including the term 'phenomenology' into the general title of his key work and only at a very late point in the publishing process the general title was changed from 'Phenomenology of Knowledge: Fundamental Features of a Theory of Spiritual Forms of Expression' into 'The Philosophy of Symbolic Forms' (Krois and Verene 1996, xvii). Connecting Neo-Kantianism with Hegel is not as unlikely as it may seem at first glance. Hegel's criticism of Kant – his rigorous dichotomy of perception and ratio – is in line with the criticism voiced by the Marburg Kantians. And just like Cassirer regards the whole of reality as being experienced from a perspective of meaning, Hegel argues that experience is always mediated (*vermittelt*). History offers us yet another point of both agreement and difference. Kant envisaged a universally valid truth – universal synchronicity – whereas Hegel put the emphasis on history, or diachrony. As opposed to Hegel, Cassirer does not regard history as ever coming to a close but will nevertheless, in agreement with Hegel, suppose to be one principle universally underlying *all* historical forms of relationship towards the world: mind, spirit, Which in Cassirer's case is not to be conceived as an entity, a substance, as Hegel is supposed to do (1996, 165). However, in Cassirer's view this history includes a genealogy and even a teleology of the symbolic forms – an internal development, receding from a subjective and concrete stance towards an objective and formal, functional attitude, to be viewed as a progression, a liberation.

Cassirer attempts to reconcile the two extremes, by maintaining the general validity of principles while giving due credit to the broad and varied quality of culture. This ambition is not that remarkable, considering that all of the post-Kantian philosophy is actually run through with this issue. At least three options present themselves: there are only stories (historism), *or* among the wide variety of stories, there is only one truly valid story (Enlightenment) *or*, as a final option, one single valid story lies concealed *within* this whole range of stories (Hegel). Cassirer chooses to embrace the final Hegelian option which, in light of Cassirer's somewhat restricted, conflict-avoiding personality, is hardly a modest ambition – he is indeed the most Hegelian of all Neo-Kantians. Ultimately, it is not a program than can be completed by a single person, no matter how much learning and life experience this person may bring. This is exactly what might make this project so appealing: Rather than ever being completed, the appeal lies in its quality as a programme that is destined to be fragmented in its execution and can never aspire to full completion.

The 'factual stories', that which has occurred, are conceived quite broadly by Cassirer. As was mentioned before, initially he includes myth and religion, art, language, and science. The idea is to establish a historical or diachronous order of things, a 'genealogy': First there is myth and religion, then language, then modern science – although 'cross-connections' can be identified, as will be discussed later. Later he adds arts, technology, morality and law, and history, each of which is elaborated to some degree. The list gives the impression of a rather mixed bag, and in the Cassirer literature – quite understandably – there is some debate going on about the exact number of symbolic forms. Should we regard them as an open or closed? Krois (1987) makes a case for openness, Lofts (2000) argues in favour of a closed set. There is enough evidence to suggest that Cassirer was still in doubt as to which knowledge practice should rightfully be called a symbolic form. Still, only language, myth and religion, and science are given full elaboration. Before the question of the exact number of symbolic forms can be addressed, we first need to look at the criteria that are supposed to be met for a cultural domain, as a knowledge and action system, to qualify as a symbolic form.

Three characteristics. Not every claim to knowledge, either in its broad or narrowed-down sense, will be able to meet the necessary criteria. In order to reconstruct Cassirer's line of thought, three prerequisites must be fulfilled. First of all, it should bear the hallmarks of revealing reality: its design should be fundamental enough and its orientation broad enough to make it global as well as world-making. Secondly, a symbolic form must be essentially social, being accepted as a self-evident knowledge/action practice shared by a broad community. Thus, language, science and religion all presuppose the presence of a community of language users, science practitioners, etcetera. In the case of language this is quite evident, as it institutes a community. Cassirer assumes (GW 16/2003c, 280/1946, 61): 'For it is language that makes his existence in a *community* possible; and only in society, in relation to a "They", can his subjectivity assert itself as a "Me"'. Yet this prerequisite would also apply to other forms, sometimes referred to as life forms (which is explicitly true in the case of myth). Each symbolic form is therefore a socially instituted life form: a social structuring practice, which thus provides social stability (Kreis 2010, 307–328). This means that a symbolic form has therefore a normative quality: It 'is', but more than that it 'is valid', be it only within its own specific domain. Both language user and science practitioner can be held accountable for their actions and words, in respect of their claims to justice, standards of correctness, possibly even in terms of veracity ('do you really mean what you're saying?'). What is essential here is the acknowledgment *that* standards of a particular type are at work, and that their specific content will vary according to time and place whilst functioning in their own right – to match the general quality of a symbolic form.

Summing up, the three characteristics of a symbolic form would then be as follows: (1) offering access to reality, (2) the presence of a social infrastructure, and (3) normative validity. On further consideration, these characteristics prove to reflect the nature of intentional phenomena, be it on a higher level of generality. Indeed, as was explained in Chapter 1, intentional phenomena are characterised as being (1) interpretative, (2) socially embedded, and (3) essentially normative. Indeed, these qualifications apply not only to the level of intentional phenomena, but also to each of the three levels of the human condition. A key concept in this respect is that of a *rule*. A rule defines a standard against which phenomena can be interpreted and that holds sway within a particular social order (Mooij 1991, 69–87). For example, in the world of sports, based on a set of regulations (i.e. the standard) developed by a specific community, an infinitesimal difference of a couple of milliseconds might be conceived as being decisive in distinguishing between winning *or* losing a competition, (+ / –), along with all its associated trappings of flag display, ambitions, disappointments, frustration, etcetera. The physical event remains a phenomenon of nature, but it becomes transformed into a rule-driven cultural phenomenon. Thus, the establishing of rules does not merely touch the very core of intentional phenomena, but it actually marks the transition to a state of culture. Of course, this does not qualify sports as a symbolic form, but this example will make clear what a symbolic form is actually about – unifying multiple levels of revealing reality (intentional phenomena, their hierarchies within a world, and their nomenclature). Indeed, the same qualifications can be found here, be it on a higher, more generalised level, namely that of the symbolic form. The sports example also demonstrates what culture actually *is:* its arbitrariness, the cutting off as well as the bonding that it brings, the madness, the excess, etcetera. More than just Goethe, culture also includes Formula 1 car racing.

The number of symbolic forms. Rather than just one symbolic form there are multiple forms – which follows logically from the concept itself – but their number is not limitless. So what is a symbolic form, and what is not? The three characteristics represent the criteria that a candidate must meet to qualify as a symbolic form. Essentially, language as a whole does meet these criteria (but the more detailed discussion later on will have to make clear if this is truly the case). Language is the gateway to reality, and access is provided based on grammatical, semantic and pragmatic rules that all language users – all members of a particular language community – must obey. The same applies to the mythical and religious conception of the world: Reality manifests itself in a particular way, while there is also a community adhering to religious standards. Modern science would qualify as well, considering that nothing falls outside its scope, while imposing a unique set of demands that must be met by the scientific community. Here, a symbolic form differs from its actual specification. Any given religion, language or science is of course not a symbolic form in itself, but instead offers a specification of its associated symbolic form. So where does this approach leave philosophy? Cassirer fails to address this issue – according to his line of thought, philosophy does not represent a symbolic form because, although its scope covers the whole of reality, it does not aim to reveal reality as such. Philosophy is a reflexive discipline that focuses on the conditions of possibility of access to reality whatsoever. The same would be true for ethics as a normative, reflexive, philosophical theory, not providing specific morals but reflecting on the possibility of a moral point of view as such and in its diversity (Kreis 2010, 449–455). Indeed, ethics may not qualify as a symbolic form, but morality and law may do so whether conceived as a symbolic form in itself or conceived as being part of the symbolic form of language – in a broad comprehensive definition (see below). In both cases, 'anything' can be perceived from either the perspective of morality or the perspective of law. Having its own socially embedded and binding form of access to reality, technology also appears to satisfy the symbolic form criteria; or being part of modern science conceived as a symbolic form (see below). It is obvious that we in all these cases are dealing with highly generalised and open forms of access to reality, with issues of demarcation – 'can this still be called science, is this still religion, is this art?' – that cannot be addressed in an unequivocal or procedural manner.

And what about art? Cassirer's mentioning of the arts may need some explanation. Although at first Cassirer only refers to art as a symbolic form in passing, his qualification is quite consistent (GW 24/2006b, 149–183). Why should this merit our attention? Because it means that he endows art with the function of revealing reality. Rather than offering an image of an already established reality, art reveals the way things are and the way people live their lives. Just like language and science provide us with an schematized or abbreviated form of reality, so does art offer an intensified and substantiated type of reality, revealing the shapes of things and of life through images, sounds, rhythms and gestures rather than through concepts: 'It is one of the ways leading to an objective view of things and of human life. It is not an imitation but a disclosure [...], an intensification of reality' (GW 24/2006b, 155). This function is a common trait shared by all art forms and genres through the ages, connecting historical art forms and genres with the 'aesthetic experience' that also falls within the scope of art: offering an authentic form of disclosing reality. This is precisely where Cassirer's and Kant's paths diverge, one may assume. Kant distinguishes sharply between what he calls 'aesthetic universality' and 'objective validity' (which belongs to our scientific judgements). With Kant, the judgment of beauty is not the product of a defining (*bestimmende*) faculty of judgement that would lead to determination of the object, but is produced by the reflexive, contemplating faculty of judgement – according to the classical and still prevailing interpretation of Kant. This reflexive capacity considers the already formed object and world, putting it in a new perspective, but does not constitute a world itself in its objectivity. However, Cassirer argument is: The artist chooses a certain aspect of reality, but this process of selection is at the same time a process of objectification (GW 24/2006b, 158). As a result, art *does* offer knowledge and insight and even leads to the truth. In doing so Cassirer might even have been more close to Kant than one might suppose. Indeed actual studies in Kant undermine the assumed sharp dichotomy between objectification and reflection within the classical interpretation of Kant, proposing a new reading of the *Critique of Judgement.* (Kuypers 1972; Henrich 1994). Indeed, Cassirer (GW 8/2001, 261–346) developed his own philosophy after having reread thoroughly Kant's Third Critique, the *Critique of Judgement* – and after having edited for the first time the original Introduction of Kant's Third Critique (which was lost until then). However it may be, Cassirer's unique proposal proved to be fruitful. It was later on adopted and referred to by, for example, Suzanne Langer (1953) and otherwise by Nelson Goodman (1978), both being directly influenced by Cassirer.

In fact, there are other views of art that bear similarities to Cassirer's view. Here are some keywords. Although not intentionally, Merleau-Ponty (1964, 32) offered a substantiation when explaining his views – or at least we might be able to distil one. What a painter or a sculptor does – he mentions examples like Cézanne, Matisse, Klee and Rodin – is show the creation, the birth of man and of objects, even before they have actually become 'a thing' or 'a man'. Indeed, art offers an intensification of reality. The visual arts, to which he actually refers, explicitly shows this act of birth. What a painter does, is to show the birth of seeing, not in the form of an object but as something that unfolds in tandem with the act of seeing a painting. Just like Merleau-Ponty unwittingly sharpens Cassirer's views on art, so does Ricœur (1978), who as a thinker is close to Cassirer (Adams 2015) presents a related view as well, without actually realising it. Art offers an alternative form of 'seeing-as' as well as an alternative form of 'being-as' ('voir-comme', 'être-comme'). Finally, we should mention Gadamer's views on art. These are also closely related to Cassirer's views in the sense that, unlike Kant, he sees art as an true form of access to reality. However, where Gadamer (1985), in his book 'Truth and Method' ('Wahrheit und Methode') in line with Heidegger, recognises a difference in hierarchy and contrasts the 'truth' of art with the 'method' of science, Cassirer rejects such a contrast. He postulates that both art and science lead to truth – although different paths are used to attain it. Indeed, where Gadamer recognises an opposition between 'truth' and 'method', Cassirer, in line with Cohen's Neo-Kantianism, claims: 'truth *is* the method' (GW 16/2003d, 483). Truth is the outcome of the method which, in the case of Cassirer, does not rely only on logics and ethics, but on the diversity of the products of the human spirit, including myth, religion and art.

Cassirer's approach. Examples mentioned so far include myth and religion, art, language, ethics and law, science, technology. At its very heart lies – based on an obvious hierarchy – the threesome of myth and religion, language, and science. To each a part of the principal work has been devoted, and they will be discussed in more detail in the next section. But first we need to outline Cassirer's approach, which has already been mentioned in passing. How exactly does he address the issue of the relationship between factuality and general validity? As we saw, Cassirer proceeds along familiar Neo-Kantian lines by taking the fact of culture as a starting point for his inquiry into its possibility: 'The course of our investigation leads us, as always trough the world of forms, through the region of the objective spirit, from where, by a process of reconstruction, we seek access to the realm of subjectivity' (PsF III, 74/67). Indeed, the view that dictates how things are perceived cannot be perceived as if it were a thing itself. Instead, it needs to be reconstructed (PsF III, 345/300). That defines the transcendental method, as being adopted by Cassirer as well (PsF III, 49–63/45–57, 119/107, 345/300). To this end, Cassirer employs a variety of empirical data (taken from religion, ethnographics, linguistics, natural sciences), while not actually engaging in science as such. What he does is take the facts (as they present themselves at a given time) as a starting point. His ambition however is to describe, based on this material, the conceptual infrastructure of a mythical world, a linguistic world and a scientific world. And, more precisely, to offer a categorical analysis of the various symbolic forms by describing the fundamental categories that inform the associated forms of consciousness and that serve to structure the corresponding worlds. We may want to compare it cautiously to what Kant refers to as 'objective transcendental deduction': the justification ('deduction') of the applicability and validity of categories, thus creating a field of objectivity, of validity. The deviation from the project is not found in its actual nature, as was observed before, but in the expansion of its territory (which once again brings the need for a modification in this approach).

The solution he offers to the basic problem, that of facticity and universality, is essentially quite simple. The basic categories in which symbolisation takes place are universal – referred to as 'qualities' – but each take a specific shape, based on the corresponding symbolic form: They are 'modalised'. He uses the paired concepts of 'quality' and 'modalisation' to bring out the *invariant* basic structure *as well as* the historical *variation* of experience (PsF I, 27–29/95–97).

Both components are essential: paying tribute to historical variation and to universality. It is Cassirer's Hegelian vein, once again. Each symbolic form constitutes in its limitation a valid access to reality, which limitation brings another symbolic form into being. Describing these forms of revealing reality in a historical and systematic way turns Cassirer's 'The Philosophy of Symbolic Forms' into a counterpart of Hegel's 'Phenomenology of the Spirit', as has been demonstrated. Yet, it has been worked out in a Neo-Kantian fashion – a categorical analysis. The fundamental question would then present itself as to what he considers to be valid categories. Here, he follows the well-established path of Neo-Kantianism. His orientation is on Kant, but only loosely so. Fundamental categories would be space, time, number, causality and subject. They return (invariantly) in each symbolic form, while variably acquiring a different filling in. Obviously, the spatial concepts of the myth, of the life world and of modern mathematics differ widely among each other, but they do present themselves as a variation on the theme of juxtaposition, of 'next to each other'. The same would apply to time: modalisation of time thus produces variations on the theme of 'after each other' as well as to causality. Indeed, myth has its own form of causality (for example, in the sense of magic), which differs from the causality associated with the life world or the modern natural sciences. Moreover, we may distinguish categories that are not universal but that would only apply to one special symbolic form. The thing-attribute relationship defines both language and the life world, but is absent in the case of the myth and of science in its purest form. A typical difference with Kant is – as was observed before – that Kant does not qualify space and time as categories (of thought) but as forms of intuition. Also, 'number' and 'subject' (the 'I' in language, in myth) cannot be met with in Kant. Particularly noteworthy is the introduction of the subject as a category. Kant does leave room for a subject, but it is a different type of subject: the subject included in 'I think' (*Ich denke*), which is supposed to accompany all representations, without which any representation would be possible, thus safeguarding the unity of experience as well as its objectivity. Cassirer's role of the 'subject-as-category' is fundamentally different, however. This subject is correlated to a specific symbolic form and, being functionally linked to a specific type of symbolic forming, cannot not exist outside it. As a result, 'the' subject will be broken up into a variety of subjective conditions, each of which is linked to a particular symbolic form: the subject existing within language, within myth, and within science, respectively.

Modalisation is the second tool employed by Cassirer (next to category or quality). It turns out to possess a 'logic' that leads from concrete to abstract. This 'logic' is more or less embedded in the hierarchy that exists *among* the various symbolic forms: from the concrete quality of the myth, through language, to abstract science. The same route, the same 'logic' or genealogy, can be identified in the trajectory followed by the categories *within* a given symbolic form: again from concrete to abstract, with the body fulfilling a key role, namely as point of departure. This is well illustrated by the category of the number. Initially tied to the body – the counting of the fingers or toes – a number goes on to be objectified, eventually taking the form of a formal quality, removed from experience, only conceived as being thought. A similar trajectory, with the body as point of departure, is followed in the development of spatial orientation, in causality, each of which, through objectification in language and formalisation in mathematics and natural sciences, is increasingly detached from the immediate bodily perception. Indeed, in this logic we see a genealogy, a dialectics at work. Either a specific symbolic form or a level of symbolisation within a symbolic form will turn out to be insufficient, inadequate, paving the way for a new level of symbolization, an other symbolic form. Equipped with these conceptual tools, an analysis of the various symbolic forms will now be possible.

2.6 Myth and Religion, Language, Science

Language. Language was the first symbolic form explored by Cassirer. This may be surprising in itself. The sequence adopted by Cassirer to describe the symbolic forms respectively (when compiling his chef d'oeuvre) is obviously not congruent with the historical development leading from myth to language and on to science. Indeed, the relationship is also more complicated, the more so because language fulfils a pivotal role in the overall structure. This may also explain why it is the first symbolic form dealt with by Cassirer. By doing so he conceives language as the fundamental form of revealing reality. Although language has obviously been a topic of interest throughout the history of philosophy, from Plato to Leibniz, this is more or less a first in terms of endowing language with a constitutive function. Earlier attempts in this direction had been made by Herder (1844–1803) and Von Humboldt (1767–1835), to whom Cassirer readily refers. Kant had made no such attempt, for which he was criticised by Herder early on. Cassirer however, attributes a key role to language, relegating myth and science to a secondary position. Which is understandable: Man had been able to survive without modern science for quite a long time, and would most certainly have been able to do so in the absence of myth, but it simply could not have done 'without language'. Indeed, language has cross-connections with other symbolic forms, which it actually underpins. Thus, more than just one of the symbolic forms, language appears to be the symbolic form par excellence, serving as a role model. Cassirer may not have stated this explicitly, but his philosophy is certainly run through with this notion. Here we recognise the fundamental ideas of the so-called *linguistic turn*, which has put such a firm mark on 20th-century philosophy. True to form, however, Cassirer is reluctant to draw far-reaching conclusions.

In line with his trusted approach, Cassirer relies mostly on the linguistics of the time, with its strong historical and grammatical overtones. This introduces a limitation, considering that he obviously was unable to take account of paradigms developed later within the linguistic sciences. Subsequently, they are the structuralist linguistic movement introduced by Saussure (from the 1920s onwards), Chomsky's transformational-generative approach (since the 1960s), and finally the multitude of empirically flavoured movements, with their strong emphasis on the social component of language (also in reaction to Chomsky, who chose to disregard this component). This limitation is inevitable, being embedded in the prerequisite to take the fact of language as a starting point, to be clarified by linguistics. (A phenomenology in Husserl's sense would start with its own phenomenology of language – not so Cassirer, however.) It is remarkable though that Cassirer should have included all three approaches, in his own unique way. In fact he was anticipating structural linguistics that he was effectively ignorant about and which was still in its infancy. What connects him with Chomsky is the latter's 'rationalism' and the presupposition of a fundamental capacity in man. With Chomsky, this is the innate language competence, while Cassirer speaks in terms of a generalised symbolic function (which he conceives in a more functional way, less 'ontical' compared to Chomsky). What sets him apart from Chomsky, whilst connecting him with the orientation that emerged after Chomsky, is his focus on the social component of language.

What leaps to the eye here is the strong affiliation with the structural approach. Only a couple of years earlier, Saussure's (1986) lectures had been published under the title 'Course in General Linguistics' ('Cours de linguistique générale'), and only later, while seeking refuge in the United States, Cassirer would meet the great champion of the structuralist movement of the time, Roman Jakobson (who would later become a close friend of Lacan's). From Cassirer's perspective, language is a system of signs, with sign and system functioning as correlative concepts, and a linguistic element or sign acquiring meaning only within the context of overall structure. This might well qualify as a structural approach, and the fact that we may recognise some degree of similarity to later structuralism can hardly be surprising, considering that Cassirer describes the culture and the mind in terms of a system made up of relationships, its terms referring to each other (Cassirer GW 24/2007c).

Obviously, he is not practising a historical or structural form of linguistics, nor a philosophy of language. Again he takes 'the fact' as point of departure – in this case the fact of language, more particularly the fact that a lingual articulation of the world exists, which would allow him to inquire into the possibility of access to reality. In his view, what is essential for a language to qualify as such is possessing the function of objectification, of making a statement on the state of affairs. This is the underlying principle of the type of access of reality brought about by language. A sign language or a language that limits itself to expressing emotion only would not be a language in that sense. A language does not qualify as such until it offers the capacity to represent the state of affairs, to make statements such as: 'The grass is green', 'I have a bicycle'. At the heart of language lies the proposition or statement. The possibility to make a statement in the first place – the propositional function, that of objectification (*Darstellung*) – is therefore vital to the function of language. No language can be imagined without this particular possibility. This can be inferred from an 'ideating analysis', such as: 'We cannot imagine language in any other way than as being fundamentally propositional'. Language can be imagined without expression or even without formalisation, but not without objectification as its outcome, because then it would lose the function attributed to it.

What underlies this function of objectification? It is based on the generality that is inherent to language. A limited set of language means (words and rules) offers an infinite number of possibilities. Then again, Cassirer argues that language does not provide the primary form of universality, which function is fulfilled by the pre-linguistic consciousness, namely by means of 'vortices' or 'nuclei' in the flow of consciousness (as was shown in the foregoing). These are the first means of representation, the 'first universals'. However, this potential is exploited and optimised by language through positing characteristics (*Merkmalsetzung*). Adding markers asserts its unity but, much more importantly, it generates a unity that did not exist before. Thus, language posits (*setzt*) therefore its own general quality and meaning – the primacy in language lies with meaning. Indeed, we may speak of a semantic theory of language, revolving around content of meaning, rather than the formal syntax or social interaction of pragmatics.

The second question that Cassirer must address would be whether the lingual relationship towards the world might actually produce potentially valid knowledge. With Kant, the categorical structure – the relationship of phenomena towards the forms of intuition (of space and time) and categories (such as causality) and apriori judgements – is supposed to safeguard this. Loosely orientating himself on Kant, Cassirer demonstrates that language fulfils this function, adding as it does a categorical structure through the categories of time, space, number and subject. For what is specific to language (and the life world) this adds the new category of thing-property relationship. A substantial part of the first book of 'The Philosophy of Symbolic Forms' is devoted to the inquiry into the categorical structuring introduced by language, including the mode of counting, spatial definitions and the various interpretations of time ('the times'). And as is to be expected from Cassirer: including a wealth of material. A new element compared to Kant is the introduction of the subject as a category: in this case the subject being implied in language. This position is opened up by the introduction of the personal pronoun, for example, but there is more. The subject in language may also show itself in the form of a possessive pronoun as well as in the conjugated forms of the verb, etcetera. This in itself proves that the subject-in-language can manifest itself subtly, in a variety of nuances, allowing a whole gamut of 'subject involvement' to be expressed, which will differ for each language or language group, and by extension also for each culture or region. Ordinary language thus becomes the essential tool of nuance, enabling forms of I-involvement, of commitment, of intentional commitment to be represented.

This does not alter the fact that the propositional function of objectification (*Darstellung*) is essential to language – it is its core task. But it has other functions as well. For example, Cassirer introduces the function of 'below' and 'above': 'Below' the objectifying level we find the level of expression or imitation (the 'sensuous level'): 'ouch' as an expression of pain, or the word 'boo' to describe the sound made by a cow (imitation). A sheer expression does not yet represent language, but language does have an expressive function ('help!'). Even the interjection, a sentence made up of just a single word ('help!'), the 'holophrase' (often mentioned by Lacan), is still a sentence, and is therefore part of a structure, ending up being incorporated into the attribution of meaning. The sphere of expression also includes what Cassirer defines as the sensuous aspect of language: vocalisation, intonation, which often represents a Gestalt itself with mimics and bodily expression. Most likely it connects language and the use of language with prelingual behavioural patterns, which go on to be embedded in the texture of language. (Cassirer pays little heed to the role of motor functions – it is particularly Gehlen (1966) who will take this up in his later, more empirically flavoured anthropology). Also the mood of the life world – its easy-going or refractory quality, as the case may be – will be reflected in this layer of language (of mimics and pantomimics). There is also an 'above': Superimposed on the propositional, objectifying level we find the level of pure relations, finding its full manifestation in logic. And just like pure expression does not yet represent language, neither does pure formalisation. A purely formal language needs common language, if only appearing at its fringes, to be empirically embedded and interpreted.

As mentioned before, the three levels found *within* the symbolic form, in this case language – expression, objectification, formalisation – correspond to the mutual distinctions *between* the symbolic forms – myth, language, science. Like any symbolic form essentially is made up of three levels – expression, objectification and formalisation – for each symbolic form one particular level will stand out as being the core function of the corresponding symbolic form. We saw that for language this is objectification, for myth it is expression and for science, pure meanings or formalisation. This concludes the discussion of language, so now we will move on to myth and modern science.

Myth and religion. Myth, with religion following on, will emerge from the level of imitation or *Ausdruck* (expression). This is where both its roots and its core function can be found. Just like language takes up a special position, so can the introduction of myth as a symbolic form come as a surprise – its status, that is, not the fact itself. However, in modernity we witnessed the world of philosophy gradually taking interest in myth, which ended up in Schelling' s project of a philosophy of myth in the 19th century (PsF II, 4–16/3–10). This interest in myth and religion was evident from the rise of hermeneutics as well. The dominant force of the natural sciences effectively discredited the world image created by myth and religion, whilst at the same time the emerging humanities supplied religious studies with the tools required to interpret or explain it as a historical phenomenon. This would lead, for example, to the project developed by Bultmann (1964), a theologian who set out to transform religious tenets, based on a mythical mode of experience, into a modern discourse – the project of demythologisation (since the 1920s, in Marburg, where Heidegger was lecturing). But that was a different question from the one raised by Cassirer. Cassirer was not merely interested in the fact of myth as a historical phenomenon or in its 'translation' or 'actualisation' into modern-day idiom, but in testing its validity (from a Neo-Kantian perspective), in the inherent validity of myth itself.

What certainly helped him answer this question was the presence of the Warburg library in Hamburg, where he was lecturing at the time. The library owned a great deal of relevant historical material, which did much to stimulate his efforts. As in the discussion of language, he used the material available at the time, which may cause the documentation to appear somewhat dated. And yet the question itself is as relevant as ever: the supposed validity of the mythical form of experience. The myth may have lost much of its authority in modernity, but this is *not* true for the mode of experience on which the myth is based and which is still fully at work today – in fact, it is 'of all times'. While language is connected with the propositional experience, the myth is tied to the non-propositional experience (or pre-predicative experience). Demonstrating the legitimacy of this mode of experience is the second new contribution made by the project of the symbolic forms. The second volume of the main work is devoted to this pursuit. For reasons of space, this second volume will be discussed more succinctly than the first (devoted to language). In fact, this summary fails to do justice to the work itself, which is particularly rich in quality, with Cassirer truly coming into his own.

The essence of the mythical world can be summarised briefly as: The world has an human 'face'. Particularly in a period of time where the myth (including religion) has effectively vanished as a valid symbolic form, we can form ourselves an image of this mythical form of life and yearn back to it. This feeling of yearning is understandable, with the myth offering a perspective that is quite inescapable, as man is being faced with the bleak alternative of living in an anonymous and infinite universe. The mythical world offered something different instead: a world in which man seems himself reflected, a world with a human face. Rather than representing a structure made up of anonymous forces, events taking place in the world have a dramatic quality, in which magic is a dominant force (Mauss 1954). Then the Sacred enters stage and the drama gains substance through the presence of powers, of superhuman forces called gods which, either personified or not, have human characteristics and engage in relationships with man (and vice versa). These gods manifest themselves in privileged places which for that reason are shielded or secluded. This is what brings the notion of the sacred (*sacer*) into being: the space that must not be entered, the words that must not be spoken (Otto 1929). By virtue of the sacred being introduced, next to it we see the profane emerge. This distinction between the sacred and profane reflects the essence of the mythical world, commonly to be made in the field of religious studious (especially in Cassirer's time). But he goes a step further, reinterpreting this distinction as being a dichotomy, a mean of symbolisation. Indeed, at the heart of the mythical mode of experience lies the specific form of symbolisation found in the sacred/profane dichotomy. This is what Cassirer refers to as the basic opposition, the *Grundgegensatz* (PsF II, 87–97/73–82). Likewise, the mythical form of symbolisation works with oppositions, for the very reason that each form of symbolisation is about separating and distinguishing, as is written in *Genesis*. Indeed, according Biblical theology 'create' in Hebrew ('bara') means 'separate'. Complementing Cassirer, the process is accompanied by the creation of a void, in this case as the result of a commandment, a ban referring to the sacred: 'Thou shalt not….' It encircles a space, it creates a void. Hence, this form of symbolisation pervades human actions and life as a whole. And it produces a community because of the social bond it forges, while offering direction of action and stabilisation of feeling as well. Thus, myth represents a symbolic form.

However, in a mythical world even this separation is of a relative nature. In its turn, the sacred, the superhuman, supernatural power pervades the profane, manifesting itself in privileged places (rather than being perpetually absent or removed). Indeed, the sacred participates in the profane, shows its presence there, or crosses its path. Also Christianity offers, in the field of monotheistic religions, a clear example of these paths crossing in the doctrine of the history of salvation versus the profane history. In fact, the Eucharist, or Holy Supper (in the Lutheran tradition) offers a clear example of the kind of presence involved in this type of representation. It is just ordinary wine and bread, but then again it is also the flesh and blood of Christ. Rationalism is forced to offer an explanation based on thought constructs ('transsubstantiation', a transition from one substance to the other), but it poses no problem at all to the mythical mode of experience. There is a real presence ('presentia realis') corresponding to a phenomenon known to all. Objects that once belonged to a person may represent this person to such an extent that the object itself reflects the presence of this person in a materialised form (like in a piece of jewellery, or a pen). And when this person has gone, it is often difficult for people close to him to 'get rid of it', because it may feel like one is actually getting rid of the person who owned it. Thus, on the one hand the piece of jewellery represents the person (before their death), while on the other, (after their death) he or she becomes part of this object, as a symbolic figure by virtue of their personal characteristics, that which together makes this person what he or she was. The types of examples signify a first step towards symbolisation, we could say, namely the creation of a matrix. A separation is introduced, but only in part. Rather than witnessing a transition from one substance to the next one, according to the Roman Catholic doctrine, we see a symbolisation or representation carried through only halfway. From a genealogical perspective, it represents a halfway step. Yet more than that, it a form of symbolisation in its own right, in its own way.

Cassirer designs the inquiry into the mythical form of revealing reality, in the same way as his inquiry into language, which is why a brief summary will suffice here. This form of revealing reality, is essentially expressive or intuitive. It proceeds along Gestalts and images and is not discursive, as was discussed in the foregoing. What we see is a coalescing or coinciding of image and object, where a separation between image and object is introduced as well as negated. The next question, that of validity, leads us to the categories. Again we recognise categories of space, time and number as well as of causality, of subject. The category of thing-and-attribute, however, is missing, belonging as it does to propositional language. The time of myth refers to a primal time and is circular in nature; its spaces are interlinked, while its causality refers to magical intervention. This is all about us, not about the individualised me.

Cassirer argues that out of the myth came religion and, ultimately, a purely monotheistic form of religion, which is or is supposed to be critical of the myth. This process purification is referred to as the dialectics of mythical consciousness. The monotheistic represents the end of the myth as well as of religion (through a ban on images, which might well be regarded as the hallmark of monotheism), by highlighting the empty space of 'I am who I am', and by introducing the element of the future in the concept of time within religious consciousness. Notwithstanding, monotheism remains firmly rooted in the mythical mode of experience: the human face of the cosmos expressed through the existence of God. Conversely, the human face itself can be seen as divine, representing a new variety of this religious form. The face would be sacred ('sanctus') in that it becomes impregnable, as understood by Levinas (1969). And so we leave Cassirer's range of examples, but certainly not the underlying notion. Indeed, even a 'religion of the face' is still a form of religion, rooted in a mythical mode of experience: the vulnerability, not of individual man, but of any human being. It's true, mythical consciousness is not confined to the prehistory of man but, according to Cassirer, actually constitutes the first layer of all human experience. Cassirer (PsF III, 88/78) likes to cite Hegel: 'The features which the spirit seems to have left behind it are also present in its depth'. This applies here to the sphere of 'aisthèsis', of perception preceding the objectifying intuition through language: the human aspect of the cosmos, the physiognomy of the landscape. Just like the mythical form of representation precedes the objectifying form of representation, so is it followed by its formal form, which came into its own fully in modern science.

Science. Science is the third and formal form of access to reality, with most of the connections to direct perception being severed, whilst refraining from the ordinary perception of the life world – unless it takes place within the context of a theory-driven experiment. According to Cassirer, the central operation is about formalisation, introducing 'pure meaning' (*reine Bedeutung*), Lacan's 'small print'. They generate their own formal world, one that is different from the life world: H_2O for water, A/B/O for blood. This formalisation leads to a specific type of making for the world (*Gestaltung zur Welt*). Shaped by his Neo-Kantian background, he is not primarily concerned with offering a historical explanation of the rise of modern science. However, he will emphasise the role of mathematisation in this endeavour, in a modern as opposed to a premodern approach. If a clear caesura were to be introduced between premodern and modern natural sciences, Cassirer would choose Kepler rather than Copernicus: the transition, not from geocentric to heliocentric, but from the circle to the ellipse.

Within this form of access to reality, the phenomena are obviously categorically structured, but each category takes its own shape, with space, time, number and causality being modalised. No longer is the number part of the life world or the individual body – it is now being posited. As a result, Cassirer would stress the fact that mathematical numbers are formed as a series departing from a single unity, the number being conceived as a thought construct (in line with Dedekind's theory of numbers). In doing so, he distances himself from the (then current type of) formalism in mathematics (Hilbert), which reduces the number to a number-sign without any meaning, while also renouncing a Platonic view which holds that numbers would exist in an ideal world (Frege). Mathematical symbols are not empty letters, nor are they ideal objects – they are elements forming part of a structure. This means that mathematics is not about objects but about structures, about types of formal structuring (PsF III, 440–442/383–385). This conception of the number and of mathematical entities in general is obviously closely related to the fundamental traits of his own brand of philosophy (as is invariably the case with Cassirer): the primacy of thought, of form, which also finds its expression in his functional theory of mathematical concepts as a structuring principle, as was indicated in the foregoing.

These fundamental ideas are also reflected in the concept of the nature of science. Science is not inductive, it does not build on data nor on 'big data' – bearing in mind that 'big data' are also constructs. Gathering and analysing 'big data' means gathering information, but that does not necessarily make it a scientific effort, although it may be seen as a 'partner' to science. Science requires the presence of a theory, from which the object is constructed as being loaded with theory. Yet also a scientific theory sets itself up for failure when pretending to offer a truthful reflection of reality. What it does is provide a thought construct, a model based on which predictions can be made and which can be built upon. Theory thus becomes a construct, relying as it does on an agreement and functioning as a tool. Much more than classical Neo-Kantianism, Cassirer adopts a dynamic scientific approach, keeping an eye to scientific history and the possibility of a paradigm shift. We recognise a kinship with Duhem's instrumentalism as well as well is with the conventionalism championed by H. Poincaré (Cassirer actually refers to both), and with later American pragmatism but also with T.S. Kuhn's paradigm shift theory. Thus phrased Cassirer's view are also in line with the French tradition of comparative epistemology adopted by Bachelard, Ganguillem and the early Foucault.

A qualification of the distinction between natural sciences and the humanities would be in order here (in line with the Marburg orientation). Also the humanities – the cultural sciences – presuppose a departure from the self-evident qualities of a life world, focusing on data ranges and generalities, albeit of the form type rather than the causality type – think of 'the' Renaissance man, 'the' narcissistic personality. They also require object constancy, except that the object is not the physical object but its meaning (of a cultural object). In the final reckoning, in the field of humanities it is also all about establishing series (*Reihen*): (s_1, s_n). This constitutes an important and useful starting point for any type of humanities, even including its individualising varieties: A trait does not become a trait unless it is repeated. And yet this may not provide a satisfying alternative to historism with its strong emphasis on the unicity of the fact. Moreover, the unity of science intended by Cassirer is a fragile one, certainly not the robust type of unified science represented by Neo-Positivism (or its present-day varieties). Thus, the distinction between cause and form ('form' taken in the narrowed-sense, opposed to cause) remains unchallenged, and it is precisely this distinction that set the humanities apart from the natural sciences. However, the unity of sciences proposed by Cassirer is of a highly generic nature, as it merely covers the unity of science as a symbolic form, which can hold all manner of oppositions: conceptual, procedural and historical, as well as in terms of social context and function, etcetera.

The primacy of theory in Cassirer's scientific view leads to an open approach to science, as was demonstrated in the foregoing. Practising science may be equal to formalising, but not to establishing causal-deterministic relationships between phenomena. Functional, teleological explanations in regard of living nature would be perfectly acceptable also not in line with Kant (GW 5/2000b, 204–252; Krois 2004). The same applies to bio-semiotic or bio-semantic orientations, or to conceiving physical nature as being controlled by symbols or maybe even as being teleological in nature (De Mul 2013). Only post-factum, not beforehand, can it be determined whether a theory was practicable: an apt metaphor, a useful symbolic ideation. The temporal form of truth, we could say, is that of the 'futurum exactum', the perfect future tense: it will turn out to have been true. And yet: A possible positive outcome must not lead to the conclusion that life itself would be interpretative, or that matter itself would be coded. They remain visions, ways of representing reality. They are symbolic ideations, metaphors which may or may not prove fruitful. Once again it shows that this idealism is not a triumphant idealism, with thought producing (*erzeugen*) reality, but rather that it cautions us: They are only ideations, mere models, anything but the reality that we might know. Also science falls short as a representative system, finding itself powerless to say 'what is'. This would then apply to any form of access to reality. Cassirer (2005, 260) summerises: 'To put it in paradox we may say that man in spite of all his efforts never succeeds in coming into real contact with the thing themselves. He is always in pursuit of reality and in pursuit of truth – but both of them seem to recede from him'. There is always symbolic ideation: The process of seeing precedes that which is seen. And seeing, in whatever form, is partial, perspectivistic, inadequate.

Indeed, rather than applying an immutable hermetic code, symbolising or representing means applying a system of representation that is insufficient to mirror reality, whilst offering a disclosure of reality.

2.7 Symbolisation: Three Sources and Three Modes

The process of representation ends what came before, replacing it by a mediated presence: 'No being is tangible or accessible except through meaning'. (PsF III, 345/299). In this mediated presence, something will appear as being present through a reference to what it is not itself (another mental event, an image, a word, a formula, etcetera). From this, *three* characteristics of the process of representation or symbolisation result. Quintessential is the *as* figure: x *as* y. By necessity, anything will be conceived *as* being something *else* as well. Cassirer (PsF I, 33/100) points out very clearly: 'every [...] element of consciousness is represented in and through another'. Because of this consciousness, the mind, in whatever form, is constituted as a system, a whole, to be supported by a formative principle. Secondly, by virtue of this *as* figure, symbolisation is also *differential* in nature. Indeed, any qualification allows a different one: x *as* y ... *or as* z. This turns symbolisation, thirdly, into a dynamic process: x *as* y, *or as* z, ...and so on. Which is maintained as it unfolds. Thus, reality is disclosed, relying as it does on an empty space (...) created by the symbolic itself, with terms mutually referring to each other. Only from and within the symbolic realm can reality appear as distinct entities, being different from each other. Cassirer (1996, 31) comments rather evocatively: 'Outside this clearing, reality remains in eternal darkness, an undifferentiated and infinite primordial ground [...] Reality can only be delivered from this darkness by the pure energies of geist, by a kind of creative work'. And myth would then be its first outcome, with language following in its wake.

Radical metaphor. This leads to the question how the symbolic function, taking the form of myth and language, manifested itself for the first time. No longer a (transcendental-)philosophical question, as has been discussed so far, this has turned into an empirical issue – with the caveat that its empirical causes are impervious to concrete empirical research. In the words of Cassirer, it marks the transition to a different genre, a different state of being. Indeed, there is not only a categorical gap between nature and the symbolic, as it is actually the symbolic (e.g. the Spirit) itself that creates this gap and its associated unique categorical field of culture, of the objective mind (GW16/2003c, 301/1946, 87). This manifestation of the works of culture, of *culture* as a work, is what can be called a genuinely 'original phenomenon' ('Urphänomen'), a term coined by Goethe and adopted in a modified sense by Cassirer, while expressing the irreducible character of the phenomenon of culture (PsF III, 98/87). Notwithstanding, Cassirer made an attempt to analyse it, be it in an speculative manner. As a matter of fact, for a long time the inquiry into the origin of language was even rejected on account of its allegedly unscientific nature. In fact, Cassirer makes a first attempt, building partly on the traditional biological anthropology that goes ultimately back to Herder (1744–1803), who saw man as a creature characterised by a biological deficit ('Mängelwesen'). It has become something like a self-evident truth within the philosophy of man, from Hegel to Nietzsche. And in the traditional biological anthropology of the 20th century, man is accordingly conceived as a creature that lacks, from a biological viewpoint, natural adaptive qualities, thus assigning man a special position within the animal kingdom. Indeed, organic life, animal life, is not conceivable without the presence of adaptive qualities, without any form, e.g. organic form, biological form – although the question how life "achieves" form, how form comes to life, remains insolvable (1996, 15). Which is exactly why *life*, such as culture, is an original phenomenon ('Urphänomen') as well (Möckel 2004). In man, however, this adaptive quality of life is lacking, in the absence of any natural alignment between inner world ('Innenwelt') and outside world ('Umwelt') – as Cassirer's Hamburg colleague J. von Uexküll (1909) described it (and to whom also Lacan refers repeatedly when discussing this issue). As a result, this non-alignment between stimulus ('Merknetz') and response ('Wirknetz') leads to a stimulus surplus, a state of excess tension.

Following this line of thought, Cassirer views the origin of myth fundamentally as a discharging of that tension-loaded state through the forming of an image, a mythical figure or deity representing this tension (for example, as a god of food or fertility). By extension, the origin of language may also be conceived as the transformation of a tension-loaded state (e.g. a natural cry) to something that is foreign to the experience or even quite disparate: a word, a sound carrying meaning, expressing a thought or an emotional state that did not exist in this form before: a *radical metaphor* which is a condition of the very formulation of mythic as well as verbal conceptions (GW 16/2003c, 302/1946, 87). Both images and words break open the more or less closed circuit of stimulus-response, interlacing it with a world of symbols, a symbolic world which implies a radical metaphor, a transmutation. Decisive for man is only the symbolic, not the organic (Möckel 2009, 216). This achievement implies not only a transition to another category but actually the creation of the category of the symbolic itself. That is a huge step: a step from the immediacy of life, a fundamental caesura. Indeed, myth, like art or objectifying knowledge, arises in a process of separation from immediate reality, actually raising a *barrier* against it (PsF II, 30/24; PsF III, 326/284). Even stronger terms are used: 'Their function, as we have seen, is rather a process of almost violent separation and individuation' (GW 16/2003c, 277/1946, 57; GW 15/2004b, 196). The result would be that the spirit in its relation to life, without turning against it, always stands in opposition to it, reaching beyond the primordial ground of "life". That means that life itself can never be the source of the symbols in which reality is first comprehended and understood, in which it "speaks to us" (1996, 30–31). This raises the question about the possible nature of this source.

Three sources. To identify this basis or source he reaches back to the concept of original phenomenon ('Urphänonemon'), which he derived from Goethe but which he fleshes out differently. In the 1940s Cassirer (1996, 127–190) devoted a number of key sections to this topic, which were not published until much later. In Cassirer's conception, Goethe distinguished three fundamental domains of reality, as it is given to us: (1) the sphere of each life, of being a continuously moving flow or stream, which nonetheless represents a unity (monas); (2) it goes on to step outside itself, interacting with reality and with others; (3) it is ultimately objectified in works that remain and that transcend the life unity's life span. Nonetheless, Cassirer does not conceive these three domains as spheres of reality (existing inside or outside ourselves) but rather as perspectives on reality, only from which reality can be disclosed. Consequently, they are given a different name – he speaks of 'basis phenomena' rather than 'original phenomena'. They do not refer to reality itself, but to its conception or its disclosure from each of these perspectives. Indeed, in processing Goethe's concept, Cassirer (1996, 136) remains faithful to his own philosophical principles – which holds that basis phenomena are functions rather than entities. Quite plastically, he summarises their specific character as follows: They are the windows of our knowledge of reality, by which the phenomenon "reality", i.e. reality as a phenomenon, discloses itself. They are the fundamental modes of mediation, through which reality reveals itself to us; they are the look that we cast upon the world; they are the eye, so to speak, that we open up; and in the opening of the eye the phenomenon reality, reality as a phenomenon or as a world, discloses itself to us (1996, 138).

More than that, he adds his own *justification* to this tripartite division of perspectives, which takes the form of a phenomenological analysis (1996, 136–153). Life inescapably presents itself to us as a unity (monas), as an I (the sphere of "life" itself, the I-Phenomenon). As a next step, it will meet with opposition from a non-I, external reality, another, a you, thus introducing it into the sphere of action and reaction, the You-Phenomenon. In turns, this leads to the production of lasting works with an objectivity of their own (the sphere of the

Work, the It-Phenomenon, e.g. the spirit of objectivity). As a result, every basis phenomenon will offer nothing more than a window that can be and needs to be filled and made concrete in all spheres of reality. Indeed, a basis phenomenon is not a concrete phenomenon itself, but may generate concrete phenomena. It is not a phenomenon but a phenomenon *function*, in the same manner that a propositional function ('Satzfunktion') is not a proposition itself, but may generate true propositions, subordinated to it.

Thus, they can find a concrete application in the scientific domain: in biology (living and living together); psychology (the trichotomy of feeling, willing, and thought); and in linguistics (Karl Bühler's organon model of language – its expressive, evocative, and representational function). Particularly instructive, however, is the application in the field of philosophy, to the extent that any basis phenomenon can inform a unique type of disclosure of reality (1996, 166–190). Indeed, it can be effectuated from the I-perspective, along the path of intentionality, from the You-perspective, which includes the shared sitation, and from the It-perspective, which contains the objective structure of the myth, language, science – from the objective mind. This tripartite division (I-You-It) corresponds precisely – and this should be taken as a side remark – to the three levels of the human condition as described in Chapter 1: intentionality (Husserl), situation (Heidegger), and the objective mind, or structure (Lacan). From a chosen perspective (I-You-It) – from lived experience, a shared situation, an objective structure – meaning is added, which is a prerequisite for gaining any access to reality – e.g. to life itself, the external real, and to the primordial Other (the above was published initially in Mooij 2018). Whatever the case may be, this outcome resonates with the first component of symbolisation: its *sources*, semantic fields. Besides, there are the *modes* of symbolisation as well: the form of the image, the form of the word, and of the formula.

Three modes. From the point of view of the three modes, reality is represented by means of images, of words, pure meanings: intuitively in an image or Gestalt, discursively in words, formally in a pure meaning, a formula. They correspond to the three partial modes of the symbolic function, i.e., expression, objectification and pure meaning (*Ausdruck, Darstellung* and *reine Bedeutung*), as was shown repeatedly, with their outcome in myth, language and science (PSF III, 518–525/447–453). These three partial functions or basic modes of representation, will now be discussed, no longer focusing on their outcome – (*Ergebnis*) in myth, language and science – but rather on their function: how exactly they produce this outcome. The arrangement remains the same, as well as the basic terminology. Leaving behind the cultural domains, the arrangement will be reflected in the three layers of experience, the three specific ways of representation contained therein. In this description devoted to the modes of knowledge, the sources of knowledge will not be given be any detailed attention but will only be mentioned in passing.

Expression. Expression (*Ausdruck*) associated with cultural domain of myth, will also be reflected in the primal layer of each mode of experience: the human face of the cosmos and the physiognomic aspect of perception, its Gestalt quality. Cassirer speaks here of the sphere of expression, which in its turn comprises three functions. Firstly, it has the function of accomplishing contact-with-reality, which leads to the awareness of 'there *is* a reality to be in contact with' – not in the sense of 'I am facing a reality as an object', but rather out of an awareness of belonging: There is a reality, something to be in contact with, of which I am a part and from which I cannot distance myself. In this plead for an ontological realism we may hear an echo, once again, of the ontological realism associated with early Romanticism (Frank 2002). Here reality is not actualized through the mediation of the phenomenon, but is present in full actuality *in* the phenomenon: 'Here being [...] reveals itself to be in simple existence'. (PsF III, 76 /68). For this reason, Cassirer would typify this sphere as being 'immediate'. An understandable choice, in light of the highly primal character of this level of experience, and yet it may lead to the mistaken belief that, in Cassirer's views, this type of experience would be non-representing at all. And yet it is *also* representing. According to Cassirer (PsF III, 326/284), the expression, the Gestalt perception and ensuing action – is already representing, in the broad sense of representation he favours: 'expression [...] already reached out beyond immediacy – for did not remain within the sphere of mere presence but sprung from the basic function of signification'. In that sense, the expression also offers a form of representation, thus rendering it non-immediate, just like any other level of symbolisation. This representative character is also evident from the fact that the expressive form already includes contrasts: the sacred/profane opposition in the myth, the day/night opposition of the Gestalt experience. This highlights the very difference between Gestalt representation, in Cassirer's view, and what today is commonly referred to as pattern recognition: Gestalt representation is, while being a representation, already differential of nature.

We might argue that pattern recognition is vital to animal organisms, which after all respond to more or less fixed patterns of sound, colour and smell – ranging from closed stimuli to open signals – while it also includes responsiveness to signal-meanings. What lies beyond is a staggering wealth of visual patterns and sound patterns, and associated sensitivities. And yet the Gestalt experience of man is different in nature, by virtue of its differential design – sacred/profane, day/night. The experience of the moon coming and going in the night affords a pattern, while the moon can also be seen *as* a face, which thus makes it a Gestalt (a whole characterised by internal oppositions). This also becomes evident from the so-called Gestalt laws of the Gestalt psychology, according to which sensory ordering takes place based on resemblance/difference, far/near, open/closed oppositions, offering the possibility of a Gestalt switch (rabbit/duck). At the level of the Gestalt experience, 'difference' in terms of oppositions therefore already manifests itself. This demonstrates that the Gestalt experience severs the relationship to brutal reality in one fell swoop, for the very reason that it offers a representation: seeing is seeing *as*. In this sense, the thesis of the so-called isomorphism between Gestalts on the one hand, and patterns in physiological and physical events on the other, suggested by a few Gestalt-psychologists (Köhler 1992; Katz 1961) would not be very plausible.

This brings us to a second characteristic of the Gestalt representation. Although the Gestalt experience offers some form of representation, it is a partial one, a representation carried through 'halfway' (as has been mentioned before): It is a proto symbolisation, in which the separation has unfolded only partly. It is an intrinsic consequence of the *medium* in which this representation occurs. Indeed, the image may offer a representation, but it does so in the form of a likeness, through mirroring. When the cosmos, along the road of magic, shows itself with a human face, it reflects man himself, mirroring his face. The features of the physiognomy will bring this to bear on the entire world of perception: Leaves are dancing, a car looks aggressive. At this level, the observer sees himself. This brings us to the final point of the Gestalt representation. The world of the Gestalt and the image show themselves as a whole, in a closed form. Thus, myths and religions tend to close themselves off and become totalitarian – it is all part of their design. This is true not only for ancient myths, but also for modern-day world images including totalitarian ideologies – but even modern science if that aspires to be an ideology by functioning as an ultimate rationale of everything. This is what Cassirer (2007e) would later base his criticism of modern ideologies on. And this is also how the later Lacan will highlight the aspect of totality of the sphere of the image, which he calls the imaginary. The image confronts us with an inner, unfragmented coherence or consistency (*consistance*). Conversely, if a world tends to be 'consistent', we find ourselves locked in the register of the image, in which the world closes itself and shows itself as a closed world, But this interrelated quality does not detract from the primacy of the sphere of expression, from a genealogical point of view. Indeed Cassirer asserts (PsF III, 69/63): 'The understanding of expression is essentially earlier than the knowledge of things'.

Objectification. Where the function of the expression supports the contact-with-reality (bearing in mind that this primary contact is not truly immediate and does involve some element of distance), the function of representation in a narrowed down sense (*Darstellung*) creates effectively distance towards reality as well as a higher level of separation between the representative and what is represented. Objectification is a more appropriate term. Indeed, object-constitution now becomes possible, with the object gaining autonomy as being objectifiable, as being 'opposite'. The objectifying representation thus functions as a fulcrum in the process of representation. The world is no longer given as a whole, but has become articulated. This is brought about by the *medium* of this function, namely the word, or the articulation into words, which has an effect of 'breaking'. Indeed, within their structural coherence, words refer primarily to each other and have to pass through that network of meanings to refer, as a next step, to objects situated outside which are actually formed themselves as a result of this attribution of meaning: That is a house and it is *not* a shed. Essential here is negativity, the gap, the hole existing between the terms mutually, and subsequently between the terms and the world. Instead of, or rather next to, the primary contact with the world through the image, leading to the experience of totality, we find objectification, the word leading to the experience of brokenness. In the terminology of the later Lacan, instead of or next to the experience of consistency (*consistance*) which is inherent to the image, we find the hole (*trou*), which is inherent to the word. And yet both forms of representation – the intuitive and the discursive – also imply each other. The word breaks open the closed state of the image, whilst a caesura can only be placed in a field that has a unity of its own. Having said this, Cassirer again made a rather unfortunate choice when naming this partial function of objectification in language – he speaks of 'representation', ('Darstellung') without qualifying the term. Not the best choice of wording, considering that representation as such lies at the heart of the symbolic function in all its manifestations. Objectifying representation would describe the process much more aptly.

Formalisation. Formalising or signifying (Truwant 2015) is the third partial function, which generates a third type of meaning: pure meaning (*reine Bedeutung*). Here the connection with intuition and the life world is severed, and formal theory has primacy. Water is not water coming from the tap but H_2O, even if it is actually water coming from the tap. Cassirer (PsF III, 345, 346/300) would emphasise that, in addition to discontinuity there is also continuity between common language and formal theory, while formal theory emerging from common language: 'Here the world of pure meaning adds nothing new in principle to the world of representation, but only unfolds what is already potentially contained in this world'. And yet there is a fundamental difference, because formalisation will ultimately lead to a voiding or evacuation of the life world as a whole, as a result of the construction of formal models that may or may not turn out to be correct. Which is precisely where the significance of the formalising approach by modern science lies. Cassirer followed the path of the then current theory of science to appreciate the significance of the general symbol concept (relying on Hertz and Duhem). Yet essentially this conception was already embedded in Marburg Neo-Kantianism and its fundamental notion that reality can be revealed through numbers. Ultimately, it is a Platonic idea that mathematics generates the world of nature. Likewise in line with the Marburg orientation, Cassirer will therefore argue that modern science, even from a historical perspective, represents a form of applied Platonism – as would later be subscribed by Lacan as well.

Modernity. Obviously, formalisation covers a wider field than just modern science – a point Cassirer chose not to elaborate. Indeed, this does not merely constitute *the* basic invention of modern science, but also of modernity as such, we could say at a stretch. Husserl (1970, 301–314) spoke of idealising, but the term 'formalising' would be more apposite. Both presuppose the existence of a life word, in relation to which we could speak of idealising, of formalising. However, the latter term reflects the essence of what is happening and the repercussions vis-à-vis the life world much more effectively: the caesura. Through formalisation, the ties with the life word, the 'intuition' in Cassirer's terms, are severed, which is the central point. As the ties with the traditional relationships in the life world are cut off, they are replaced by new, formal and artificial relationships. Indeed, in modernity, this process is unfolding not only in the field of science, but also in the political and economic domains, etcetera. In science, water becomes H_2O. In politics, a governance based on family relationships gives way to a system of representation, taking the form of a representative democracy ('one man, one vote'). In economy, traditional ownership yields to its formal variety, which takes the form of the freely negotiable share. Thus, economy becomes monetary economy. Lacking any content, and being essentially empty and interchangeable, money even turns out be an apt metaphor for modernity as such: indeed, from substance to function (Simmel 2011, 351, 179). Otherwise, traditional relationships are maintained, although sometimes in a modified form. Cassirer's view may offer a specific contribution to understand the tension thus created between 'system' and 'life world', which since Hegel has been the common thread in modern social philosophy. Not in Heidegger's anti-Modernist sense, nor in the embracing of modernity by a belief in science (which as a result may function as a myth), but rather in a complex to-and-fro process between modern science, the life world and the world of myth and religion. He who banishes one form of religion (e.g. religious practice and believe) does so at the risk of religion emerging in a different form. Indeed, the theory of symbolisation is a reliable safeguard against any form of absolutisation. And still, however broadly conceived the theory of symbolisation can never be a panacea. The point it tries to make is that absolutisation will always detract from the *as* figure which is inherent to any form of symbolisation or representation. Any perspective cannot be aspire to be more than one out of many perspectives on reality. By definition, other perspectives will always be possible and even necessary. The inadequacy of each representation or symbolic form creates the need for multiplicity while expressing its relative quality.

The inquiry into power. Despite all openness, one question or type of questions remains yet unaddressed: the inquiry into the cause of the shift, the change of perspectives or within a perspective, in the form of the rise and fall of partial perspectives and paradigms. Cassirer describes this essentially as an internal affair and outlines its conceptual infrastructure, disregarding the inquiry into external control. And yet the concept itself could point us in the right direction, namely through the social embedding of any symbolic form. This social embedding refers to the social interactions and, by implication, to the inquiry into power. Science would be a case in point. Current science reflects currents fundamental views, which for some reason are prevalent at that particular time. It is these fundamental views that determine what are acceptable and legitimate questions. This is also reflected in the practical field. Science is a unique form of access to reality, but it is also a corporation. We need not discuss this in detail. What matters here is that this component, summarised as the component of power, can be made to fit into the concept of a philosophy of symbolic forms. Philosophy as a cultural philosophy would therefore be open to cultural sociology. Indeed, this connection between content and context need not be described in terms of internal or external, as the so-called external element is already part of the concept of the symbolic form. Cassirer (GW 15/2003e) pointedly ignores this point, as becomes evident from his historical discussions. In his otherwise brilliant history of the Enlightenment the social context is largely neglected. And yet this aspect is part of the design, as with Hegel in a more speculative fashion. A number of avenues can be followed to fill the gap, and Foucault's (1970) historical analysis of discursive practices certainly offers some pointers. A more empirical approach was favoured by the French sociologist Bourdieu (1974), who also refers to Cassirer. Rather than speaking of symbolic forms, Bourdieu prefers to use the term 'field' to denote science, arts and politics. Each of these objective fields correspond to a unique form of subjectivity, which in line with art historian Panofsky and before him Thomas Aquinas, he refers to as 'habitus' – the state of mind required in a particular field. The habitus bridges the gap between individual and field, turning him into a scientist, artist, etcetera. Making reference to Von Humboldt, Bourdieu (1974, 143) uses, as does Cassirer, the term 'inward form' ('innere Form'). Thus we see many parallels with Cassirer's scheme: a symbolic domain and a corresponding consciousness – field and habitus.

The difference is that Bourdieu designs this scheme from a sociological angle, complementing cultural theory with cultural sociology. He examines the various specifications of the different types of habitus, in intellectual and artistic movements, etcetera. In the course of his empirical endeavours he encounters the phenomenon of power, which actually lies at the heart of culture. A person can participate, to a greater or lesser extent, in cultural capital (social status), social capital (networks), or the linguistic capital in the field of the symbolics of society, with all its inertia. He who was born a pauper, may become a prince, but there will always be something of a pauper left inside (and vice versa). The triumph of the paradigm is also the outcome of social and economic struggle. Which, as a final point, also puts paid to the caesura between validity and genesis ('context of justification' and 'context of discovery'), a core issue of classical Neo-Kantianism, in a similar way as with Cassirer. Validity applies only within a given apriori, but even this apriori is historically relative. In line with Bourdieu, we find that the qualification of the apriori also has a societal basis and is linked to prevailing balances of power. Its broad discussion on an empirical level falls obviously outside the scope of this section, as here we are only concerned with the legitimacy and possibility of this question within the contours of Cassirer's concept.

2.8 A Symbolic Form in the Making?

As was mentioned before, Cassirer offers a rather muddled answer when it comes to defining the exact number of symbolic forms. In fact, to the three forms discussed before he adds: the arts (invariably), technology (later), law, morality, history, sometimes economy. It is not a particularly satisfying list, and he uses its elements loosely and with precious little system to it (in a similar way as Bourdieu, who applied it to a different set of terms). We could also say that, contrary to his own ambition, this conception of the symbolic form is hardly a functional one, treating symbolic forms as separated cultural domains in a substantive sense. In concert with the three-fold subdivision of the symbolic function, however, we may recognise a similar tripartite system of symbolic forms, emphasising the 'manner of forming', the functional side of a symbolic form. Indeed, there is no obligation to follow Cassirer in his developmental, teleological, or even Hegelian perspective on the human spirit. Neither a stratification within human consciousness nor a genealogy of symbolic form would imply an undervaluation of the strata or any teleology in substance. Also in these matters, a functional perspective seems to be more appropriate. This leads to what might be termed an open system, a conception that is actually closer to Cassirer's line of thought than his own list: Basic coordinates do exist, but their content may vary.

These three partial functions, one may argue, underlie and constitute the core of each of the three clusters of symbolic forms that generate specific meanings. Each partial function goes on to develop into a specific symbolic form, representing its core, which leads to three distinct symbolic forms or systems of meaning. Following on from the threesome discussed before (myth, language and science) they produce *three clusters* of symbolic forms: the cluster of (1) myth and religion and art; (2) the cluster of language and language-dependent culture – culture conceived in the usual way as morality, law and political order, and finally (3) the cluster of science and modern technology. Joining them up in this way can well be defended based on Cassirer's own principles. Myth, religion but also art share a central role, namely that of the Gestalt experience, of the image: *mimesis*. Including morality, law and the political domain, language shares the central function of *objectification*: This is a house, that isn't yours but mine. Both science and modern technology are grounded in *formalisation*. Each of the three clusters therefore correspond to their respective partial functions of the symbolic function, offering three modes of symbolisation or representation: expression, objectification, formalisation ('Ausdruck, Darstellung, reine Bedeutung'). It should be borne in mind that a symbolic form may have a single partial function at its core, but this does not lead to the switching off of the other partial functions within a symbolic form. Had this been the case, then the concept of a symbolic form would become rather flat. The threefold distinction *between* the symbolic forms therefore returns therefore *within* each symbolic form, as was noted before. But this would then also be true for any of the clusters of symbolic forms. For that reason, each symbolic form or each cluster of symbolic forms is layered, and this stratification enables a factual development, adding an index of factuality to each symbolic form. This also reflects the Neo-Kantian principle of proceeding from facts, from culture itself. We find that modern science on the one hand is the outcome of an inner logic, while on the other it is a result of coincidence, with its genesis being tied to a historical and cultural context (the creationist concept of Christianity with the associated secularisation of nature, late-Mediaeval nominalism, the Platonist movement of the early Renaissance, early technological developments, etcetera). It makes that every symbolic form, whilst having an internal logic, is just as well associated with an index of factuality, which means it can become obsolete or lose its binding power.

Thus, the arts, with their gamut of forms and genres, qualify as a symbolic form, as they also reflect the threesome of imitation, creative design and formalisation ('Nachahmung, Manier und Stil'). At its basis lies the aesthetic experience, which is grounded in the experience of mimesis, of the image, of the Gestalt experience, finding its elaboration in the factual and historically shaped and highly diverse realm of the visual arts. Cassirer (GW 23/2006b, 157) writes: 'Aesthetic experience [...] is pregnant with infinite possibilities which remain unrealized in ordinary sense experience. In the work of the artist these possibilities become actualities; they are brought into the open and take on a definite shape. The revelation of this inexhaustibility of the aspects of things is one of the real privileges and one of the deepest charms of art'. However, it seems that 'the arts', following the period of modernism are increasingly disintegrating into a multitude of experiments in the field of representation, with the possible outcome that they cease to qualify as a symbolic form, on account of no longer meeting the criterion of general binding. Most notably the modern forms of arts appear to be characterised by hyper-reflection (Sass 1992). This doesn't cause art to disappear, but it does change its character to being only experimental and non-binding (Danto 2013). The same question will be raised whenever a new and experimental work of art is presented to the world: Can this still be called art? The question poses itself because 'this new thing' seems not to form part of well-known movements or traditions. An answer can therefore only be provided – according to Cassirer's functional conception (applied to art) – only in retrospect, once it has become apparent that this work of art has eventually become part of a new series, exemplifies a new type and can therefore be slotted into what might qualify as a new tradition or movement.

A similar pattern can be observed with religion, which is also becoming increasingly reflexive: I believe that I believe (Vattimo 1999). Religion, too, has lost most of its binding power in modernity. The schemes of life it offers are no longer considered appealing. And yet religion, 'even if we are no longer convinced Christians', may still remain in a reflexive form in post-modernity – as an aesthetics of the rite or an ethics of the face of the Other. Moreover, Christianity has at its disposal a formidable three-some, following Cassirer's trichotomy. Religious practice includes the mythical rite of the liturgy, the spreading of the Word and living from the Spirit. Also the Christian God appears in a three-fold manner. First there is the transcendent mythical God who created order and legislation, next there is the God of historical reconciliation, and finally there is the God in the guise of the Holy Ghost, as a model for action and desire, manifesting itself in the psychic reality as well as in the public domain – in the subjective and objective mind. Apparently, Christianity still has some potential left – the symbolic capital of a mythical, narrative and signifying nature – to nourish and inform life. Also on a global scale, Christianity and other religions remain firmly present. And yet concerns about the sustainable quality of religion and art – even the question itself – raise yet another question. After all, each symbolic form comes, notwithstanding an internal logic, with an index of factuality. Might we expect a new type of symbolic form to emerge in the 21st century, from a unique type of representation, over time, but still conceivable from an inner logic?

A fourth symbolic form? After all, there is yet another type of symbolisation, left unaddressed by Cassirer: objectification *of* symbolisation. That could be imagined as a fourth partial function: symbolisation of symbolisation. It is not Cassirer but his first teacher in philosophy, George Simmel (2011, 491) who paid attention to this domain: the physical condition of the objective mind, i.e. the *objectified mind*, the mind's physical objectification, in its diversity, including the universal medium of exchange: money. Simmel claims that the life-style of a community strongly depends upon the objectified culture and the way in which the objective mind determines the subjective mind. Indeed, with the emergence of money, as a universal currency exactly covering everything, we see a new form of subjectivity arise within modernity. From the perspective of language and myth, word and image – Cassirer's perspective – we can distinguish at least three types of objectification, of objectified mind: writing, printing and, we can add, virtuality. First and foremost, the objectified mind takes the form of writing (Ricœur 2001, 131–182). The written word is not a duplicate of the spoken word. Indeed, there is no such thing as phonetic writing. To quote Derrida, it is a supplement, adding something to create something new. Removed from the actual speech setting, the word or text becomes autonomous. The speaker steps back, relinquishing his authority on determining 'what is written'. As a result, the audience, no longer confined to those hearing his words, expands into a general readership. Now it is up to the reader and future generation to define the exact meaning of the words written. Thus, writing offers the first level of symbolisation of symbolisation, of tele-presence, a presence of something that is absent. And this can only be effectuated because the dialectics of presence/absence are embedded in speech itself, with the word being a 'presence shaped by absence'.

The invention of book printing led to a second level: The tele-presence had been subjected to a process of enormous broadening in the geographical space. For the very reason that reproduction is no longer tied to manually copying a limited series, instead taking place in great numbers, mass distribution becomes possible. It is not just the expert who has an opinion – anyone can voice it now, identify meaning. (This development may well have contributed in no small measure to the rise of modern science, which is structured as a community of peers, as well as to the development of today's representative democracy in a narrowed-down sense.) A third level occurs in modern information technology (tele-phone, tele-vision e-mail, internet, skyping, social media, and what else the future may bring). Part of it is still tele-presence (telephone, skyping), another part isn't: The distinction between presence and absence – this is mine, that is yours – is increasingly becoming blurred (Eggers 2013). We can no longer separate the original from the copy: The e-book does not exist in an original form. The corporeal presence (*lebhafte Gegenwart*) still emphatically present in the case of the book – it feels good, it smells good, etcetera – has vanished. More than being presented in a virtual form, its very existence is virtual. Consequently, this third level runs parallel to that of modern science. (Also in modern science, the object is virtual, the object of study merging with the models produced: the atom does not exist as an atom, but only as an atom model, DNA takes the form of a model, etcetera. Also the object of modern science is becoming increasingly virtual and evasive, reflecting the strength of modern science.)

So what is the status of this 'fourth symbolic form' as writing, as printing, and virtuality? Is it found at a meta level (symbolisation of symbolisation) or at the material infrastructure of the symbolic forms mentioned before (objectification of symbolisation) – the letter, the page, the screen? *Or* maybe it has its own unique status as a symbolic form? A case could be made for either option. In favour of the first option pleads the factual state of dependence on the aforementioned symbolic forms: It functions as an addition. And yet functioning as an addition or supplement it can actually produce a transformation, allowing to function as an autonomous (fourth) form. Even when writing and printing may be not successful while claiming the status of a fourth symbolic form, virtuality may succeed. In favour argues the fact that it leads to its own unique type of making for the world (*Gestaltung zur Welt*), taking the form of a tele-presence, of virtualisation and far-reaching transparency, bringing its own type of social interaction, impact on life, on the form of subjectivity or identity, etcetera. Indeed, Simmel's claim, elaborated in 'The Philosophy of the Money', that the entire life-style of a community depends upon the objectified cultures, seems to be justified. Where life prior to massive tele-presence was characterised by continuous separation and micro-separation, this separation has been removed to be replaced by a continuous and instantaneous universal accessibility, an abolition of distance – Heidegger's (1962, 105) 'de-sever' (*Entfernen*) or Simmel's (2011, 514) diminution of distance, both shifted up to a higher gear, although not necessarily the highest. This is eminently reflected in the mild panic experienced by a person who finds they have forgotten their mobile phone. It brings discomfort as well as feelings of being lost, being out of reach. Then again a person switching off their device may also feel relief for being 'out of reach', only in a different sense, because the mobile phone also ties us down, keeps us enchained. The same applies to the ongoing process of mirroring ourselves on others who we are following (and who apparently, for some reason, like to be followed). This virtual interconnectedness (which is not particularly virtual, for we know exactly what the other is doing and where he is), is bound to impact the nature of subjectivity and identity. The same would apply to the parent-child relationship, with the parent being aware of the child's school performance even before the child knows itself. And of course we will see new places, new forms of taking-distance and allowing-distance emerge, without this (perhaps not so) virtual over-involvement, where people allow each other more freedom. But when, where, and how? Within the present context, this point should not be addressed in any detail and will merely be mentioned. There is yet another reason why it cannot be discussed: It is too early yet, because developments are still ongoing, also technologically. Notwithstanding, this whole technological and social development is very close to what Heidegger qualifies as *Framework* (*Gestell*), while describing the modern world as being locked in by technology and where all things have to be 'enframed' in a certain way in order to exist (Heidegger 1978a, 9–41). What will come out of it? Does it encourage anarchistic tendencies, like we seemed to be witnessing in the early stages of the internet, or will we move towards increasing supervision and monitoring, where the separation between private and public domain becomes more and more fictitious? In the latter case, the state of separation and obscurity will be eliminated as a mode of experience and as an actual possibility, which is likely to have a major impact on the then current form of intersubjectivity. Indeed, representation feeds off the dialectics of absence and presence that it institutes. And when the universal tele-presence puts an end to the pool of absence, this will have far-reaching cultural and societal ramifications. A new form of totalitarism might arise, one that is less politically driven and more sophisticated than the 20th-century model (GW 25/2007e), whilst not being all that different in a more fundamental sense – the abolishment of the dialectics of absence and presence. To which could be added the marketing of almost everything, with money becoming the denominator of all values in societal life (Simmel 2011). From this perspective modernity has lost its focus on self-determination, in favor of control on a global scale. But it is too early to draw conclusions. After all, only in the wake of the scientific and technological developments of the 19th century did Neo-Kantianism find itself in a position to qualify science as a symbolic form in its own right, attributing to it the weight of a specific making for the world.

The matter as such – a fourth form of symbolisation – was also raised for a more general reason, as it may illustrate the degree of fruitfulness of this approach. Which can be described as follows: First there are facts, and only after a fact – the factum of a cultural development – has been established, can we take the step of inquiring into its possibility and rationale and, by extension, its implications for the way of life, the form of subjectivity. In this light, the Neo-Kantian approach, as modified by Cassirer, is not a thing of the past, of the 20th-century, but can be brought to bear on 21st-century issues. In its own unique way, it may shed light on the social ontology of the present and the near future (De Mul 2010).

There is yet another reason why this matter – the significance of the objectification of symbolisation, as exemplified in writing en printing – has been raised: It marks the transition to the chapter on Lacan. Three issues deserve attention. *Firstly*, Cassirer is not assigning preponderance of the objective mind over the subjective mind, with the subjective mind being alienated in the objective mind – as advocated by Simmel. It will be a major topic with Lacan, who highlights the alienating power of the symbolic order. *Secondly*, Cassirer underestimates the importance of the physical condition of the objective mind, i.e. the objectified mind, and pays very little attention to writing (PsF II 278/238) and other systems of notation, and most certainly turns a blind eye to its associated philosophical problems. He can hardly be faulted though, considering that the matter only became topical in the footsteps of structural linguistics and in the context of French Structuralism. Here, the emphasis shifted to the material infrastructure of symbolic systems: initially with Lacan, later with Derrida (1967). With Cassirer, 'meaning' is the central category, reflecting the main theme of this chapter. Symbolic forms are systems of representation that generate different types of meaning. Lacan however stresses what lies beneath: the signifier. Cassirer's (PsF III, 345/299) ambition was always to conceive being from meaning: 'No being is tangible or accessible except through meaning'. Admittedly, he devotes attention to the sensory, to the material, but only in the context of form/matter: form and meaning have primacy. *Thirdly*, it turns being itself, reality, into a meaning-concept. Here, the real outside the symbolisation is left out of the equation. 'Being', reality will eventually merge with the sum of intersubjectively validated symbolisations, rather than something being behind symbolisation and hidden by them. Cassirer is most certainly not an ontological idealist: Man still has to rely on matter, on what is offered by the senses. He is also not a Hegelian, in the sense that reality would ultimately have to be logical – we cannot know its true nature. And yet the concept of the inaccessible real existing outside us he rejects as a valid concept, unless used as a border concept – as contrary to his basic views: the functional nature of human mind.

Lacan chooses a different approach on these *three* counts – the alienation, the real and the signification/signifier issue. Admittedly, most of his basic scheme runs parallel to Cassirer's, as was mentioned before: the imaginary order and the symbolic order (including the formal approach) in Lacan's sense run in parallel to the functions of expression, objectification and formalisation in Cassirer's sense. And yet, contrary to Cassirer, within his concept of the symbolic order Lacan makes room for the category of the signifier (giving it primacy, rather than signification) and he introduces a separate category for what he calls 'the real', while attributing to the symbolic order a primacy over the subject's state as well. The connection between these three additions or corrections will become clear in due course. This will also explain precisely why the choice was made to juxtapose the problem of symbolisation as dealt with by Lacan with Cassirer's approach. This may demonstrate that Lacan actually *formalises, corrects* and *deepens* the issues raised by Cassirer. Formalisation refers to the attention to the level situated below the semantic level: the content of meaning and the formal signifier change places and priorities. Thus, the 1966 volume *Écrits*, which made him famous, opens with the essay 'The purloined letter' ('La lettre volée'), which offers a comment on the eponymous Edgar Allan Poe story (Lacan 2002, 11–61). Summarising, the contents of the stolen letter, its meaning, have no bearing on the consequences, which are actually caused by the letter itself regardless of its meaning (which after all is not known). The correction pertains to the point that symbolic forms are not really modes of expression produced by the mind, but are experienced from a single subject as being imposed from the outside, determining action and experience. With language as example par excellence. Deepening it means analysing the consequences of cultural and language dependence on the state of human existence: subjective dividedness, with the associated issues of desire and pleasure. Ultimately this leads to understanding the real as a traumatic remainder. It means that the real ceases to be a 'border concept', as with Cassirer, instead becoming a 'concept of the remainder', of what remains after the process of symbolisation has formed the subject itself. To summarise: Where Cassirer, as an all-round philosopher, chooses to 'broaden', offering a theory that is supposed to encompass all aspects of culture by defining its symbolic infrastructure, the psychoanalyst Lacan prefers to 'deepen' in respect of individual subjectivity: defining the infrastructure of the subject as an effect of symbolic structuring.

CHAPTER 3

Lacan

Cassirer and Lacan come from two fundamentally different worlds. Cassirer was a scholar of the traditional kind who was active between the two World Wars. He worked from a well-defined philosophical tradition, framing it in his own unique way in response to the changing times. Although Cassirer was hardly an unknown name in the French cultural world of the 1950s, Lacan fails to make reference to Cassirer in any of his written and oral work, notwithstanding the fact that by his own admission he was familiar with Cassirer's works (Mooij 2008). The ambition of juxtaposing Lacan with Cassirer is not to identify any actual influences, but is rather aimed at highlighting those issues that they both addressed, going on to explore Lacan's elaboration of them: representation, symbolisation. In line with Kant's views, Cassirer found that reality cannot be known per se, *an-sich* – it may exist detached from ourselves. After all, we cannot relate to anything without contributing our own involvement. We symbolise, represent reality, but symbolisation cannot be sheer duplication without man's contribution. Rather than simply copy reality, we conjure up a specific image of reality. Any form of access to reality will therefore be mediated by symbolic systems, which means there is a range of forms of access rather than just a single one. As a result, access to reality is plural by definition as well as being mediated by symbolic forms such as language, the order of the image, and science. Taken together, these perspectives produce culture. In that sense, Cassirer also owes a great deal to Hegel: General culture stamps the single individual, who in turn is stamped by the cultural domain he finds himself in. For a person to be able to speak English, the English language must exist. So what does culture effectuate besides, and essentially? It introduces a caesura, separating us from immediate life, from being, thus putting immediate access out of reach. And it is this very state of exclusion that enables him to move forward, creating a variety of cultures, while having a desire for knowledge, more knowledge, and even more knowledge. It all follows from the thesis that man is a symbolising being, an *animal symbolicum*, gifted with speech.

So how does Lacan fit into all this? Well, Lacan *also* chooses this as point of departure. Man is a talking animal and carrier of the symbolic function, which for symbolisation has to rely on external orders including those of the image, of language, of science. From there, Lacan (2002, 284) calls a psychoanalyst a practitioner of the symbolic function. Indeed, he was a psychoanalyst, not a

 | DOI:10.1163/9789004373662_005

philosopher, who worked from a specific tradition, namely that of Freud. It is in the very act of retrospection that we find that the central concepts espoused by Freud retain their central position with Lacan. Adding his own reinterpretation, he referred in the 1950s to that as 'a return to Freud', *retour à Freud*. So what form did this reinterpretation take? He put the psychoanalytical field of concepts in a framework, namely the one outlined here. He had been exposed to it by the French philosophy of his time which, certainly in the eyes of Lacan, was strongly influenced by both Hegel and Kant. In addition, there was the emerging Structuralist movement as well, which put the theme of symbolisation firmly on the agenda. And one point emphatically made by Lacan was that man's cultural mode of existence had implications for man himself, for his subjectivity. It leads to subjective dividedness, creating a desire, a state of separation from the real. This would eventually become a central theme in his work, next to the theme of the nature of language.

3.1 A Return to Freud

Who was Lacan? Lacan could rely on a profound knowledge of the history of philosophy, with his preference for the idealistic tradition running parallel to that of the Marburg orientation: Plato, Descartes, Kant, Hegel, the modern logicians. As a notable divergence, he also had a fondness for Aristotle (who, by contrast, was not particularly highly regarded by the Neo-Kantians). Lacan was also well versed in contemporary philosophy, both the continental tradition (Heidegger, Sartre and Merleau-Ponty) and, in later years, the analytical school. Rather than adopt a specialist approach, he dealt with philosophy in a creative or perhaps even aggressive way, thus highlighting a yet unrevealed aspect. If anything, Lacan was a highly receptive and responsive thinker, unlike people like Husserl (who, to all intents and purposes, invented his own brand of philosophy). Anything but the reticent thinker, he was closer to the image of the old gypsy: always shopping around, looking for elements that suited his purpose – but he wouldn't just pick anything. First and foremost he was an avowed Freudian, in a most fundamental way. Freud adds a solid foundation to his work: He shares Freud's 'discontent in culture', adding a new level of intensification. It makes that Lacan's interpretation of the human condition becomes even more fragmented and poignant than in the case of Freud. Man suffers from his existence, from the experience of separation, from its sheer weight (*douleur d'exister*). Thus, Lacan painted the Freudian line of thought on a new canvas, adding his own signature. In doing so, he draws on concepts of other psychoanalysts as well, both of the first generation (K. Abraham,

S. Ferenczi) and of the second generation, to which he belongs himself (E. Jones and above all Melanie Klein). In this project, he integrated a multitude of seemingly contradictory motifs, in the same vein, as Freud *and* Klein, Descartes *and* Heidegger, Kant *and* Hegel. What leaps to the eye is the way he connects the *structural* with the *existential*: Lévi-Strauss *and* Sartre, Hegel *and* Kierkegaard. Indeed, we should not forget that Lacan while being deep rooted in the Structuralist movement, is strongly influenced by Sartre as well (Leguil 2012). His aim is to fully bring out the antinomies in human existence as well as identify mutual relationships. This makes him a connecting, synthetic thinker, although one could easily be led to believe otherwise. It is for a very good reason that Badiou (2012, 32) refers to him as 'our Hegel'. In fact, Lacan does owe a great deal to Hegel, with whom he shares the same focus: on the tension existing between the individual and culture, between the subjective mind and the objective mind, with the objective mind, or culture, strongly defining the subjective mind. This means that Lacan cannot be understood without his context, his kinships and sources. Failing that, any interpretation of his work is likely to become one-dimensional and plain. And yet it does make clear why Lacan, no philosopher by training, had a profound influence on French philosophy. Lacan cannot be fully understood when his ties with philosophy are disregarded. And yet until his last breath he would remain a (more than) full-time practitioner as a psychoanalyst as well as a psychiatrist. Consequently, Lacan cannot be understood without considering classical psychopathology. Both as a person and a psychoanalyst he would not shy away from the sleazy and rough-and-tumble aspects of life – quite the contrary, in fact. Freud's philosophy, structuralist linguistics, philosophy in general and his vast clinical experience enabled him to pursue his own chosen task of acquiring a psychoanalytically informed insight into the highly complex structure of man, of any man – *le sujet*. At its heart lies the notion of a void within human existence, as a result of man's dependence on culture and language, which denies immediate access to the real, relegating it to the realm of impossibility with the real being capable of affecting man in a traumatic way, from both the inside and the outside.

Historical background. More than any other thinker or philosopher, Lacan puts emphasis on context. This is actually embedded in the theory itself: Man is fundamentally dependent on culture, and therefore on the environment and situation he finds himself in. This would also be true for Lacan himself. Much more than in the case of Cassirer, an explanation is required: not so much for the sake of clarifying the problem of symbolisation, but rather to gain proper insight into Lacan as a phenomenon. Lacan would only find recognition rather late in life – starting with the publication of his a selection of his articles published until then, *Écrits*, in 1966. He partly had himself to blame for this, as his writings were few, most of them being inaccessible or hard to trace. This all changed overnight, in the year 1966. His influence was already considerable in small circles, but now his fame rose quickly, both in France and abroad, his work gaining academic stature particularly in the Anglo-Saxon world (Rabaté 2003). The gradual publication (also in English translation) of his *Séminaires,* held annually between 1953 and 1980, contributed in no small measure to this. This seminar, actually a series of lectures, represents the actual core of his work. Included in his *Écrits*, these articles actually constitute a review of the 'current state of affairs'. In 2001 a second collection appeared, *Autres Écrits*, which includes articles published since 1966 and those left out of the 1966 publication. It made little impact, if any, as its contents seemed to come from a distant planet, light years away from today's views. Times had changed, and so had we. Notwithstanding, Lacan did contribute to the shaping of French Structuralism between the 1950s and 1970s, while in the wake of this period he actually witnessed a new rise in popularity. His ideas were now more readily taken up and digested – a rather surprising development that could not have been foreseen in the 1970s and 80s. In light of the arcane, inaccessible quality of his work, its broad recognition, even on a global scale, is quite amazing. Moreover, Lacan's quintessential Frenchness is often not regarded as a redeeming quality. The – intentional – inaccessibility of his work has multiple causes: Lacan aspired to be an enigma, and certainly not to be transparent. This lack of transparency would become his trademark, his 'unique selling point'. It was also the product of a lack of didactical skills – even the most basic of matters he managed to give an unnecessarily complicated twist. Although fluent in speech, writing never came easily to him. While his speeches were dominated by verbosity, his writings were quite elliptical. Finally: The problem of accessibility is also the product of the approach itself, which brings that the reader cannot remain passive but is forced to engage actively with constructing and implementing the meaning of the words. Initially, this inaccessible quality may form a barrier, but once overcome it will have an appeal that is inherent in every hermetical text, an increased level of appropriation brought on by a sense of 'I managed to work it out'. As a result, this lack of accessibility becomes a driving force rather than a deterrent.

Outline of the work. Obviously, a hermetical body of work spanning three decades can be approached in a number of ways. Lacan was 'our Hegel'. And yet, in the final analysis, the content of this diversity should not be overstated. The differences are there, but they only exist within a limited framework, although they are sometimes magnified. We must also not forget that the *Séminaire* is essentially a report of a series of lectures. In a lecture, the teacher often tries things out, only to abandon or modify them later. In light of this, any pretension to distinguish a multitude of phases fails to do justice to internal dynamics – the details aren't really that important. What is essential here is recognising that it is the same vision unfolding repeatedly and in different ways, in different contexts. Thus, over the course of many years, a complicated body of work accumulated, with well-defined contours. From the early 1950s onwards – when he made his first public appearances – he introduced the three orders discussed in Chapter 1: the symbolic order, the imaginary order and the order of the real. Obviously, his philosophy developed over time, which means asking relevant questions on the distinction of periods would be justified. A useful periodisation would be the following. Prior to his first public appearance, Lacan focused mainly on the domain of the imaginary, while starting with his first public appearance (in the early 1950s) he would frame the symbolic in conjunction with the imaginary and the real as a central theme, giving priority to the symbolic. From 1964 onwards, he would increasingly 'formalise' this schema (although some degree of formalisation had been present before). This would produce the rather inaccessible seminars of the late 1960s and early 1970s, actually constituting a reflexive reworking of what already been substantially developed in the 1950s and early 1960s. Lacan speaks (2006, 291) appropriately of a logification of the psychoanalytical experience: his aim in these years. It may be considered to be a second tour of his return to Freud, by harking back, returning to Descartes, while tirelessly contemplating his *cogito sum* or considering Pascal's wager, with Pascal being a major source as well. In this very period Lacanism as a movement of thought was borne. Notwithstanding the difference in approach, these two periods may be taken together, being referred to as the 'classical Lacan'. The years, from 1973 onwards, see him cast his position in the form of questioning his own theory as well as partly rephrasing it. This period may be referred to as the 'later Lacan'. This dichotomy between the classical and the later Lacan will be used throughout this work. The exact dating would then be 1956–1964, 1965–1973 for the classical Lacan and 1973–1980 for the later Lacan. Of course this distinction can be further refined, and a dating at micro level may well be useful.

However, introducing a sharp contrast within the classical Lacan, between Lacan focusing on the signifier and Lacan turning away from this effort, would produce an opposition that cannot really be maintained. Indeed, the triad of the imaginary, the symbolic and the real remains a dominant force, although the design of each of these categories will change with time. Initially, the imaginary is oriented on the mirror stage and narcissism in the sense of Freud – turning the 'image' into a central figure – while at a later stage it takes on the broader meaning of anything that constitutes a whole or Gestalt, which can be qualified as consistency (*consistance*). The concept of the symbolic goes back to linguistics (Saussure) and cultural anthropology (Lévi-Strauss), in the heyday of Structuralism, later on being developed in a both formally and logically way. The central figure of thought is the 'signifier', with its associated concept of formal difference. Ultimately, the domain of the symbolic is being summarized as including that which creates a hole (*trou*). The real at first covers a broad field related to 'reality', but soon it takes on the specific Lacanian meaning of 'impossibility', a concept that is gradually elaborated. More and more, the emphasis is on the intangible, which Lacan typifies as something that is turned off, is placed outside (*ek-sistence*). Meanwhile, Lacan remains a Freudian, at least he intends to be one. Indeed, his threefold approach, (symbolic, imaginary, and real), applied to the psychic reality, runs perfectly parallel to that proposed by Freud: superego, ego, id (Über-ich – Ich – Es). These three instances relate to internalised, originally external ideals and commands, to the I-figure, and to the drives. Moreover, a threefold approach has been common since Plato and Aristotle (spirit-soul-body), with Lacan associating his triad with that of Aristotle (Lacan 2005, 146).

What must not be forgotten is the fact that for Lacan always the 'circumstances', the external situation, is extremely important, as was mentioned before. This we see reflected in his work, also at a substance level. Different contexts require different approaches and different institutional crises are being reflected in in his theory on these very moments. Moreover, Lacan was not a teacher with a steady audience, but he had to attract his audience through his 'performances'. In the early 1950s, at the Sainte-Anne psychiatric clinic he addressed a small circle of psychoanalysts, most of them not fully trained, and other interested people. Although inspirational in themselves, inevitably the full content of his speeches was far beyond the grasp of most of his audience (considering that these were clinicians with busy schedules). In the 1960s, the glory days of French Structuralism, the École Normale Supérieure became his new arena. In the students of this exclusive educational institution he found a more understanding group of listeners. And he offered them the menu of the time: a formalistic brand of structuralism. What this young audience didn't have, however, was clinical experience. Finally, in the 1970s, Lacan's central venue would the main hall of the Law Faculty located at Place Panthéon, where Lacan spoke to an amazingly large audience in increasingly cryptic or elliptical terms. Although failing to grasp the essence of his words, they were somehow affected by them – which may explain why Lacan was always talking to a packed house. But once the affective resonance had gone, people would no longer come.

Substance-wise, the system would change just about every year, at least a little bit, without the resulting changes and addition fundamentally disrupting its continuity and coherence. Quite the contrary in fact – even in the later years, after 1973, when the transition started to become apparent, its core elements remained intact. This transition was the outcome of his rethinking of the relationship, the nature of intertwining of the three orders, in which he re-emphasised the impossibility of the Real (a term that has occasionally been capitalised since), of the sexual. Attention shifted to the dramatic aspect of the Drive and the self-reliance of an unthinkable Real. He liked at that time to speak of the 'real to the second power', (le *Réel comme Réel, le réel à la puissance deux*). The three orders he distinguished – the symbolic, the imaginary and the real – were now regarded as being equivalent. One was not put above the other in some privileged way, there was no supremacy of the symbolic, *nor* of the real. What we see here is not a return from Lacan to Freud, but a return from Lacan to Lacan. He moved his audience by talking in rather sceptical terms about his earlier work as well as psychoanalysis and its therapeutic possibilities as a whole.

Finally: In addition to a later Lacan there is also an earlier Lacan (within the time frame of his public appearances, between 1953–1980). This is the Lacan of 1953–1956, who had already defined the basic contours of the three orders (the symbolic, imaginary and real), but had not yet quite worked out the concept of the signifier (Lacan 2002, 237–322).[1] We might even speak of a 'Lacan of the signification', where reconciliation and integration in the style of Hegel and also Cassirer are still believed possible. According to his early-1950s views, language does produce a loss in reality, but this loss can still be undone: After all, a 'full speech' or 'parole pleine' is still believed possible – until the introduction of the concept of the signifier put an end to this notion. It can well be maintained that Lacan is always working on one central theme, which is addressed in a variety of ways (Assoun 2004, 13). The central, overarching theme appears to be 'the lack' or *le manque*, the caesura taking place in everyone's life. Most likely, he experienced this in his own life, finding it difficult to deal with it. Yet it is the central theme, one may argue. Even the shift to the Real, at the very end, is an answer to the complaint that was often heard: 'always this lack'. Indeed, Lacan had often been accused of neglecting reality in his emphasis on the role of language. In respect of classical structuralism, this would be a correct finding – for methodical reasons, no comments were made on the relationship of language with reality – but in the case of Lacan this criticism was not justified. Most likely, the emphasis in the Lacan reception of the 1980s on the 'Real' had the aim to exonerate Lacan from this essentially unjustified criticism. Indeed

1 Whenever reference is made to the English translation of the *Écrits* by Bruce Fink (Lacan 2002), reference occurs to the pagination of the original French edition (Lacan 1966), also being listed in the English translation.

Lacan's central theme is the relationship between the symbolic and the real: its deficit, the absence of such a relationship (dys-harmony, not being attuned). Obviously, accents and elaborations will vary over time, which makes it eminently possible to latch on to a particular period and elaborate on it. Some may feel more attracted to his earlier work, favouring a more exalted interpretation, an effort to which Lacan, with his affinity with the Baroque era ('the world is merely pretence') certainly gives cause. After all, Lacan was steeped in the world of Christianity and Catholicism, influenced especially by the Augustinian tradition: Augustine, Luther, and Pascal (M.-F. Lacan 2010). He considered Luther's idea of the dereliction of man and his abandonment to be a very true expression of the core of psychoanalytic experience (Lacan 1992, 114). In contrast, others may feel more attracted to later periods, where the formalisation he had always aspired came to full fruition. Over the course of many years, J.-A. Miller has attempted, quite successfully and in a most sophisticated way, to take the ideas of the later Lacan, which had partly remained fragmentary, elaborating them, putting them in a retrospective context, systematising and implementing them. What we saw emerge here was a vast body of work with an unmistakably unique quality (Miller 2014). And yet Lacan managed to cover both worlds: the world of the Baroque, with its veils and mirrors, of semblance and reflection, *and* the world of modern science and formal symbolisation. Rather than address them consecutively, he *juxtaposed* them, albeit with different accents. Even his over-rigorous formalisation has a rather Baroque quality, conjuring up images of a pace of mirrors: what is *Spielerei* and what is not? This Baroque side (Lacan 1975, 102) probably also plays a part in the reluctant reception of Lacan's work, and maybe also in the reluctance it sometimes produces.

In the face of it all, Lacan remains remarkably consistent and dedicated. With all the changes in the development, the basic scheme of the imaginary, the symbolic *and* the real, in the last phase redefined as *consistance, trou, ek-sistence*, is retained throughout. In the following, the basic coordinates of his line of thought will briefly be discussed, while aspects of periodisation will only be addressed in passing, if at all. What here is referred to as the 'classical' Lacan remains central. Within it, the full emphasis is on the question of symbolisation. This chapter will therefore not refer to the numerous areas – philosophy, sciences, the moral tradition, the psychoanalytical tradition – on which he commented. This means that the significance of Lacan for psychoanalysis will only be mentioned briefly, in passing. Nonetheless, limiting ourselves to the problem of symbolisation in relation to that of language does not constitute a real limitation, because that is exactly where the specificity of Lacan's philosophy, its very core, lies. That is where we find his original contribution. Just like Cassirer introduced the *linguistic turn*, so does Lacan and

French Structuralism represent its high point. However, Lacan is not so much concerned with the structure as such but rather with the relationship between language and its structure on the one hand, and subject on the other. The influence of structuralism puts an emphasis on the notion that language, seen from the perspective of the language user, comes from the outside, and this 'coming from the outside' has severe implications for the language user, for man 'as a subject'.

The design of this chapter is as follows. The first two paragraphs will outline the contours of Lacan's theory: Here the emphasis is on the exterior quality of culture vis-à-vis the individual, or man. The next two paragraphs (dealing with the language sign and symbolic identification) elaborate its formal aspect. The same theme returns, only now taking on a more formal quality. The relationship between Lacan's and Cassirer's conceptions of language and symbolisation will also be discussed. As a result, the tone of these paragraphs will be rather abstract. The paragraph dealing with the real, also in conjunction with the problem of symbolisation, rounds off the discussion of the classical Lacan. The next three paragraphs dealing with the later Lacan will examine what exactly is added by Lacan to his previous work, including a discussion. The aim is to flesh out the classical Lacan even more. Indeed, this distinction between the classical and later Lacan is a common one, and is running parallel to the distinction made, in other terms, between a first and second classicistic period (Milner, 1995, 77–116). As mentioned, the emphasis in the present Chapter is on symbolisation. This issue will not exhaust his work, far from it, but does constitute its core, which is contended here. Therefore, the aim of this Chapter is not to present an overview of Lacan's work, far from it, but only to offer a specific reading, an interpretation of its main theses: The concept of symbolisation provides their inner coherence. This interpretation will be elaborated concurrently with the exposition of the main theses. In the final paragraph, an overall comparison is made between Lacan's thinking and that of Cassirer, thus putting two different conceptions of symbolisations and their context next to each other. This also points forward to the final Chapter 4.

3.2 The Autonomy of the Symbolic Order

Lacan's basic intuition is that man lives in a physical universe, whilst in order to survive he has to rely and is dependent on culture. Culture is a second nature that traverses the first nature, thus culturally transforming biologically determined needs. Man is cultural by nature, a view that is wholly in line with Cassirer's, while being endorsed by Lacan (1992, 54) as well: 'it is obvious that the things in the human world are things in a universe structured by words, that language, symbolic processes, dominate and govern all'. An essential difference, however, is that Lacan regards culture as something that, from man's perspective, comes from the outside and to which he will have to submit. Here, 'man' is not a producer of culture that helps him reach his destination, but an individual that is completely dependent on culture and on the environment he finds himself in, one that he feels uncomfortable in and does not fit him like a glove. The parent-child relationship and, more generally, the relationship between man and his environment, is defined by asymmetry, by misconception and misunderstanding, which is structural in nature and therefore inevitable. Which inescapably leads to conflict. As mentioned before, this is part of Lacan's core message.

The three layers of the symbolic order. How does Lacan flesh out this notion? Initially, his views were in line with those of French 1950s and 1960s structuralism, which highlighted the significance of external culture and its embedded structure (in one fell swoop disqualifying the then current Existentialism). Lacan joins this effort, distinguishing three layers in culture that he brings together in the concept of the 'symbolic order': (1) language, (2) kinship relationships, including the role of a third-figure, a father-father and (3) social institutions and social groups with their norms. Though not rigorously maintained by Lacan, this threefold distinction can well be defended in light of the three illustrious names backing it up: Saussure for language and linguistics, Lévi-Strauss for family relationships (including marriage and parentage) and Durkheim for social institutions and the social bond, the social ties. They share a common ambition. Saussure conceives language as a system that is autonomous in respect of the language user. This produces an opposition between language as an external system ('langue') and individual speech ('parole'), with priority being given to language as a system. Lévi-Strauss would apply this notion of an underlying structure informing individual choices to the field of cultural anthropology. He discerned the workings of a fundamental ban on incest, which may take different forms in various cultures, but is in fact functional in each culture and marks the transition from nature to culture. Lévi-Strauss's approach appealed strongly to Lacan (2002, 276), and he would go on to apply it to the field of psychoanalysis, to the maximum extent possible. Until his dying day, he would think highly of Lévi-Strauss, both his work and as a person. This is quite understandable, considering that his cognizance of Lévi-Strauss' work would prove crucial, adding great momentum to his own work (Zafiropoulos 2003). Indeed, Lacan is indebted to him (1958, 205–226) for introducing the threesome of the symbolic, the imaginary and the real. After all, what is played out in the background is the French sociological tradition of

Durkheim and Mauss, which would become a major inspiration for the Structuralist movement as a whole (Zafiropoulos 2001). Rather than view society as the sum of individuals, it recognises a social order or the sum of social institutions. Removed from the individual, they constitute an enforcing framework for individual action. Durkheim even speaks of external coercion imposed by social institutions ('contrainte extérieure'), a notion that to some degree is eagerly embraced by Saussure as well as Lacan. Moreover, as a social order, society has a symbolic quality to the extent that a participant in social interaction represents an institution: A carrier of authority represents authority, a teacher represents the educational domain, a father symbolises fatherhood and a punker is a punker for representing the punk community (through his attire). The outcome of an institution through individual action would be a so-called social fact: individual behaviour or experience intrinsically determined by social institutions.

Thus, the concept of the symbolic order consolidates the contributions of Saussure, Lévi-Strauss and Durkheim into one single concept. Though not adding much new, it solidly anchors the concept and represents a solid synthesis. It is given the name: the Other (O). Also, there are similarities with Hegel's objective spirit, another major inspiration for Lacan. And, not to forget, for Cassirer. Also with Lacan, the culture, the objective mind, is the medium in which man has to take shape, but with Lacan the objective mind is primarily *opposed* to man as the Other, and the alien. For one thing, we find ourselves in a different, much more conflict-ridden world than in the case of Cassirer or even Hegel. Even though Hegel has a keen eye for conflicts and tragedies in the world as well as between man and world, a synthesis or reconciliation is at least virtually within reach. Not so with Lacan. The unsolvable opposition between man and world, between subjective mind and objective mind, is a crucial figure of thought for Lacan, with which he must have had first-hand experience himself.

There is yet another reason why the symbolic order is referred to as 'the Other': It represents a formal concept, namely that of an 'order as such', which being an order will be formal or symbolic by definition, in a narrowed-down sense, but takes different shape empirically, depending on time and place – in the words of Cassirer, it is modalised. The concept of the symbolic order can therefore not be equated with its relatively static variant current in the conservative and restorative 1950s (when Lacan introduced the concept). Substance-wise, equalising the two would represent a misconception, disregarding as it does the formal character of the concept as well as Lacan's overall ambition. Nor can the concept of the objective mind in the sense of Hegel (1991) be made equal to its empirical specification in Hegel's time, as elaborated in his 'Elements of the Philosophy of Right' of 1820. The same would be true for Lacan, albeit in a slightly different sense. Which does not necessarily imply that a clear distinction between the symbolic order per se in its formal structure and its concrete implementation has always been made by Lacan. Particularly in the early days of Lacan's teaching, this distinction may be a bit hazy at best.

The biological lack. What is the point in emphasising man's state of dependence on language as an external and autonomous structure? This highlights another basic concept developed by Lacan. Man's biological make-up is bound to fall short in the sense that he has no natural behavioural patterns to fall back on, for which reason he becomes dependent on external control: the order of the image and that of language. Thus, from day one onwards, man lives in an unnatural world, which is supposed to help him compensate for the biological deficit of natural adaptation.

Lacan thus subscribed to the main thesis of the biological anthropology of the first half of the 20th century: Compared to 'the' animal, man is characterised by 'paucity of instinct', an open attitude to the word, an eccentric position and a biological lack. Here he referred to the theory of the Dutch anatomist Bolk, who considered brain development in man compared to primates as being retarded, leading to malleability – comparable to what would later be defined as the 'plasticity of the brain'. Lacan (1973, 16) liked to quote the Hamburg biologist J. von Uexküll, a colleague and friend of Cassirer's, whose work he also liked to refer to (Cassirer 2006b, 28–29). Based on his studies in the field of comparative anatomy, Von Uexküll argued that in the animal world we find a comparatively stable match between inside world and outside world, between *Innenwelt* and *Umwelt*, which has been disrupted in man.

Moreover, for the fragmented state of man, Lacan often referred to Hegel (Lacan 2002, 345). With regard to the 'biological lack' he could also have referred to the biological anthropology of Arnold Gehlen (1966), who argued that as a result of a lack of biological control, man has to rely on external control from social institutions that may help to 'unburden' him. Finally, there are connections with the views of biologist-cum-philosopher Helmuth Plessner (1975) laid down in his thesis on the natural artifice of man. For Lacan (1992, 54), man in that sense is bound to be artificial by nature, living as he does in pre-fabricated linguistic culture that offers him stability: 'man is caught up in symbolic processes of a kind to which no animal has access'. This artificial quality most definitely applies to his sexual nature, which is referred to as 'perverted', considering that it will always pass through the mould of language and culture while being underpinned by fiction and fantasy. Therefore, sex is bound to be counter-natural. As late as 1975, he still defines perversion as the 'essence of man' (Lacan 2005, 153).

This statement actually represents more than a provocation, because it adequately sums up Lacan's view on man: Man is primarily alienated in culture, which has far-reaching consequences, as nothing is natural and stability is thin on the ground. It reflects Freud's basic idea of the primitive situation of the child as being characterised by helplessness ('Hilflosigkeit'), because of its biological insufficiency, in line with Heidegger's idea of thrownness or dereliction, to which Lacan adds dependence upon the Other ('détresse humaine'). These connections become manifest and concrete in the experience of the young child, which at birth is quite helpless, being wholly dependent on the support from others. Lacan (1992, 114) even embraced Luther's idea of the dereliction of man and his abandonment as being a very true expression of the child's experience at this stage.

Three-phase entry. Here we see a return of the three components of the symbolic order: language, relationships – more specifically, the parent/child relationship – and finally institutions. It is of course essential to understand how the symbolic order can enter inside the *vécu*, the lived experience of mental life (Lacan 1972, 194). The first layer, the first step is that of language. In the experience of the child, language comes from the outside, causing it to grow up immersed in language, in a 'language bath'. For its interpretation of what it experiences, it has to rely on this external agent. Incapable of interpreting its own physical tensions, it requires them to be named or symbolised, which means – and this is fundamental – they cease to be what they are, as they are transformed to become part of the interaction. In response to diffuse crying, *le cri*, it hears: 'let yourself be fed' (*laisse-toi nourrir*). What happens here is that to a physical quality meaning, a social meaning, is added (Lacan 1991a, 238). Crying is interpreted as a demand, while the physical milk takes on the meaning of a gift, while the meaning itself will always be tied to matter. A cry *as* a demand, milk *as* a gift. *This is* how Cassirer might have formulated it, and so did Lacan. However, what Lacan adds to it, is the element of alienation, displacement, and of restraint. This is where Lacan puts the emphasis. After all, it is the mother who has the initiative, who sets the tone – the tone of language – taking the form of a demand: 'let yourself be fed'. What Cassirer describes as the 'origin of language' – an inquiry that Lacan will not make – returns here taking the form of a question about the 'leap into language' of the child. In the process, the natural sounds produced by a baby are transformed to acquire the stamp of language, in which it is born a second time. The same applies to the milk that is physically ingested, with the meaning of a gift added. This process of stamping runs deep: see Cassirer. The sensory material acquires a symbolic form (in Cassirer's terms) which also constitutes a limitation, a 'symbolic castration' (according to Lacan). A concrete meaning is added while, moreover, the transformation of the crying into 'let yourself be fed' turns the child into a 'you'. As well as a 'you', it becomes a 'he' or 'she', a somebody, or rather: a single somebody. On top of this, in the transformation the child has to submit to 'the language as such' as well as to the specific form of 'this language' – its unique grammatical features, its idioms, the dialect of a region, city or village. And there is always a jarring element.

Indeed: Who says language, says 'the Other'. It is not just language itself that interprets, it is also the Other, the actual Other who, in the language at his disposal, interprets the child's behaviour. The child exits in and through other people, because of which the child is inscribed as being for others (*être pour autrui*). Thats is an obvious reference to Sartre's concept of being-for-others, with Sartre being a major source for Lacan as well. As a result of his being-for-others, the child falls into the grip of language *and* of the Other: the Other's discourse (Lacan 1966/2002, 655). The Other, the maternal Other or parent, has the power to impose his or her interpretation, being able to 'explain things' – the Other lays down the rules of the game. The superior power of language is thus doubled by the Other's omnipotence, the Other's privilege (Lacan 2002, 691). According to Lacan, a child will therefore never experience itself as being omnipotent, attributing as it does from its own impotence, the omnipotence to the other. This is why the other is capitalised: the Other, with a capital O. (Lacan points out that the child often thinks or might think that the Other can even read its thoughts.) Thus, the subject, the child, does not own language but initially it is language that takes possession of the child. It is 'occupied' by language as well as by the Other. This alienation takes on a second form in the confrontation with the law – the incest prohibition according to Lévi-Strauss's broad interpretation – which in the experience of child comes from the outside, in the form of an imposed ban. Again a limitation is implicitly at work here: The child is male *or* female from the perspective of sexual difference, and in line with that it is also given the name of either a boy or a girl. Indeed, the child is supposed to behave in line with its gender: Boys should play with car toys or knight figurines, not with princess dolls, while the reverse is true for girls. Thus a substantive gender quality is thus added to the formal sexual difference. What exactly does it mean to be a boy or a girl, not only in the eyes of the mother or the first Other, but in the eyes of the others as a whole? What expectations and ideal images are there in society? This leads us to the third step, the third layer, that of the others and of social institutions. Enter social institutions such as fatherhood, motherhood, being-a-daughter, being-a-son, and all its associated ideals of the other. They come from the outside, and can be read in the eyes of the Other, looking at the child with approval or disapproval. Because the child is strongly dependent on the Other, most of the time it will try its best to live up to those ideals. Thus, the ideals and commands originally coming from the outside take root in its inner world: from its family, and from the ruling social order and normative discourse. The child submits to this, threatened by the loss of love, likewise the adult submits under the threat of social expulsion or loss of a job. This is true for a static society as well as for a dynamic society. The fact that rules of conduct may vary does not detract from the finding that such rules will always apply. In that sense, there is no essential difference between traditional rules of behaviour of any group in society on the one hand, and the range of fluctuating codes that differ among groups and time periods on the other. Anyone taking part in social traffic, regardless of its nature, has to appreciate this to some extent.

Lacan would emphasise that identities thus obtained invariably come from the outside, the Other, thus introducing an element of alienation that ultimately goes back to the alienation effectuated by the entry into language (Lacan 1986, 211–213; 2002, 840). Man is even considered to be an hostage of the symbolic, having to sacrifice his own being (Lacan 1991a, 322). In contrast, Cassirer (2005, 261) would never speak in such terms – it constitutes a key difference. Although with Cassirer subjectivity also develops in stages, through myth, language and science, this he refers primarily to as self-realisation rather than alienation. Cassirer (PsF III, 44/39) writes: 'The entering of the ego as a spiritual "subject" into the medium of the objective spirit constitutes not an act of alienation but an act of finding and determining itself'. Indeed, Lacan will never disregard the index of alienation, which means that acquisition of identity is always associated with a loss of being: The external order has its own autonomy, taking its own course. Lacan would therefore compare the autonomy of the symbolic order to what Freud calls the repetition compulsion (*Wiederholungszwang*). He also speaks of *automaton* (Lacan 2002, 39) with the autonomy of this *automaton* leading to a strong *antinomy* between this order and the subject, as we have seen. However, if the subject were to stay trapped inside, it would have a status similar to that of a manikin. At this level, people become mere puppets of the symbolic order, domesticated sheep earmarked by the symbolic order. For man to escape this state of alienation, a second movement is needed, to lead out of it. Once we have entered there has to be an exit too; after alienation there is separation. However, it is culture, Otherness itself that allows for separation as well. That will be discussed in the following. This second step of the dialectics of culture will be discussed now.

3.3 The Dialectics of Desire

Thus, culture and language stamp the individual, but only up to a point. This is because, by definition, language leaves gaps and is never unequivocal in its expressions. These gaps are associated with an essential characteristic of language: its general quality (which was also emphasised by Cassirer). Language is made up of general terms, and falls short in terms of providing the right word in a specific instance, here and now. Moreover, it does not merely label 'what is', casting as it does 'what is' into a mould, giving it a shape it did not have before – this is what Cassirer tells us, and so does Lacan. Lacan would also argue that language is inadequate when it comes 'to revealing the state of being'. It simply lacks the terms required – what is expressed by the symbol Ø, to be read *here* as the falling short, the inadequacy of language. This applies to the state of being of the subject as well as the object.

Still, this inadequacy works out positively rather than being an obstacle. Indeed, the inadequacy of language makes it possible to escape from this overwhelming power, preventing the child from coinciding fully with what it is claimed to be. The child is not merely what it asks, or what is asked of it, but also what remains unfulfilled in the fulfilling of the demand. The fulfilment of the demand leaves a remainder, which in turn nurtures desire. This has a major implication for the subject's state of being: its duplication, provoked by language. It creates an inner state of dividedness between the 'subject of the statement' and the 'enunciating subject' (Lacan 2002, 800; 2013, 37–55). You are what you are said to be. That's what you *are*. But then again you're not. It is in the 'not', in what was initially unsaid, in the excluded subjectivity – the subject of the act of enunciation – that the unconscious can be situated. According this view, what's-not-being said, what's-not-understood, is not irrevocably left out, but shows itself in factual statements and in the subject's actions, for example in the life choices which may not be understood at first, and can only be grasped much later. That which is unconscious, or repressed, has not vanished altogether from the symbolic circuit, but does present itself, be it without a label. It often takes a long time to find out what form that label should take.

La Chose. The inadequacy of language applies not only to the subject side, but also to that of the object. Language likewise falls short in terms of naming the object. Lacan (2002, 319) liked to quote Hegel's expression (or attributed to him): 'the word as the killing of the thing' ('le symbole comme meurtre de la chose'). This applies in general: The introduction of the signifier does not only kill a single thing, but ultimately the not-yet signified real as such. As a result, the real, being itself, will be effaced, crossed out, because of its being represented by signifiers, that actually replace it: 'the signifier instates lack of being ["le manque de l'être"] in the object-relation'. (Lacan 2002, 515). In other words, being lost, the pre-symbolic state causes the emergence of a void that did not exist before, and consequently also the possibility of filling it, which did not exist before either. For clarification, Lacan (1992, 149) draws on the image of the jug or a vase ('Krug') used by Heidegger. The matter from which the vase was shaped, the matter of signifiers, envelops a void, namely that of the inside of the vase, which through representation is shaped, with the clay losing its density in the process. Lacan writes rather evocatively: 'Thus, emptiness and fullness are introduced into a world that by itself knows not of them'. A central void (*vide central*), lack of being, emerges, with the desire also coming to the fore, taking the form of a desire to fill the void. Lacan calls this original emptiness/fullness *la Chose, das Ding*: the real that suffers from the signifier, an inflicted incision, an emptiness. Several references are contained in this complex notion. Lacan is playing with references to Freud's first Other (*Nebenmensch*), Kant (*Ding an sich*), Heidegger (*das Ding*), and ultimately to Eckhart (*Ding*, Soul).

Seeing that Lacan had referred to Heidegger, he might also have referred to Sartre (1966) – whose major work 'Being and Nothingness' was an important source of inspiration to him. Indeed, to a certain degree Lacan's real runs parallel to Sartre's concept of the being-in-itself ('en soi'), both of these being defined as 'identical with itself', as an undifferentiated opacity, without otherness or difference, without connection with the other: 'It is what is' (Sartre 1966, lxvi). However, in the case of Sartre it is consciousness that introduces negativity ('not') and difference as well, with the 'thing' being lost in the 'not': no-thing-ness. Consciousness introduces the gap ('trou') into the 'being-in-itself' ('en soi'), which loses its density as a result. With Lacan, it is not consciousness but the signifier that introduces the gap ('hole') into being-in-itself, into the real. Indeed, the nothingness created by consciousness (Sartre) runs parallel to the void created by the signifier (Lacan). Consequently, with Lacan (1981, 168) empirical reality is marked, from the very beginning, by a 'symbolic nihilation' ('néantisation symbolique') – also with a clear reference to Sartre. Next to it, Lacan follows Sartre' s second step, with the nothingness giving rise to the emergence of a desire for being ('désir d'être'). However, with Lacan it is the void which gives rise to the emergence of an essentially primitive and original desire: the desire to close the gap, to fill the emptiness created by the signifier, to fill the bottle of the Thing. That makes the concept of the Thing ('la Chose') inherently ambiguous: it is the void *and* the void being filled as well. Here Lacan turns away form Sartre, instead turning to Augustine. Indeed, Lacan (1992, 171) refers to the central place of the Thing as an 'intimate exteriority' or an *extimacy*, with the Thing appearing as filled lack, without any lack. Inevitably, the notion of an intimate exteriority, of *extimacy*, reminds us of Augustine's inner God, the mystery of the soul, defined in his *Confessions* as being '*ex intimo* corde meo' (4,13), 'interior intimo meo' (3,11): being more inward than my innermost self, and a transcendence, a beyond as well (emphasis added).

Bearing in mind that Lacan, in his own words, from his adolescence onwards had been an avid reader of Augustine's works, we may truly understand Lacan's (2002, 656) phrase: 'the true subject of desire is nothing other than the Thing, which in and of itself is what is closest to him while escaping him more than anything else'. Indeed, Lacan's concept of the Thing ('la Chose', 'Ding') as being an intimate exteriority reminds us strongly of Augustine's concept of God as an 'interior intimo meo': being more inward than my innermost self. It is its transcendence that explains why the Thing is called by the the name of Sovereign Good ('summum bonum'), or is called 'real' as well. The *real*, the *ens realissimum*, is what lies beyond, being impossible because of that.

Indeed, the Thing does not exist empirically or factually, it is merely a non-existing 'mythical' figure, an object out of reach, its non-existence resulting from the fact that it is not yet symbolically processed. When it comes into existence, it appears only as veiled, while being represented as something else, particularly as a work of *art*, an empirical object that has been elevated to the dignity of the Thing, whilst being an object that remains close to It. And this conception of art (as elevation of an object to the dignity of the Thing) is a concise rephrasing, in fact an inversion of Freud's naturalistic conception of sublimation as a form of desexualisation. Indeed, it is worth mentioning, as a side note, that precisely here Lacan (1992, 195) refers to Simmel (2011, 77–96), Cassirer's first teacher in philosophy and his theory of art, because of its crucial concept of an 'object out of reach'. The sublime in Kant's sense *and* sublimation, the elevation towards the Thing, could be put on an equal footing. And yet distance towards the Thing has to be maintained, the object of pure love *has* to remain out of reach (Le Brun 2002, 307–319).

This becomes apparent from another presence of the Thing: the mythical body of the mother, also being an original exemplification of this emptiness/fullness, the primordial Other. The mother, the Sovereign Good, is a forbidden good, that needs to be kept at bay: Such is the foundation of the moral law. Obviously, the primordial Other does not exist empirically or factually either, but is merely a non-existing 'mythical' figure, its non-existence resulting from the fact that it is not yet further symbolically processed (1992, 145). In its representation, this immediate presence with the primordial Other (as the not-barred Other) will be lost, as a result of which we see a factual divided Other emerge, one that carries the mark of representation, of castration, limitation. Next, this immediacy is left behind, leaving a hole that enables empirical relationships to be established.

However, the attraction of the primordial Other remains. This is a major theme with Georges Bataille, and it deserves mentioning that he and Lacan had struck up a close friendship, Lacan's second wife Sylvia having been married to Bataille before her second marriage with Lacan. In his discussion of the desire of a lover to rather kill than lose his beloved Bataille (1986, 20), he points out: 'only the beloved can in this world bring about what our limitations deny [*interdisent*], a total blending of two beings, a continuity between two discontinues creatures'. Again the beloved one is supposed to accomplish the unfragmented presence, the continuity and merging of two beings in order to effectuate the immediate presence with the primordial Other ('la Chose').

The attraction of the primordial Other – leaving aside the question whether it is forbidden or impossible – is counteracted by what will become Lacan's major theme: the severing of the bond, the discontinuity, the difference. Why? Because culture and symbolisation as such are made up of cutting, curtailing, drawing a line, thus saying 'stop right here'. It is Lacan's (1992, 87–104) version of the Moral Law, which he traces back to the Decalogue: 'Thou shalt not', the ban on incest in its broadest sense. Therefore Lacan (1992, 23) can rightfully say: 'the presence of the moral law is that through which the real is actualised' (i.e. presentified). Because of the presence of the Moral Law, the impending invasion from the primordial Other ('la Chose'), the fullness of immediacy, can be frustrated. This threat of an invasion, what Freud referred to as 'death drive', now manifests itself in its true form, and its driving force is what Lacan would later refer to as 'Jouissance'.[2]

And when depicting this deadly 'Jouissance', in a film for example, the character of the 'alien' from the science-fiction genre would definitely fit the bill, being something of a completely unfamiliar order entering the world, to be ranked in the order of death, of devouring. The film 'Under the skin' by J. Glazer, after Michel Faber's eponymous novel (2000), illustrates this quite wonderfully. A somewhat enigmatic, unworldly but strangely attractive women drives around in a van in the Glasgow area, addressing random men who respond to her sexual advances, never to be seen again. It turns out she as an alien man-devouring creature, a black female, swallowing every man who crosses her path. Hardly a male fantasy, it goes even further, reaching down to a deeper, more fundamental level: not just that of the fantasy, but what actually precedes it. Again we find: It is only fiction, a mere representation of something that *cannot* be represented, falling outside the domain of representation. Also an 'alien' is nothing more than a representation, and can obviously never be the actual devouring entity. Not until 'Jouissance', the mother body in his devouring guise,

2 This death drive, or primary masochism, has two manifestations, according to Lacan: the return to and from 'Jouissance' as a tormenting pleasure, *and* alienation without separation: being marked by the signifier without any progress, which at best would lead to a puppet's life, at the Other's beck and call without any chance of owned desire. Indeed, two types of primary masochism, to be distinguished from all other forms of (secondary) masochism offering a way out of a situation.

is lost, can we enter into a relationship with a loved one whose body and body parts can become objects of desire (without the fear of being devoured).

By virtue of its grandeur, addiction would be a case a point. Trying to overcome it appears to be always a very difficult struggle. Take the protagonist in John O'Brien's novel *Leaving Las Vegas* (and the feature film of the same name), who finds himself unable to leave Las Vegas. Similarly, the protagonist in Thomas Mann's novel *Der Tod in Venedig* (on which the film *Death in Venice* of Lucino Visconti was based) is unable to leave Venice as a place of death, even though he has always led a life of rough discipline. He lacks the inner strength to oppose the forces of death. In his play with death, a specific brand of Romanticism, of *Romantic Agony*, is not far away (Praz 1970). It is also possible that not the inner strength but the will is lacking. We see this happening in forms of counter-culture, or counter-music, expressing itself in the form of rage or melancholy, in situations where the symbolism of death is strong while personal death is often but a step away (with many suicides): I'm out of the game, I don't *want* to join in. The more moving the art, the more it engages with this barrier separating life from death and destruction. This may be a romantic notion of art, putting art and death closely together, but it is certainly a view of art in its own right. This reflects a whole different manifestation of the death drive, which has many faces, although the irrevocable outcome is always the same. No matter how much misery it brings, how much resentment it may provoke or how mundane it may look, we will be hard put not feeling impressed by sheer self-destruction, by this 'Jouissance' of not-joining in.

The object a. This general presence with the primordial Other is excluded through representation. Representation breaks up the unity, a loss that Lacan specifies as a loss of a specific part, defined as object *a*: a body part fulfilling an intermediary role in the two-unity, the breast for example. But what exactly is meant by 'breast'? Initially, it is the actual breast from which the child will be *weaned* after a certain period of time. In a more fundamental way, the breast itself will then be lost. This loss is enclosed in the invitation 'let yourself be fed'. It does not take the shape of the breast that the mother *gives to the child* and that belongs to the mother, but of the preceding breast that belongs to both, also to the child: 'the plan of the separation, which makes the breast the lost object involved [*en cause*] in desire, passes between the breast and the mother'. (Lacan 2002, 848). At this level, the child is not separated from the actual mother's breast (here, there, tangible) but from the breast that *is* at a more primitive, more fantastic level, i.d. the level of the Thing: at a level where the mental separation between mother and child has not yet come to pass. Once that caesura has been made, once physicality can be represented as corporeality, as 'my body' as being opposed to 'your body', this intermediary sphere, this fantasy breast, is lost, excluded. What remains is the reminder of this process, the constitution, the extraction of an excluded object. Which is what constitutes the factual, actual breast itself – as an *effect* of representation. Remember Cassirer's thesis: through representation, immediacy, the sphere of immediacy, is excluded. This is what is played out here and now at a primitive, elementary level. For that reason, the term of lost object may be used but is in fact inappropriate. After all, it does not concern an actual, so-called partial object, far from it. That would be a neurotic interpretation, failing to appreciate the context of representation of its genesis, its being structurally excluded (Lacan 2004, 197). The nature of this concept can only be clarified from the perspective of representation. Indeed, the essence of representation is cutting off (*coupure*).

The lost object of the breast now becomes the prototype of object *a*. The act of being lost, of being excluded, makes that the child can desire for a breast, becomes attached to a breast. After all, a human subject can only desire for something it does not have, something that it lacks – the lack as a precondition for desire. It's Lacan's thesis of putting desire on a par with the gap, the lack of being, the loss of life. Desire implies distance, a gap in which it can exist: The question of desire is that the fading, the unconscious subject yearns to find itself again (Lacan 1972, 194). This loss, would create the possibility of longing for a particular breast, in addition to which there are other breasts that might bring satisfaction as well. It can only be encircled, it merely adds contours to actual objects, insofar as these come to its place. Without the breast being regarded as intrusive, as threatening, as though it were the excluded breast itself. Indeed, it is excluded, for internal reasons, not accidentally but inherent to the process of representation leaving a remainder. In a sense, the actual object themselves become satellites orbiting around that primordial, excluded object *a* keeping them in orbit. Like the loss of the original breast may lie at the heart of the desire for a particular breast.

Moreover, other partial objects than the breast may fulfil a similar role, in relation to those body orifices where something goes in or comes out, is being separated or cut off. Thus, Lacan (1986, 174–200) eventually defines four figures of the object *a* as lost objects. To the breast (feeding) and the scybala (gift, purification) he adds the voice and the gaze – the props to be found in the Other's desire. Here we are not talking about the voice as a source of meaning – no, this is about sound and sonority, the meaningless pieces of sound, the subject's highly singular soundtrack. And the gaze is not the look as such, the meaning giving act of seeing, but the non-seeing gaze in the Other, as has been *seen* by the child: its material quality, its expression, the glance. A person may be attracted by the look of an eye, or by a the sound of a voice. This other person will then have 'it'. An empirical object may then embody the excluded object, resulting in one object being served up as another object through a kind of alchemic or metabolic process, a process of symbolisation. It *is* an ordinary breast, and then again it *is* not, it *is* also something else, something that is out of reach which, while being out of reach, is present as well – in a real presence (Le Gaufey 2009, 126). This real presence is quite comparable with the kind of presence as real presence (*presentia realis*) involved in the Eucharist: It is just ordinary wine and bread, but then again it represents, it *is* also the flesh and blood of Christ, albeit at a remove (see Chapter 2). Similarly, the excluded object nurtures desire, but some distance will have to be maintained. Indeed, once the excluded object comes too close, it will appear as something extra-mundane, as an erratic object, not embedded in the world of perception, taking the form of a hallucination, for example, of a pseudo-empirical object. One may speak of the formations of the object *a* (Nasio 1987, 75–107).

The drive. It appears that Lacan's theory of object *a* offers a revision of Freud's conception of the drive which holds that drive can be split up into partial drives, each focused on a distinct part of the body. Indeed, the activity in the subject that Lacan (2002, 849) calls 'drive' (*Trieb*) consist in dealing with these lost objects in such a way as to recover from them, to restore to himself, his earliest loss. With the result, the drive representing sexuality in the unconscious, is never anything but a partial drive. Therefore, this theory represents a recalibration of Freud's drive theory. And yet where Freud considers the drive to be something that *connects* man with nature, Lacan (2002, 834) by contrast sees drive as that which *separates* man from nature. Being a partial drive with a partial object, according to Lacan (2005, 17), drive is not an extension of the natural body, but rather the effect of the retrograde impact of language on the not yet symbolically processed body, a conception sustained till the end, with the drive being an echo within the body caused by the presence of speech. Its object being put at a distance, cannot exist as an object, only as a configuration, a shape, an object *a*, something that cannot ever be reached and can be encircled at best. It simply falls outside the scope of what can be represented. Consequently, the object *a* can be qualified as 'real', namely in the specific sense of impossible to reach and being inexorable as well (Lacan 2013, 565). This is nicely illustrated by the example of Michelangelo Antonioni's 1966 film 'Blow Up', based on a novel by Julio Cortazar (Leclaire 1991, 155). Unwittingly, a photographer witnesses a murder, which only becomes evident after a dead body has become visible on an enlarged exposure of one of his photographs. An investigation turns up nothing – the body seems to have been lost without a trace. Here, the lost object becomes the equivalent of the vanished body, which is encircled through the drive taking the shape of a look-drive or scopic drive (but no longer exists empirically). Therefore, the adequate depiction of the lost object is not an excess, but a void, an absence, a lack, which is the cause of desire itself (Lacan 2013, 441).

Torus. Likewise, the arts (cinema, painting, lyrics, for example) are capable of evoking that which falls outside the scope of language. But Lacan wouldn't be Lacan if he had made no attempt to formalise this impossible relationship. To this end, he employed models taken from mathematical topology (which indicates what remains constant during plane transformation). Remarkably, Cassirer did engage in a similar endeavour well before Lacan (without any demonstrable or plausible influence on Lacan being at work). Cassirer uses Felix Klein's topology to clarify the emergence of the constancy of the object of perception – object constancy – to visualise what is not intrinsically visible (PsF III, 177/157; GW 24/2007). Equally remarkable is the fact that also Merleau-Ponty (2001, 260–264), an intimate friend of Lacan's, draws on topology, namely to explain his notion of a brutal, savage state of being ('être brut', 'être sauvage'). Thus, in his turn Lacan uses this topology to represent the object loss in order to envisage what cannot really be envisaged: emptiness, e.g., the empty space of a mustard jar, Klein's bottle, *cross-cap*, etcetera. Another example is the *torus*, which might be compared to a tyre, an inner tube or the rim. The tyre itself contains two spaces, two cavities: the first one being the cavity where air is pumped into, which in turn encloses a second cavity where the wheel is fitted into (or the central space). An imaginary figure moving across the surface of the tyre in circles will eventually arrive at its point of departure, to complete another full circle. The spiralling journey across the surface of the tyre symbolises the sequence of signifiers articulating a demand (supported by the hollow space inside the tyre): 'I want chocolate, can I have a banana, and so forth'. At the same time, the trajectory of the demand encircles the tyre's circumference with the central empty space inside it: that is the central void (*vide centrale*). It represents the lack left by the loss of the immediacy, taking the form of *la Chose*. Here, the tyre becomes one of the links in a chain, considering that the rim of the next chain-link passes through the central void. The individual lack of each person connects them, links them, 'chains' them together. This would be true at a general societal level – supply and demand – but much more strongly so at the level of intimate relationships (partner relationship, parent-child relationships). Thus, each demand will be driven by a concrete lack, whilst at a deeper level it is nurtured by a fundamental lack, an unconscious desire, circling around the hole (*trou*) left by the loss of immediacy. Throughout the philosophical road travelled by Lacan (2005) his fundamental model of man remains that of the *torus* – the inner tube, the rim, or the chain.

Desire being mediated by the Other's desire. In the genesis of desire, it is not only language but also – and even more so – its inadequacy that plays a crucial role. First and foremost, language causes immediacy to be lost – the lack of being represented by the term Φ, the symbolic phallus. This will make the child dependent on the Other who speaks, the language of the Other. The Other expresses what the child feels, is supposed to feel – it is what it is said to be (*laisse-toi nourrir*), as was shown before. With time, however, the child will find that the Other and the Otherness are not unequivocal. It now thinks, when being addressed by an adult person: 'He is saying this, but he may well mean something else'. The child finds out about the gaps left by language, about its enigmatic qualities. 'Off to bed, right now', sometimes does not mean 'off to bed, right now'. 'So what does it mean then?' The child discovers that the language is not homogenous, not closed, but is open to interpretation: Language is not a closed system, not a code with 'a = a' invariably meaning 'off to bed = off to bed'. Cassirer would have said: Language does not mirror reality. In the same vein, Lacan's basic assumption is that language turns out to be defective, consistently failing in an essential way to adequately name, to mirror, what is: (Ø). Insight into the inadequacy of language will enable to child to escape the alienating effects initially introduced by language. Insight into its inadequacy has yet another effect, in one fell swoop putting paid to the Other's alleged omnipotence: the Other is no longer in full command, things are not necessarily the way the Other says they are: no longer is the Other's word law: so again (Ø). Then there is a third effect: the Other's inadequacy gives access to the child's own desire. The confusion about what the Other asks raises the question as to what the Other actually wants, which finds expression in the question: what is the Other really after, what does he really want, what role am I supposed to play, what is expected of me in this world, am I welcome here? What is this lunatic asylum that I find myself in? The inadequacy of language unlocks the demand, thus opening up the dimension of desire, which also causes the child to experience the Other as having desires and being a creature of the lack: a third meaning of (Ø).

Initially, or fundamentally, this lack in the Other will be experienced as being undefined, as a huge gaping hole, because of the child's state of distress ('détresse') or helplessness ('Hilflosigkeit'). Lacan (2013, 27–30) never fails to stress that. Indeed, we are far removed from the image of the 'good enough mother', which offers us a far more peaceful picture of the early mother-child relationship (Winnicot 1965). Indeed, Lacan's conflict-ridden world aligns more with Melanie Klein's (1955) conception of early childhood: What does the Other want from me? Consequently, the child's answer will take the most general form of wanting to be 'everything', to compensate for the completely undefined lack in the Other. This means the loss of presence is restored, be it in an illusionary fashion, as a result of the child identifying with this 'everything' – what Lacan, in the 1950s, would equate with the identification with the imaginary phallus, φ. The illusion is more or less required, being the result of representation itself. The representation (from O to Ø) may lead to separation, but is also associated with the illusion that this separation can somehow be overcome. This is only an illusion, however, offering little perspective. Indeed, if taken to its full consequence, it will even prove disastrous, considering that restoring the lost two-unity eliminates the symbolic perspective – the very product of the loss of immediate presence. The impossibility of restoring the unity with the maternal body, the primordial Other, Lacan defines as 'Name-of-the-Father', the hallmark of *culture*, representation as such – just like the symbolic phallus, Φ, signifies an initial loss, an original lack, the desire as such, the hallmark of *language*. The Name-of-the-Father suggests another place, a third figure placed outside the desire of the first Other, Ø, (often the mother) in relation to the child, from which this desire can then be observed.

As said, the Name-of-the-Father refers to a third figure, namely the figure of the third. And yet this figure of the third is *not* the actual father – anything but, in fact: it is the Name-of-the-Father or the signifier of the Law (Lacan 2002, 583). The Law says that there needs to be space between people in all their relationships, so that one cannot be or aspire to be everything to the other. This is most certainly true for the matrix of all relationships: the mother-child relationship. Here, Lacan follows in the footsteps of Freud and Lévi-Strauss, with the latter explicitly referring to incest prohibition (to which Lacan chooses to add substance in a broader as well as more affective sense). The Law is the Law of separation, of castration implying acceptance of the lack. So what exactly is the role of the father? The father represents the Law, which is not is own invention, he merely represents it. Lacan would therefore argue that the actual father is not primarily relevant and can even be left out, as we have witnessed in all cultures, throughout the ages, according to Lévi-Strauss as well. It means that, on this level, it is irrelevant whether the actual does or does not fail ('carence du père'), because nothing more is required than a place from which he can operate and that he can occupy when he is present or is left vacant in the absence of an actual father. There are many ways to represent the Law, for example through the mother's gesturing or not gesturing, her decisions, her job, etcetera. It is the Law that allows for an actual father to be present as a father, as a caring, limiting, encouraging, giving father (Lacan 2002, 693). Indeed, the importance of the Law does not detract from the relevance of an actual father being present, in a derived sense. Nevertheless, the father is not a Legislator, far from it.

So who exactly does the Moral Law address? Not exclusively the child, as Freud believed, but everyone, and at any rate the child *and* the mother: 'Thou shalt not re-incorporate thy child', 'you must not desire to own your mother'. So what exactly is the remit of the Law? It does not take the form of a 'ban', although Lacan initially interpreted this instance as a banning agency: 'thou shalt not'. Later on, he would emphasise the fact that this 'shalt' should not be interpreted as a moral obligation, but rather as a logical one: 'it is the only way'. This process of detachment, of separation, is a precondition for developing a stable form of subject-identity. To put it bluntly, marking an empty place is a necessary and adequate condition. The Name-of-the-Father does not refer to just one person, nor a legislator, but being the signifier of the Law, to the Law of culture: it must apply for a valid culture to exist, for the symbolic function to be effective (in Neo-Kantians terms). Lacan (2002, 278) explains, in the early 1950s: 'It is in the *name of the father* that we must recognize the basis of the symbolic function which, since the dawn of historical time, has identified his person with the figure of the law'. As a result, its effect is not just limited to a particular religion or cultural period, but is as original as is the symbolic function, although some particular religions might serve as an example. Lacan relates the idea of the Law, of symbolic castration, to the content and scope of the Decalogue (1992, 99–101) and – still in the 1970s – to the Christian idea of redemption as well (2005, 85). In its universal *function*, it may represent an ultimate term, but it is by no means an ultimate truth or entity, marking as it does the functionality of the representative system as such through its open character. Therefore, it needs to be observed and lived performatively by anyone who wants to be part of culture. By the same token, the term symbolic phallus does not refer to 'phallus' as an entity, but instead encapsulates the rule of desire, which manifests itself in the mode of a lack that cannot be undone and that signifies each individual's life. This also applies to the Name-of-the-Father as signifier of the Law. It is a term that can take different forms while invariably marking the empty space left by the mother (Lacan 2002, 557). Essential here is the empty place itself, certainly not being tied to a traditional family structure, and actually being compatible with a range of variations, but the way in which it is signified will obviously have implications as well. In many societies – certainly strongly patriarchal societies – the biological father, as a non-mother, is the obvious choice for representing the law. And yet the concept of the Name-of-the-Father does *not* refer to a father figure or paternal authority figure, and it was Freud's misconception to let the two coincide (in the oedipal complex) – this is how we could briefly summarize Lacan's contribution to this debate. What matters in this context is this fundamental law of the culture, which is why Lacan never fails to try and reach beyond the level of the anecdote, of factual stories (including that of the forbidding father), in order to identify formal relationships that can be fleshed out through factual stories. The term

Name-of-the-Father should therefore be conceived in that formalising sense, which explains why Lacan used an formula when introducing the concept. Using a formula, is to indicate that it is about a formula.

Likewise, the Desire-of-the-Mother is *also* a formal term that takes shape empirically in a variety of ways (by a mother, or anyone else). The Name-of-the-Father *and* the Desire-of-the-Mother are therefore correlative terms that are both essentially formal. Also the Desire-of-the-Mother can take different shapes and forms. But what is this desire, what is it about and what does it want from me? Initially the child will situate the desire on the side of the mother, which is not difficult to experience for the child, considering that it starts with 'let yourself be fed' (*laisse-toi nourrir*). This already holds the promise of temptation. The idea is that the child will position itself as the object of the Other's desire, trying to be everything to her. It is the indefinite quality of the desire of the Other, whilst being opaque from the child's perspective, that compels the child to keep all options open, in order to be everything to her.

The fact that the child's desire is mediated by the Other's desire might thus lead to a deadlock: a permanent state of imprisonment in the desire of the Other: alienation. For the child's desire not to be kept imprisoned in the world of its mother, not remaining alienated in its desires, it is required that this desire is *also* focused on an Other. This therefore requires the presence of an empty space, in which a second Other (next to the first Other) can appear. The Name-of-the-Father opens up this place, thus functioning as a third instance – where the Name-of-the-Father, as mentioned before, does not constitute an empirical ban, but is rather enclosed in the internal dialectics of the dialectics of desire, instituted by culture itself. The dialectics of desire resumes a dialectics of culture. Nonetheless, the Law, the Law of culture, being valid is merely a necessary but not an adequate precondition for the genesis of desire. A law needs to be effectuated through making a *choice*: I do it or I don't, I comply or don't comply. Lacan (1986, 212) would never tire of highlighting the need for this moment of choice: either/or. The space required is created by the Name-of-the-Father as an external figure in respect of the Desire-of-the-Mother, as a vector for delimiting and balancing that. From that place, each and every father can fulfil his important tasks, while being both a limiting and and encouraging, caring, giving father (2002, 693).

Phantasm. From this vantage point, the subject, the child is able to explore the contours of this desire of others, of the Other: What exactly is my role in this desire, to him or to her. The coming/and/going is not a physical movement, but is symbolically charged, is meaningful. It also shows that the Other has someone or something else outside the child, a condition that the child apparently cannot meet: 'How far can I go before the Other has enough of me?' A classic example is the fantasy of attending one's own funeral, watching one's own disappearance: 'How would the other react if I were to disappear?' and so on (Lacan 2002, 844). Once the child has probed this desire, as a next step it can relate towards to it, for example by being what (it thinks that) the Other is missing. Here the significance of the lost object comes to the fore, in two ways: either the subject identifies with this object *or* it will start looking for the object in the Other. If it chooses to identify with the object, it offers itself to the Other in order to complement him. Thus through identification with the breast as the excluded object it will attempt to feed the other or to devour him, and through identification with the scybala, it makes itself available to the Other to be pushed around or insulted; then again, through identification with the voice, it may attempt to make itself heard. Alternatively, it may look for the object in the Other: being fed or even devoured by the other, showing itself to the other, submitting to its authority. In both cases, either actively or passively, the child or the adult finds gratification (of lust), a fulfilment of its drive in the circuit with the Other. In the process, the phantasm will also function as a wall of defence against the other, against the unbounded and unlimited quality of the Other's desire, which thus acquires substance and framing: *that* is what she, what he, apparently wants from me.

The construct of the phantasm will produce a range of modalities to satisfy lust: This affects me, this does not. And to the extent that an actual person embodies a lost object (object *a*) – in a particular cast of the eye, the sonority of the voice, a particular kind of generosity, of tyranny – one may choose to engage in an affective relationship with this person, if this person more or less fits the construct of the basic phantasm, not be conceived as a single phantasm but as a matrix, as indicated earlier. Thus, the phantasm underpins the desire, adding a specific contour to the desire. It is an unconscious framework, the *format*, in which and through which is determined what is attractive and where the lost objects, which control the drive, should be positioned. It brings stability, whilst being a paragon of stability and immutability. The phantasm is the fatum, the fate or (*Triebschicksal*), to quote Freud. As is commonly known, man will not easily be able or prepared to relinquish the urge to satisfy its drives, which ties in with the function of giving consistency to the phantasm. Any modification will therefore first and foremost be experienced as loss of self. However, the underlying basic phantasm adds consistency to the experience, which is the very reason why it is not given *in* the experience, but needs to be reconstructed based on the individual's experiences and actions – wholly in line with Neo-Kantian views. Fantasies may be experienced, but their underlying structure cannot (Lacan 2002, 842–844).

At any rate, working out what exactly is the object of desire, brings a lot of 'fuss', in every sense of the word. With time, the protagonist will find how to meet the criteria of the object, namely by eliminating those who fail to meet them. The identity of the object of desire, of 'what you really want', will initially be unclear or 'opaque'. It is not until a person recognises what the other person apparently does not want, that things will become clear. In either case it involves a process of interpreting the desire. Yet, this desire does not form an entity with its object, does not exist as such. It only 'exists' in transit, in a lived and interpreted form. Man is a creature of the lack, of the desire, that does not know its own desire – nor that of the Other (who does not know it either). This non-transparency, this state of subjective dividedness, does bring the need for reflection, however: what is it that I want, what does the Other want? Reflection is needed, but how can it be brought about? Where does the possibility of reflection originate (obviously within the context of this line of thought)? Once again, language will come to the rescue, in a sense. Besides creating dividedness, it enables reflection as well as the possibility to live with this dividedness rather than perishing from it.

Reflection. We could say that reflection is inherent to the theme of language and desire. Admittedly, Lacan did not turn 'reflection' into a big issue. And still it does become relevant in the transition from demand to desire, in the inquiry into the demand as such, reaching beyond itself to point to desire. Implicit in the inquiry into the structure of the demand in its relationship to the desire of the Other, is a process of reflection. The reflexive function, the ability to reflect, has been addressed before, in Chapter 1. By way of hypothesis, the ability to reflect was reduced to two capacities afforded by owning a language: negation – 'what is' may also not exist – *and* perspective change – to view 'what is' from the perspective of the other. Complementing this explanation, on may assume that both capacities go back specifically to the i*nadequacy* of language. For the very reason that language is not a one-dimensional, hermetic code, it affords room to modalise the experience, to think away what is – I don't like it – as well as for a intersubjective structure – what does the Other really want? Indeed, Lacan chose not to elaborate the theme of reflection, but reflection does play an essential role in the transition from the dimension of the demand (the code) to the dimension of desire (language in its inadequacy): What is the Other after, he is saying this to me, but what does he want? (Lacan 1986, 214)? In other words, just like the inadequacy of language enables a phantasmatically supported desire, so does it create the possibility of reflection – the two go hand in hand.

Anxiety. In addition to installing desire and the possibility of reflection, the lingual state of existence has yet another consequence, namely in terms of anxiety. Again, there is a relationship with the inadequacy of language. It is for a reason that Lacan (2004), devoted an entire Seminar to the theme of anxiety: *L'angoisse*. He referred to a specific form of anxiety rather than the vital reaction to a more or less life-threatening situation. What is relevant here is the reaction to a threat to the subject position: an existential type of anxiety. In a sense, the genesis of anxiety comprises two stages. The first one is that of the trauma, the state of helplessness ('Hilflosigkeit') – the nature of the trauma is not pre-established, and whether we are dealing with a traumatic experience depends on the possibility of symbolic, psychic processing. Indeed, the inadequacy of language and therefore of any individual mode of psychic processing makes the occurrence of traumas inevitable – in particular if the structural anchor points of the symbolic are involved. This inevitability is structural, originating as it does from the inadequacy of language and of any symbolic processing system. It represents its potential, structural failure. However, the processing may succeed in integrating what was traumatic before, in order for the unprocessable to be processed. Should this option of broadened processing fail, then anxiety will result from too close a proximity of non-integratable reality. Consequently, anxiety in the sense of fundamental anxiety is not brought on by the threat of a defect (e.g., dismissal or disease), although it may be the initial trigger. It comes into being in cases where the possibility to frame the material defect does not exist or, to put it differently, in the absence of the possibility of a lack (Lacan 2004, 80/2014, 65). A certain void is always to be preserved. Anxiety comes into being, if this void is totally filled in – if the real, the being-in-itself in Sartre's terminology presents itself in a non-mediated way. Indeed, the parallel with Sartre appears to be quite appropriated. While according to Sartre (1966, xlviii) any immediate access to being-in-itself would result in boredom and nausea, with Lacan such an immediate presence of the real will cause anxiety. This may occur when the phantasm, the framework of the subjective world, crumbles. It results in a trauma, an infringement, causing an anxiety being related to the emergence of the real.

In this case, anxiety is not produced by the presence of an anomaly, but is rather the result of the loss or absence of the structure itself – in the case of 'anomy', as Durkheim would phrase it (Lacan 2004, 53/2014, 42). Indeed, the structure creates the possibility for something to be, and by extension of something *not* to be, to be lacking. Once the structure is lost, however, the possibility of 'the not', of the lack, is also being lost: the lack happens to be lacking ('le manque vient à manquer'). And if the possibility of the lack no longer exists, then the non-symbolised real will come too close, becoming an 'excess', too much to bear. The excluded object *a* may acquire a pseudo-empirical substance, for example, with the individual feeling threatened by some indefinite force. This explains why Lacan argues that anxiety cannot exist without an object (*pas sans objet*), referring to the traditional anxiety theory which holds that anxiety, as opposed to fear, is object-less. Heidegger (1962, 186–187) worked out this view in his thesis that anxiety is anxiety related to 'the nothing and nowhere'. In light of this, Lacan's thesis that anxiety 'cannot exist without object' must have been intended to provoke. After all, the object that Lacan refers to is the object *a* , which is anything but an intentional object. Too close a proximity to this object produces anxiety, much like this object, when kept at arm's length, also produces desire. And just like distance creates the possibility of desire, so will a lack of distance produce anxiety – because of which anxiety and desire are so intimately related. But according to the current meaning of an intentional object, anxiety also with Lacan is object-less. Transforming anxiety into 'fear of something' can therefore be considered to be a process that gives direction, turning something unbearable into something that can be managed. Thus, phobia represents a type of processing, of symbolisation, a way out. It has ceased to be sheer panic.

Apparently, anxiety is the result of the subjective world falling apart, with the subject falling prey to unprocessed reality. The too close proximity to the non-symbolised, not psychically processed real holds a threat to one's own state of existence, which makes the violent, overwhelming feelings of anxiety perfectly understandable. For this very reason, Lacan establishes a relationship of this all-pervading anxiety with the catastrophic anxiety, emphatically pointed out by the neurologist Goldstein (a cousin of Cassirer). It is precisely this anxiety theory that Lacan refers to (Lacan 2004, 74/2014, 60; Goldstein 1934, 187–197).

Two rounds. When discussing the trajectory of the entry into the symbolic order, it has been shown repeatedly that two terms or moments in time might be distinguished: entry into the language and culture, with language appearing as being homogenous and the Other as omnipotent – alienation, followed by a distancing from it, with language appearing as inadequate, no longer as homogenous, and the Other as desiring. This brings separation vis-à-vis alienation, as well as implying the limitation or 'castration' of an alleged omnipotence (Lacan 1973, 185–208; 2002, 840–845). Thus, the figure of the two terms or moments in time – 'in' and 'out' – appears to be a constant in Lacan's philosophy, even though it may be named differently depending on context. The term 'two rounds' might be a more apt choice compared to alienation or separation, because it is more neutral, more value-free. They imply each other mutually. Without alienation, being at the mercy of the first Other, with all its intricacies and intimacies, separation is nothing more than an empty shell. Separation is engaged in a close relationship with this, down to the minutest details. The twofold movement described by Lacan, of 'in' being followed by a partial 'out', however, is a direct consequence of its initial position: the independent and autonomous status of language and the symbolic order, and the alleged omnipotence of the Other. Initially, language represents an 'outside' to which the child conforms, just like it is at the Other's beck and call – a condition that would ultimately prove fatal, or 'lethal'. That is why a partial exit or separation is needed to enable the free use of language and limit the omnipotence of the Other, leading to the 'castration' of the Other. Essentially this implies the capacity to reflect and add nuance. Separation will not cause the outside to disappear, nor does it lead to neutrality – it is merely the relationship towards the outside and the Other that is being nuanced. The Other has many sides, the notion of which alone will introduce a sense of freedom. This may not cause the fixating, 'lethal' effect of language to disappear fully, but it will become dialectalised as a result.

A similar dialectics can be identified with respect to desire. Initially, to some degree the child is a prisoner of the desire of the mother, or rather: the first Other, the law of the mother ('la loi de la mère'), according to Morel (2008), from which position it will be liberated by the added term of Name-of-the-Father, which marks an empty place outside its prison (Lacan 2002, pp. 557–558). This should be interpreted in a formal sense, as it turned out. The idea is certainly not to put all the blame on the mother, with the father coming to the rescue and being put on a pedestal – although there is some reason to think that Lacan would like us to think this (most likely he had had with his patients plenty of first-hand experience with claiming mothers). But in the final reckoning, what we see here is a formal, structural relationship: the child's biological state of dependence and, next to it, the overwhelming power of 'the outside'.

Consequently, the concept of two turns, their dialectics, can also be traced back in the formal graphical representation of the desire, the graph of desire (*graphe du désir*), which indicates how a vital need, through the formulation of a demand to or from the other, is transformed into a desire that has no end term. This *graphe* (2002, 817) is made up of 'two levels' (two, once again), with a 'bottom line' – entry into language conceived as a petrifying closed code – and a 'top line' – the genesis of a phantasmatically underpinned desire related to the enigmatic desire of the Other (Lacan 2013, 27–30). The two-term scheme is essentially a dialectic scheme, loosely inspired on Hegel, with one major difference: With Hegel, the mind actively steps outside itself, alienating itself into the Otherness to be able to face dividedness and nothingness, but also to return to itself, now enriched, reunited, reconciled. In the case of Lacan, the subject or proto subject is incorporated into the Other, thus falling into the grip of language, experiencing alienation in language and culture, but finding itself able to achieve separation by escaping through the intrinsic gaps of language, we have repeatedly seen. This adds a unique signature to the Lacan's dialectics, as it brings the need for a second, separate round, in order to allow for the possibility of some level of uniqueness and freedom. And yet this whole dialectics of alienation and separation also puts us in mind of Hegel, and quite rightly so. This was acknowledged quite early. The young J.-A. Miller thoroughly understood and reviewed this relationship between Lacan and Hegel (and in this specific regard, Hegel could also be replaced by Cassirer). Where Hegel sees alienation in the Spirit externalising itself, Lacan (1986, 215) choose to place it on the side of the subject: 'which is born in, constituted by, and ordered in a field that is exterior to him'. This reversal does not compromise the relationship in any way, on the contrary, it reaffirms it. Hegel's influence on Lacan, via his teacher A. Kojève and his friend J. Hyppolite, is substantial and well-documented as well, while being avowed by himself. It goes much further than might be concluded from his explicit references to Hegel alone (Žižek 1998, 2011). Hegel's thought may lead to Lacan's (2002, 837) figure of thought: the symbolic order as a curtailed objective mind, which is curtailing itself: 'That is my *Aufhebung* [sublation], which transforms Hegel's (his own lure) into an occasion to point out – in lieu and place of the leaps of an "ideal progress" – the avatars of a lack'. Lacan's (2001, 837) explains this daring interpretation by saying that Hegel's statements, even if one sticks to the text, always provide the opportunity to say something Other as well. As might have been shown in the dialectics of the two-term schema (Van Haute 2001).

The two-term schema does not only apply to theory, but also underlies the conception of a *psychoanalysis* as a treatment. Ultimately, the underlying scheme is that of pre-oedipal ('law of the mother') versus oedipal ('law of the father'). Moreover, the two moments do not occur once and for all, but will return time and again – also within the treatment itself. Thus, these two times (of alienation and separation) can also be analysed within the course of an analysis. The point of its departure is free association: 'just say it, it doesn't matter what'. Little meaning can be attributed to this initially, but what will ultimately become manifest is the field of expectations and desires produced by the environment, the desire of the Other (with his reliability or his untrustworthiness, overprotection, neglect, etcetera), to which the child is supposed to relate. Identifying it requires a keen ear for what is not being said but merely implied. At this stage of treatment, the psychoanalyst is supposed to be the one who knows the answers the analysant is looking for, a subject supposed to know, embodying an ideal symbolic figure (O), e.g. the analysant's own ego-ideal: the first stage of transference. At this stage, the analyst is given some amount of credit. When, in the next step, the analyst appears unable to provide the answers the analysant is looking for and seems to be at fault (Ø), the analysant, the patient, will engage in a different relationship with the analyst. He will turn the analyst into the one who is supposed, not to know anymore, but to embody the object of the analysant's desire, his object *a*, the analyst being swallowed into the analysant's world as a result: the second stage of transference (Lacan 1986, 244–275;1991a, 385–460). This creates the possibility for the analysant to encircle his own desire, the figures of his privileged object, the so-called fundamental phantasm, not to be conceived as a single phantasm but as a matrix: what Freud describes as the libidinous configuration. This will allow the enclosed pathogenic pleasure to find a way out and possibly find a slightly different form of satisfaction – or maybe a different way of dealing with it. For example, this would allow a destructive brand of masochism to be released or to be handled differently. However small the margins may be, even the smallest differences in structure might still lead to significant differences in behaviour and experience. Obviously, this is primarily a formal schema and should not be interpreted as a rigid 'format' ('a typical course') for a concrete psychoanalysis or psychotherapy (Morel 2008, 39–56).

Then again, Lacan attributes a unique finality to psychoanalysis, at least in its pure form. When carried through, the traverse of the so-called basic phantasm will take on the form of a passage, an experience of feeling lost, of bottomlessness as a hallmark of this trajectory. Lacan calls this the *passe*, a passage or moment of reversal, an experience that comes close to religious or spiritual exercises, the 'excercitia spiritualia' of Loyola – Lacan (2005, 162) himself having been raised by Jesuits (Beirneart 1985, 232). More in general, the pass while reflecting the two rounds model mentioned, could also refer to the two rounds model valid within Christian thought and its secular philosophical heirs as well: a state of alienation to be followed by redemption. Leaving this specific form and design aside, a psychoanalytical trajectory does carry elements of finality. However, it cannot be equal to the abandoning of each phantasm, of the phantasm as such – that would be pure fantasy, science-fiction (Millot 2001, 151). It would be more like carrying through, taking apart, the phantasmal foundations of psychic reality, of life, in order to identify a slightly different modus vivendi. The attitude of the psychoanalyst is not characterised by distance or speed, but rather by availability based on genuine involvement, detached or pure desire, in his inquiry into the analysant's desires and mystifications and to gain insight into their relationships towards the desires of Others – parents, brothers and sisters, and others, from which his or her own desire has been woven.

3.4 Differential Character of the Signifier

Thus far, the emphasis has been on the external, autonomous character of language and of the symbolic order originating from the outside and to which man must submit. This is wholly in line with the French sociological tradition started by Durkheim, with the emphasis on social institutions being decisive with regard to individual actions. Lacan, however – and this applies to French (Neo-)Structuralism in its entirety – is also strongly influenced by the contribution of the linguist Saussure and the significance he attributes to the concept of difference. This concept would go on to dominate the French philosophy of his time. Based on this concept, Lacan developed a specific conception of language that is also at work in the concept of the symbolic order. This will be the theme of the following discussion. What has been discussed earlier, in the paragraph 'The autonomy of the symbolic order' returns in this paragraph, in a more formal guise (also in the next paragraph, which deals with symbolic identification). Another second round, therefore, except that the perspective is now in-depth and formal rather than focusing on alienation/separation. For a thorough understanding, a comparison with Cassirer might be useful. Contrasting Lacan's views with those of Cassirer will add relief to Lacan's line of thought. As mentioned before, Cassirer points beyond himself, seeing that essentially two prototypes of symbolisation are juxtaposed. The comparison with Cassirer will therefore guide of this paragraph. The next paragraph discussing the real, also in relationship with the issue of symbolisation, will conclude the review of the classical Lacan.

Saussure told us that the language sign consists of a unity of sound and concept – 'image acoustique' and 'concept' – and is a component of the language system. Like Saussure, Cassirer saw the sign as a link between a sensory element and a particular meaning, with the language sign functioning as a component of the language system. Cassirer also considered language to be a part of a system, with the signs referring to each other mutually, the sign itself being constituted as a unity of a material sound and a concept or as a unity of signifier and signified (phrased in a modern terminology). Indeed, a sign does derive its sign-ness from its reference to other signs, and more specific from the way in which it *differs* from them. Consequently, the sign has no 'being', no substance in itself. This may be summarized in the famous words of Saussure, that the language system is merely made up of differences. This differential conception of signs aligns remarkably with that of Cassirer's. One may even contend that Cassirer, while not having any knowledge of the development of structuralism at that time, actually endorses its basic tenets. Early structuralism, championed by Saussure and Cassirer's theory of representation, appears to converge in this matter. But later on, in the context of French Structuralism, the supposed unity of a sign, as linking sound and concept, signifier and signification, form and content, became more and more problematic, because of the differential nature attributed to it. A purely functional and differential conception of the sign turned out to have major implications. Indeed, the differential nature of the sign undermines its unity. Assuming that signification relies on the interplay of signifiers means that the sign loses its intrinsic unity (as a sustained union between signifier and signification).

Signifier above signification. What replaces it is the mutual difference between signifiers, as well as between signifier and signification per se. This turns a sign into nothing more than an internal and external difference, which means it loses its unifying characteristics and raison d'être. What remains initially is a range of signifiers, which generate signification through their mutual differences – indeed, we should refer to them in the plural form, as a range of signifiers, considering that based on the differential conception a single signifier cannot exist: at the very least, a pair of signifiers ($S_1 \rightarrow S_2$) is needed. A signifier is characterised by a semantic void, to which signification is added only as part of a context. The difference with Cassirer's take (and Saussure's) on the matter is obvious. Here, the signifiers are assigned primacy in relationship to signification, which makes the category of the signifier much more fundamental or basic compared to that of signification. This does not necessarily mean that the category of the signification would be lost, far from it. Nor does the category of the sign, a word as a temporary unit of signifier and signification, of form and content, lose its value. What it does mean, however, is that an autonomous field of terms or signifiers is inserted below the level of the semantic field, supporting it like a framework. The concept of the signifier is therefore much wider than that of the phoneme, as a sound. After all, an image, a letter or a dash can also function as a signifier, which initially they do, as their precise meaning still has to become clear. Their precise meaning will only be understood in a particular context, from a particular reception, etcetera. This reflects Lacan's fundamental contribution: the significance of the formal difference preceding a substantial, semantic interpretation of this difference (Safouan 1988, 236). Limited though this contribution may seem, it does have major implications.

This significance of the formal difference carries through into the world of perception, which is also structured differentially, in fact even prior to language making its entry, Lacan would say. But while Cassirer sees the structure of the world of perception as being primarily defined in a substantial and semantic way, Lacan defines it as being primarily formal and differential. For example, Cassirer introduces the semantic opposites of 'sacred/profane' or 'day/night' as distinct units of meaning or distinct Gestalts. Lacan (1981, 169) will not contest the point of introducing these differences, but he does add a formal difference at a deeper level: the day /not-day distinction. This difference actually precedes the difference in meaning between day and night. This allows the concept of night to find its place in the lack of the day (not-day). Instead, or rather below a substantial *opposition* we can then identify a *difference* in a formal sense. Or, to quote another example: the semantic man/woman distinction is supported by the differential difference of (+ / –): having or *not* having a phallus, with 'phallus' functioning as a meaningless marker. As a next step, culturally defined meanings of being-a-man or being-a-woman (being a boy, a girl, a son, a daughter, a father, a mother) can be attached, which leads to specific ideals and forms of gender identity. The signifiers provide the formal framework, to which meaning is added, like flesh to the bone. Again: The category of signification is not abolished, but is assigned a derived status. This formal level is relevant to Lacan, because he is always looking for a formal infrastructure, one that can gain empirical, semantic substance in a variety of ways – just like the Name-of-the-Father is a formal concept that can acquire substance in different ways, as was shown before.

This does highlight a key difference between Lacan's and Cassirer's views on language, however, with the category of the signification losing its position of priority. This also leads to a new view of symbolisation in a general sense, as the thesis of equal origin of matter *and* form – Cassirer's basic theory – loses its value. We have repeatedly seen that in Cassirer view there is no matter that is not formed *simultaneously*, just like there is no sensory perception that is already determined by thought, by symbolic ideation – the primacy of signification. Lacan chooses to replace this concept by the primacy of the signifier, which is formative in itself. Apparently, both pay attention to the forming, constituting aspect of language and of symbolics as such – Cassirer being inspired by Von Humboldt, Lacan by Saussure – but they localise it differently: signification versus signifier.

Consequently, the feeble framework of this concept is supposed to accomplish that which had been accomplished before by the category of the signification. According to 'traditional epistemology' it would be possible to identify an actual cow by combining the signifier 'cow' with the associated meaning of cow. The content of meaning precedes the elements subordinated to it.

This route has now been cut off, and Lacan will have to show how this can still be done (Lacan 1961–1962, session of 6 and 13 December 1961, and 28 February 1962). As an example he refers to a bone in the shape of an awl in which prehistoric man (Cro-Magnon man around 30,000 BC) has carved notches: / / / /. Lacan had seen this bone in a display cabinet in the museum of Saint Germain-en-Laye, and it had made a deep impression upon him. Those notches, a series of dashes next to each other, has been photographed (Porge 1989, 104). They may represent a repeated event (possibly related to hunting), but we cannot be certain. We simply do not know their exact meaning and what each single dash refers to – the referent – is unknown as well. Both are parenthesised.

We only see a tally-stick, a memory aid, while in fact this represents one of the deepest roots of writing, found all over the world (Kuckenburg 2016, 109). What we do see a dash (mark, trait) that is being repeated as an other dash (mark, trait). Erasing divergences, the mark establishes a distinction between something which is marked *and* something which is not marked, the marked not being defined by so called natural pre-existing qualities, but only by being symbolically marked, having received this stamp.

Unary trait. Lacan speaks here of a 'trait unaire', unary trait. This complex notion refers to the trait made by one, not in the sense of 'turning it into a whole' but in the sense of 'making the difference' – it identifies. The tally-stick, the unary trait offers the most primitive form of symbolisation, which can be used to add structure to reality, without which no difference in that reality can be experienced. It is a translation of Freud's concept of the *single trait* (*einziger Zug*), a trait that one person takes from someone else in order to identify with this other in the symbolic field, like children take on their parents' traits (Freud 1955b, 64). Lacan elaborates this term in a much broader sense, however, namely as a primitive term of symbolisation as such: a single trait, which only exists through repetition. Here, the difference between Lacan and Cassirer is strongly highlighted (as well as with all brands of philosophy that are based on the category of the signification). In the case of Cassirer, reality is primarily disclosed from the signification, while the paradigm of the primitive symbolisation can be reduced to the *simple line* (*Linienzug*) which carries a multitude of meanings. With Lacan, reality is primarily disclosed from a *single trait* (*einziger Zug*) and here the paradigm of the primitive symbolisation is formed by at least two meaningless lines. A more concise way of illustrating the difference between these two brands of philosophy would be hard to imagine: the primacy of signification (a simple line) versus the primacy of the signifier (a single trait, existing in its repetition: two dashes). Cassirer versus Lacan is like ~ versus //. The world that is formed by being bisected by the unary trait is not yet the world of significations, of Gestalts, but one of binary constructs: marked/not-marked. According to Lacan, it is this binary, bisecting aspect that is responsible for the alienation that is effectuated by the logos, the signifier, in respect of organic life which, as it presents itself, certainly does not have a binary structure itself (Lacan 2013, 448). This structure is contributed by the unary trait. It is this trait that allows us to see something as a thing, as *one-and-the-same*, as an element of a set, range or series – even before it acquires any form of substance. But without the trait the empirical thing would be lost. Indeed, the sameness is not in the things, but in the trait, the mark which makes it possible to add things without paying heed to their phenomenal divergence. This pre-symbolic phenomenal divergence is being wiped out, effaced, in the process of symbolising (Lacan 1972, 192).

In this range, the dash is repeated, while the process of repeating generates a difference between the dashes (/, /, /, /), which is merely the result of a difference in position in the series, while at the same time we see, as a result, a unit emerge, as the process of repeating shows what is repeated as being the identical unit: / (///). It might be compared to the range of natural numbers, which are necessary to create order, an order that did not exist before, but is created from nothing, *ex nihilo*. We already saw this in the discussion of Cassirer. In the Bible book *Genesis*, man is taught how to count, in the part where it says that the world, man's life word, was created in six days: day 1, day 2, day 3 through day 6. In the process, the week is created as a series of seven days, a week that did not exist before this structure, this symbolic series, was introduced: It is being posited. And yet this series is established only retro-actively, as a result, afterwards: *nachträglich, après coup*. The two is here to grant birth right to the first one (and so on) and this *first repetition* is necessary to explain the genesis of the integer, the number as such (Lacan 1972, 191). The trait, the number repeats itself differently ($S_1 \rightarrow S_2$), generating difference and unity as well. Thereafter, the adding of this formal structure to brutal reality allows a world to be created. Only based on the unity that is proposed in the symbolic and posited by the symbolic can we identify something out there in the world as being something, as being the same: there we have it again, and there again, and there again. The structuring of objects is therefore preceded by symbolic structuring, which is one of Lacan's fundamental principles. It would therefore be the primary task of the signifier, regardless of content, to introduce a formal hierarchy or structuring, in order for phenomena to appear as phenomena.

As a result, the concept of unary trait differs from the distinction that is commonly known as *type/token*, i.e., the distinction between the type itself and its concrete realisation. In line with Cassirer, the relationship between a meaning and an empirical realisation could be taken as an example: the meaning 'cow' enables us to actually see something as a cow. The content of its meaning, the intension, ι, precedes, as a rule, the set of elements (ε_1, ε_2, ε_n) that it can hold: ι (ε_1, ε_2, ε_n). Here, *meaning* is the key term, with a difference in level occurring between the meaning and the phenomena it comprises. This is *not* the case in the conception of the unary trait. Here, *signifier* is the key term, without any difference of level between type and realisation: There are only traits, each of them only existing through its repetition, while generating sameness in the world ('another one, and yet another one'). In other words: The 'type' *itself* is a 'token', but it is a token that takes up an exceptional position, being removed from the range while driving this range from its own position outside the range, but structuring the range $S_1(S_2)$.

Signifier, object, subject. What has been argued does apply to a unary, single trait *and* to a linguistic trait (including non-linguistic traits while functioning as a linguistic trait): Both are signifiers. There is, however, one important difference between both categories (Lacan 1972, 193). The unary trait is identical with itself, while being a *single* trait, but in language no trait, no signifier can be identical with itself, because each signifier, while being an element of a set (of signifiers), is also member of many other sets (of signifiers) – through the axes of substitution and connexion. Only as a second step, through metaphorical substitution of signifier for signifier and the metonymical combination of signifiers with each other, can contextual meaning emerge (Lacan 2002, 505–506). Because of its context-dependency, meaning is essentially underdetermined and unsaturated – it is multi-interpretable and non-homogenous. By extension, all that is subordinate to it, the referents, can no longer exist as a homogenous class either. Quite consistently, Lacan therefore argues that signification (on account of its dependence on the signifier) is *unable* to bundle any referents that might be subordinated to it, for lack of focus.[3] This thesis would have a major impact. The loss of homogeneity of the signification will also cause the homogeneity of the being, of the world to be fragmented by the signifier. This homogeneity is still preserved in the Copernican Turn of Kant and post-Kantian philosophy, as in the case of Cassirer: the break between the real and knowledge which is already at work at the level designated by Cassirer (and many others, following Kant), and which Lacan considers to be an established fact. In Lacan's sense, however, this break is about a fragmentation of the world, an intensified break, because it is the signifier that is throwing a spanner in the works. Lacan (1964–1965, session of 2 December 1964) speaks of a breaking of the supposed pact of harmony between the signifier and a being, something that is. The signifier does not collect primarily (as in the case of signification in the sense of Cassirer) but but disperses – disseminates.

Then there is another thing, namely the fact that initially the signifier does not refer to an object but to a *subject*. One thing we know for sure after all, when seeing a signifier, is that a human being, a subject, had to be involved – this is not an accidental scratch mark on a rock left by nature. In fact, it represents the act of birth of symbolisation and, by extension, the act of birth of man, of the subjective mind. Lacan's prime example in this regard was the character of Robinson Crusoe from Daniel Defoe's eponymous novel (1961–1962, session 6

3 Lacan 1975, 23: Ce qui caractérise, au niveau de la distinction signifiant/signifié à ce qui est la comme tiers indispensable, à savoir le référent, c' est proprement que le signifé le rate. Le collimateur ne fonctionne pas'. (Which, at the level of the distinction between signifier/signified, typifies the relationship of the signified up to what is present as a necessary third, i.e. the referent, which is exactly what is not accomplished by the signified). The scope simply fails to work'. In other words: it is the very separation (in the sense of Lacan) between signifier and signification that incapacitates the referring function of the signification.

December; 1998, 338–340). Robinson Crusoe wipes out a footprint, a natural trace that through its wiping out leaves evidence of the act of wiping out: the footprint given as a natural trace, (1) the wiped-out trace, and (2) the trace of wiping out ('trace de pas, effacement de trace, trace d' effacement'). This is a process involving at least two moments (the wiped-out trace and the trace of wiping out): a first repetition. As a result of this first repetition, a natural trace is being transformed, in two steps, into a signifier, i.e., into a group of at least two signifiers, each of which only exist in through the differences between them. Consequently, the presence of a couple of signifiers justifies the conclusion: There was a subject. Indeed, this first repetition is necessary to constitute a subject, exactly in the same way as a first repetition appeared to be necessary to explain the genesis of the number, as seen above (Lacan 1972, 191). Indeed, it is the *first repetition*, the paired signifiers, that tells us: Here was a human being. What its exact meaning might be remains as yet unclear. A signifier does not primarily refer to a signification and, because of the undefined character of its signification, even less so to the object, the referent. Its primary reference, however, is to the *human being* who produced these signifiers: Robinson Crusoe. This primary reference to the subject leads Lacan to develop the now classic definition of the signifier: a signifier represents a subject to another signifier ('un signifiant représente un sujet pour un autre signifiant'). Lacan (2002, 840) would uphold this formula to the very last. It aptly summarises this state of affairs, but may also lead to misunderstanding, in the sense that the signifier would represent an existing subject. But again, representation is not the same as duplication in another medium of what already existed. Instead it should rather be seen as a symbolisation, a creative representation (in the sense of Cassirer). There is no existing subject that as a next step is identified by a signifier. The subject is produced by the step of identifying with the signifier, the signifier *as such*. Likewise, with a caveat we could say that the signifier *constitutes* the subject in respect of the signifier or the culture.

How should the relationship between signifier and subject be envisaged? This question leads us to the problem of symbolic identification. In its elaboration, Lacan may choose to refer to Freud (and he actually does), but he will also deviate from Freud's views. Freud does address the issue of identification, but presupposes an 'already existing subject', which may go on to identify with another person (for example, by adopting their trait). Lacan, however, calls the already formed subject into question. How exactly is it formed? Lacan decides to go one level deeper, inquiring into the genesis in terms of the subject's constitution: how does it come about? And the answer is: through identification. Lacan's concept of identification thus differs from Freud's (as well as from the way this concept is commonly used). This difference is essential. Freud simply accepts the presence of the subject as a fact. Lacan, however, goes further, by inquiring into the possibility of the fact, the constitution of the subject (much like the Neo-Kantian approach). And the doctrine of symbolic identification provides an answer to *this* question. Which means that this form of identity, of identification, reaches much deeper. It goes beyond the question of the identity that a person acquires but can also leave behind, whilst still remaining more or less the same person. Here, the nature of 'the state of being' changes. The nature of the question makes that this issue becomes a rather abstract and formal one. It can be reconstructed as follows.

3.5 Symbolic Identification

When entering the symbolic order, the subject-in-being acquires the status of a subject, provided it assimilates the symbolic elements presented 'from the outside'. Initially, there is not yet a subject that goes on to identify with these elements. Instead, the subject only becomes a subject through identifying with the elements presented by the symbolic order. Within the symbolic order, three levels or layers can be distinguished, as was pointed out in the corresponding paragraph: language, the law vis-à-vis sexual relations, and social institutions, including the social group. The process of the subject-in-being entering the symbolic order *also* unfolds in three steps, each corresponding to one of these layers, as was shown in the foregoing. This in turn leads to three forms of symbolic identification that include the three components of symbolic identity: (1) identification with the signifier per se, (2) and identification with the proper noun; to this we could still add (3) identification with group ideals – a trichotomy that Lacan does not necessarily make explicit, but he does elaborate it in much detail (Lacan 1961–1962, sessions of 6, 13, 20 December 1961; 28 February 1962).

Three components of symbolic identity. Just like occurrences can be counted (///), so can children be counted: '1, 2, 3, 4, are they all here?' The child will now start counting itself. But that is not such an easy task. When asked how many brothers it has, the child will initially respond by saying (based on an example Lacan took from Binet): 'I have three brothers, John, Peter and me'. Here it clearly makes a mistake. It considers the location from which the counting takes place, that enables counting, as being a countable object in itself, which leads it to include the location in its count. Making this mistake, it overlooks its own subjectivity in the counting activity, and consequently also itself as the counting agent. A specific step is required not just to be viewed as an object being counted, but to actually view itself as a *counter*. This layer is found below the layer of 'you are *what* you are told to be'. This deeper layer concerns the *who*, the specific location, the spot from which the counting takes place; that is where the subject positions itself as the counter, as the subject counting. Once this step has been taken a child can say: 'I have two brothers, John and Peter'. It will view itself both as one and the same *and* as one of the brothers. The two go hand in hand. After all, it sees itself as one, not because it is a whole, but because it is one, one of the brothers, from which it differs numerically, as one element within a series. In other words: I am one (occupying a place in a series) *and* I am amidst others (which also take a place in the series, albeit a different place). Indeed, the number as a trait, a *unary trait*, ensures an identity, *a numerical identity*, i.e., an identity as being counted, as being numerical different – seemingly nothing more than that. However, this constitutes a huge step, of which no animal is capable. Still the young child will take it, the child identifying with the 'unity' ('monas') of the series and with its acceptance of the idea of a numerical series itself. This results in a sameness ('mêmeté'), which would be the consequence of a signifying sameness ('mêmeté signifiante') being attributed to the child. At the same time, the child undergoes a limitation, as was mentioned before, because it also sees itself as a member of a collection, as one of many, as one of the brothers. Thus, they have all been 'marked' by the symbolic order, undergoing a limitation or castration, all of them becoming nothing more than 'one of many' – 'don't think you're better'. Moreover, you do not really *have* a number, but you *are* a number, just like a prisoner *is* the number assigned to him when entering prison life, stamped on his back. You *are* the fourth child. And yet the subject is not completely lost in this identity, because more than being a number it also occupies the position of the counter. As a result, rather than coincide with its identity, becoming one with its identity, merely one out of many, it actually escapes this fate. This means the subject appears twice: as a counting subject *and* as being counted. This produces a unity as well as inner dividedness – being the counter and being counted. The subject is divided: a subject of the statement (being counted) and a subject of the enunciation (counting). Still, saying this, this counting as an activity would not fall outside the scope of the symbolic order – it is the identification with the number, as a unary trait.

However, well before being counted and also before being able to speak, the child will receive messages and signifiers from the mother, the Other and therefrom it may take some traits or signifiers that enable it to symbolise its primordial relationship with the Other, the mother. Freud's example of his grandson who at a very early age uses the symbolic pair of two elementary phonemes (oo/aa) may be a case in point (Lacan 2002, 319). Through symbolising his mother's presence and absence (*Fort/da*), the child may then surpass its fundamental dependency towards the Other and its own distress as well – transforming a need into a demand: a demand for love, a demand for presence or absence (Lacan 2002, 691). In doing so, the child brings about a primordial identification with the signifier as such: it acquires a first signature ('seing'), a first *signum* (Lacan 2013, 23). The child has thus been provided with anchors within the symbolic. Meanwhile, its pre-symbolic state of existence is being effaced, erased. The signifier, whilst having the effect of rubbing out the pre-symbolic state of the world outside, has precisely the same effect on the subject-in-being, causing the loss of his pre-symbolic state of being (Lacan 1972, 192).

Moreover, any process of identification is part of a specific language and culture setting, in dependency of the Other. Next to identification with the signifier and with the number we see the relevance of the name and the name-giving emerge. This is quite obvious, because a name has the specific function of identifying a particular person (or thing or place) as being that particular person or place: Glasgow is Glasgow, not Leeds. Linguistics and onomastics explore its grammatical and historical aspects. Also, names are the object of study of logics. Indeed, being part of the class of so-called particulars, names constitute a unique group. The term *proper* name can then be limited to the act of giving names to man, because only man will actually appropriate their name. This proper name identifies a person as being unique, while this person will also identify with their name (which is not true of things and places). This identification leads to what might be called *nominal identity*, which is added to the numerical identity (preceded itself by the identification with the signifier as such). The state of being-one (and being-divided) is superimposed by being-a-specific-name: I am Frank. Thus, the proper name produces a second identity layer: your name, which is you. It also functions as an identifying unary trait. This type of identification is symbolic as well, based as it is on an empty term (the *name* Frank), rather than on meaning or visual appearance. Which is precisely the point Lacan is trying to make: without any meaning being involved, the name identifies, as an empty signifier. Consequently, any reduction of the 'name' to a concept or 'meaning' (Russell, 1905) is rejected outright by Lacan (1961–1962, session of 20 December 1961). In its being-without-meaning a proper name is a signifier par excellence.

Identifying with the proper name has yet another dimension, one that takes us to the third and final component of the symbolic identity: *distinctive identity*. Indeed, the proper name is given by others, namely the parents, who belong to the previous generation. Moreover, the proper name, in the form of a first name (boy's or girl's name) reflects a difference in gender. Moreover, in cultures where a last name is also given, this last name defines the child as being a member of a particular family. The proper name would then refer to family traits, certain quintessential characteristics handed down generations (such as the cast of the eye or an inflection, a particular gait). This leads us back to Freud's original concept of the unary trait (*einziger Zug*): the identification with a partial, symbolic mark. Again, they represent empty signifiers, while acquiring a semantic component as well. Indeed, they generate meaning, because of the embedded symbolic ideals and expectations, which inform the child's actions and desires. Maybe even without realising it, the child, even once it has grown into an adult, will go on realise the ideals, dreams and unfulfilled ambitions of its parents, be it in its own unique way. This uniqueness is even generated through repetition, because repetition of the same thing but in a different context would already result in a difference: a unique way. Even the attempt to oppose it – as a mother I will not make the same mistakes as my mother – often resonates with repetition. And yet: this type of identification, in this case with the symbolic ideals of the Other, would not be fixating, for the very reason that the subject can relate itself to it through repetition.

This type of identification with ideals is not restricted to family circles, but can actually be extended to include any group to which a person can belong and whose values he or she will uphold. Belonging to a group can express itself in a variety of ways, ranging from behavioural traits, tattoos – an example often quoted by Lacan – a lapel pin (e.g., of the Rotary club), a cap or a (football) shirt, a particular hair style, the colour orange during the football world championships, a specific idiom or some arcane code that can only be grasped by insiders, etcetera. Lacan (2002, 669) speaks of *insignia*. Here we might speak of a distinctive identity, which expresses itself in a trait, a physical characteristic that reflects the inclusion in a given group. This state of being included becomes evident through a person's garments, the cap or shirt, a particular arrangement of a piece of clothing – invariably we see a physical element with a symbolic differential value. Again, this is an instance of meaningless signifiers. And yet they are able to function as a very strong binder, socially as well as down to the family level. A case in point would be football clubs like Glasgow Rangers, Manchester United, Chelsea, etcetera. This binder serves to differentiate – not between Glasgow Rangers and Manchester United in terms of a substantial opposition, but the difference is found at a deeper level, being empty and formal in nature: marked/not-marked, Glasgow Rangers/not-Glasgow Rangers, or Glasgow Rangers vs. the rest of the world. The semantic content (Glasgow Rangers/Manchester United) will only be added as a next step.

This is also the field of social codes, which is made up of open systems that can be 'played with' rather than functioning as hermetic codes. The whole body of social symbolics – the often unfathomable network of codes – thus contributes to the shaping of the subject's identity, of what it *is* in the symbolic field.

Although coming from the outside, the codes bring uniqueness. Each person carries inside them the time and culture in which they were shaped in the past and in which they live today: inside = outside, the objective mind stamps the subjective mind (more than the latter would like, most likely). Together with their terms, the social codes represent a particularly strong social binder. And yet again, we do not coincide with it. It's the subtle displays of ineptitude that betrays the state of not-belonging: You'll never be one of us. It's a specific touch (button done up, tie knotted in a particular way) that is lacking. This brings out the jarring quality of this type of identity: You are it, and then again you're *not*. Obviously, this also offers manoeuvring space.

Leitmotif. More than functioning as a social binder, these traits are also the medium to which the person is actually bound. They constitute the connecting, identifying elements of the subject itself. In all its levels, the symbolic identity might be compared to a molecule (H_2O), made up of a number of elements or atoms, each of which could be equated to a unary trait ('trait unaire'), the significance of which was re-emphasised by Lacan in 1975 (Lacan 2005, 146). Taken together, these unary traits form a spinal column, or subjective and timeless infrastructure, one that provides stability and sustainability over time. For this reason, yet another comparison presents itself, as the unary traits could well be compared to what is called a leitmotif in musical and literature theory. Rather than a thematic, variable motive, we see an identical concrete material element being repeated (a particular cough, a pencil, a tune) that symbolises a particular person or situation as being this person or situation – it serves to identify. Thus, it adds structure to a narrative, a musical piece or an opera as it develops: ah right, it's that tune again (signifying a person or a situation) – each in their own way, Lev Tolstoy, Richard Wagner and Thomas Mann were masters of this art.

The same applies to unary traits. They are the characters, symbols of a character. They represent the synchronous, structural leitmotifs of the diachronic process of a person's life. Which makes them solid, sustainable and anything but interchangeable, for the mere fact that they are the essence of family culture and of primary experiences accumulated so far. Its solid quality should not come as a surprise, representing as it does the very 'being' of the subject. Indeed, a person may not have all the characteristics of the family or groups to which it belongs, but in any case he *is* part of this range of characteristics. And yet this 'being' remains obscure, out of sight ('unconscious'). From this perspective, man structurally has no view of his own subjective point of view, because he *is* his own subjective point of view, the result being that he lacks insight into his own contribution to what he experiences and does. Unfortunately, this makes that mutual relationships are essentially precarious, unless he takes the hurdle of reflection to some extent. And where due reflection is lacking, conflicts will be rampant. Man sees primarily what he has before him, but not what he *is* – entirely in line with the Neo-Kantian line of thought in the sense of Cassirer. The subjective point of view from which a person lives, from what he or she is, eludes him or her, is not given, and needs to be reconstructed from expressions and reactions of others. In that sense, conflicts can actually be useful and provide insights – indeed, contrary to what Cassirer believed.

Imaginary and phantasmatic identification. Symbolic identification does not exhaust the psychic infrastructure, because it underpins the imaginary identification, like the image in the mirror is confirmed by: 'Yes, that's you'. The symbolic ideal (*ego ideal*) also serves to delimit imaginary grandeur (*ideal ego*), marking as it does the boundaries of the amount of grandeur a person is able to appropriate. And yet they are fundamentally different, because an imaginary self-image refers to a an image, a closed entity or Gestalt (the admiration received, the car, motor cycle or equipment a person owns), whereas a symbolic identity is partial, being based on a range of differential markers, unary or singularising traits. Those traits come from the outside, creating an identity that did not exist before.

Of course, the 'matter' already existed – the body, with its tensions and emotions – but this matter has not yet acquired an 'identity'. Therefore, in the process of establishing symbolic identification, a third form of identification takes place (next to the imaginary and symbolic forms), which addresses this very aspect. Indeed, through symbolisation, the bodily tensions will be transformed as well. The primordial form of life itself, the body, the vital immanence will be lost, leaving remainder: the lost object around which the drive is orbiting. As a next step, the subject can *find* the lost object of drive in a phantasmatic scenario in another person (a partner) with whom an affective relationship may develop. Lacan (2002, 849) explains: 'there is no access to the [...] Other except via the so-called partial drives wherein the subject seeks an object to replace of the loss of life he has sustained [...].' While it can also *identify* itself with this object, thus producing a desire in the other – after a number of other conditions have been met, obviously. As a result, actual affective relationships can be established because, at a phantasmatic level, man is believed to identify with the lost object. In a quintessential way, man becomes the tone of the voice of the other, or the way that the other looked at him. He or she *is* the breast that is sucked to the point of a burn-out, *is* the patsy he invariably turns out to be. Thus, symbolic identification through a 'trait' is supported by the identification with the lost object (a), which manifests itself in a particular type of drive. Indeed, the subject is found in an intermediate field: the field between the symbolic and the real of life.[4] And yet the object of this drive is anchored in a symbolic identification, which transforms the loss and enables the drive. As a result, the drive and its object are *not* placed outside the symbolic, as a thing that might 'exist' separately. Man is run through with the symbolic: also in the domain of the body and, particularly, at the level of the drive. This notion effectively completes Lacan's subject theory. To the very last, Lacan would therefore maintain the given definition of the signifier: a signifier represents the subject to another signifier. Regardless of what a person claims content-wise, this will first and foremost say something about *him*, about *her*, about what he or she *is*.

The conceptual scheme for the symbolic identification can now be formulated as follows: S_1, S_2, \$, *a*. This could be read as follows. S_1 can represent the unary trait, or the unity of the set of signifiers, or its first element; S_2, the binary signifier, represents the set itself, or its second element; \$ refers to the subject in its dividedness and the object *a* (the excluded object) is what remains as a lack when symbolisation ($S_1 \rightarrow S_2$) takes place. Lacan would never abandon this basic scheme. In the 1960s, at the peak of French Structuralism, this would initially take the form of a strongly formalising approach, one that to this day has found resonance only in limited circles. The fact that he takes this to the extreme has rightfully earned him criticism (Brickmont and Sokal 1997). He also draws on the principles of mathematics, remarkably on those proposed by Frege. Indeed, Frege favoured a Platonising approach to mathematical entities, in which numbers 'exist', albeit only in an ideal dimension; using Hilbert's formalistic approach as an inspiration would have been the more obvious choice (Bouveresse 1998, 80).

The introduction of his discourse theory, in 1969, however, based on the four types of discourse ('quatre discours') would have a major impact from day one. Foucault had made the term discourse fashionable, but the discourse theories of Foucault and Lacan only have their name in common. Foucault refers to the underlying grid of a text or a discursive practice, while Lacan's focus is on social connections. Again, he will use the structuralist process of positions in a variety of ways, in line with Lévi-Strauss, whose philosophy is also reflected in this phase of Lacan's thinking. The significance of this conception of the *four discourses* lies in the fact that they add the dynamics of discursive speech and actions to the statics of the symbolic order. It describes four types

4 Lacan 1961–1962, session of 20 December, 1961: 'la fonction du sujet est dans l'entre-deux, entre les effets idéalisantes de la fonction signifiante et cette immanence vitale'. ('the function of the subject is in the in-between, between the idealising effects of the signifying function and this vital immanence'.)

of social bond: power, coercion, protest and subversion, which are defined as the discourse of the master, the discourse of the university, of the hysteric and of psychoanalysis, respectively (Lacan 1991b). This concept found ready acceptance (Clavreul 1978) and was also subjected to critical scrutiny, producing a wealth of (rather repetitive) literature. The concept turned out to be fertile (Verhaege 2008). For example, various types of discourse, of social bond can be distinguished (such as the discourse of power, of knowledge, of protest, of subversion), but also the strategic variety found within an actual discourse (for example, within a single psychoanalysis session: counselling, explanation, temptation, interpretation). Indeed, the discourse theory should not be conceived as a static thing. Finally, worth mentioning is the conception of the *four formulas of sexuation*, in which he had invested much time and that found its final formulation in 1972, referring back to his theory of the 1950s (Lacan 2002, 685–696; Lacan 2011, 193–210; Safouan 2013, 279–296). It can be summarised as follows. All men are subjected to castration except one: the primeval father who institutes, as being himself an exception, the rule as such founded on this very exception. Indeed, the exception institutes the rule. Women, by contrast, do not form such a set and are therefore not wholly subjected to castration, which means they are entitled to an additional, non-phalically defined pleasure. It offers a further elaboration of Lacan's basic concept regarding the phallus (Φ) as an organising term of sexual differentiation. Central to the formal aspect of its rationale is Cassirer's concept of *Satzfunktion*, or Russell's *propositional function* – φ (x). Lacan (2001, 259) obviously alludes to this, speaking of the 'propositional function Φx'. Interesting though it may be, the concepts of the four discourses and the four formulas will not be discussed in detail here, because they fail to have an impact on the fundamental issue defined here: the impact of the process of symbolisation on the subject. The theme that has just been mentioned in passing in the discussion of the symbolic identification – the physical, the real – will now be discussed in depth as a final step.

3.6 The Real: Three Domains, Three Forms

Along the path of symbolic identification we see a symbolic identity emerge, as was shown in the foregoing. It is made up of three components: I am a single divided subject, identified by a proper name, but also one member of a particular family, belonging to groups with their associated ideals. Obviously, this threesome merely offers a framework, which will be shaped differently for each person; that is what produces the *singular* identity. However, with regard to symbolisation this highlights only one aspect of the story. Symbolisation unfolds not only on the side of the subject, but also on the object's side, the side of reality: the symbolisation of the real. Lacan (2002, 388, 399) speaks of primordial symbolisation ('symbolisation primordiale') while Cassirer (GW 16/2003c, 302/1946, 89) refers to a radical metaphor ('"radical" Metaphor'). We might also speak of a *fundamental symbolisation*: the symbolisation of the real *unto* a world at large, which should be distinguished from symbolisations within the world (see Chapter 2). Within the context of this issue, reality can thus be categorised schematically based on three domains, as was shown before.

Three domains. These domains include the body, the primordial Other and, as a final addition, external reality – it also deserves mentioning that this trichotomy is not used by Lacan as such. This trichotomy can be summarised as follows. In the process of 'saying I' (also in the form of a possessive pronoun) the body is appropriated, whilst shedding the 'immediacy of life', the physical tension – de *tension vitale, la tendance, immanence vitale*, as Lacan would describe it. It is the mythical subject, the living being capable of experiencing something between birth and death, capable of covering the whole spectrum of pain and pleasure of immediate presence: le *sujet de la jouissance* (Lacan 1972, 194). The diffuse source of tension (pain) and relaxation (pleasure) is thus transformed into 'my body', to which the subject, the child can relate through interaction with the Other – 'does you tommy hurt, or are your feet cold?'. This leads to the loss of the immediate presence with the body, with life – it is 'repressed', as Lacan would call it.[5] In the final analysis, what's being lost is life itself in its immediacy. This also applies to the immediate presence with the primordial Other (*la Chose*). This will be lost as well, to be replaced by the actual Other and a place within the community – I am one of you now. And finally it would apply to the immediate presence with reality outside (*ek-sistance*, as Lacan would later call it), which is transformed into a world of time and space, into nature.

Three forms. Next to the domains to which fundamental symbolisation refers, we can distinguish three forms of the real in relation to this fundamental symbolisation. The *first* form could be described as static, while the real might be conceived as that which exists prior to symbolisation: the real that is present before symbolisation is introduced (Balmès 1999, 62; Fink 1995, 27).

---

5 The nucleus of the primal repressed relates to 'the part of this being that is alive in the *urverdrängt* [primarilly repressed]' (Lacan 2002, 693; 2013, 441). Lacan also put it like this: 'Ce qui est refoulée, c' est la vie'. ('that which is repressed, that is life') (Mooij, 2008). Soler 2011, 53: 'Faire ainsi du vivant un sujet, c'est produire cette perte de vie qui fait de l'insatisfaction le composant premier du psychisme'. ('Thus bringing a subject to life effectuates this loss of life which turns dissatisfaction into the foremost component of the psychic'.) Heidegger (1987, 112–116) coined the term 'Ent-lebung' with respect to world forming (as an equivalent of symbolisation). It is only a small step to: 'ce qui est refoulée, c'est la vie'.

A traditional example would be the stars in the sky, immutable though they may appear to be (Lacan 2013, 565). Initially, the static real is the inert, 'an sich': 'For the real is [...] identical to his existence, a noise in which one can hear anything and everything' (2002, 388). This reminds us of Sartre's being-in-itself, defined as 'it is what it is'. The *second* form relates to the static real that remains after symbolisation: 'it is the domain of that which subsists outside of symbolization' (2002, 388). In this sense, it makes the real traumatising and violent by definition, although this clash is not brought about by an incidental, avoidable trauma. Instead, it is defined by a structural quality: Each process of symbolisation will therefore develop in leaps and bounds – also in science, or in one's personal life. It appears in the form of violence, as a trauma, as an infringement, causing anxiety. Therefore, anxiety is the only possible form in which the real can appear as a phenomenon, which is why anxiety is the only sentiment that cannot deceive. Worth mentioning is that also in Sartre's case being-in-itself may appear or manifest itself as a phenomenon, albeit not in the form of anxiety but of boredom and nausea (Frank 2015, 53–94). In fact, it is one of his fundamental theses. However, with Lacan the infringement may possibly be processed further, either mentally or symbolically: initially as a traumatic fragment, and later as a more or less integrated component of psychic life or of a symbolic system. For this reason, the real has been described as impossible, impossible to know, to inscribe (*réel comme impossible*). It requires symbolisation, the signifier, a process of shaping, for it to become known or to come into existence. As a result, reality has been conceived, from day on one, as being marked by symbolic nihilation (Lacan 1981, 168).

A *third* form of the real concerns the dynamic aspect. Its impossibility does not concern the real in the sense of what may exist before or may remain after symbolisation, but rather what is dynamically instituted by the process of symbolisation itself. Symbolisation leads to the forming of a world, but retrogradely also to the institution of 'Jouissance', as its outcome. How exactly? What is also at stake is that entry into the symbolic is an activity, an *active* choice – a point that Lacan (1986, 212; 2002, 840–845) would never fail to stress. It is a 'choice' that supports the joining or rejecting of the linguistic-cultural game of symbolisation. However, it is an enforced rather than a free choice. Lacan demonstrates this by mentioning the example of a robbery. It is centred on the threatening words 'your money *or* your life', which are represented by the logical symbol *vel*. Here, 'money' stands for the unconditional enjoyment that has to be sacrificed in order to enter the symbolic; 'life' would then represent the act of entering the symbolic order, which brings about alienation. A choice will have to be made: you're in *or* you're out. However, it is an impossible choice, since if I choose life, I will get life without money, without the possibility to enjoy life; yet if I choose the money, I will lose both. Indeed, there is in fact only one feasible outcome – the choice *for* entering into the symbolic order, *for* alienation, *for* a life in a potentially meaningful world but without unconditional pleasure. Indeed, he who chooses 'life' is rewarded with a meaningful world, but will have to sacrifice the money (the 'Jouissance', the unconditional enjoyment). Still, it does allow for a limited form of enjoyment (phallic enjoyment), while producing a remainder, a surplus enjoyment ('plus-de-jouir') being attached to the drive and its object *a*.[6] That would be his gain. In contrast, he who chooses the money ('la bourse'), who chooses unconditional enjoyment, is denied access to the world as well. That is his loss. Indeed, entering the symbolic comes at a price, there is a fundamental sacrifice to be made, which effectively enables participation in social life and in the world of exchange as well.

The phrase 'your money or your life' has become, in Lacan's hands, a myth – running parallel to Hegel's dialectic of Master and Slave – concerning the origin of social life. The myth explains that exchange in social life always requires a sacrifice, a surrender in order to gain something else: the primacy of sacrifice. Because of the primacy of sacrifice, a resemblance can be identified with Simmel's (2011, 85–95), more empirical, view on social life, noting that Simmel probably was an inspiration to Lacan (Vandenberghe 1994). Moreover, the primacy of sacrifice does not only apply to social life but also to human life as such. In order to produce a work of culture (even at an agricultural level), man has to sacrifice something else first: Any production, the production of culture as such, requires a preceding act of renunciation (Simmel 2011, 87). Ultimately, what is at stake is not only the installation of social life, but the constitution of the world, with the transformation of the real into a world requiring the relinquishing of an immediate enjoyment ('Jouissance'). This real of life is repressed, as a result of an *Urverdrängung*, a primal repression, as Lacan would put it, while being represented by signifiers.[7] This primal repression of the real, the real of life in its immediacy, we might add, would agree well with

6 This allows the distinction between at least four types of jouissance: the three mentioned (Nasio 1992, 115–158), and the jouissance of the living. In addition, Lacan distinguishes three more types. This would add up to a total of seven types. A discussion of these additional types of jouissance would be beyond the scope of this Chapter. See Miller (1999), Porge (2000, 238–248) and Braunstein (2003).

7 Leaving aside the elaboration, Freud is dealing with the same problem (Freud 1957). He addresses the fixation of the 'immanence vitale' by means of an unconscious ideation, functioning as a signifier: *Vorstellungsrepräsentanz*. Lacan (1992, 74; 2002, 714) prefers to translate this term, somewhat controversially, as 'répresentant de la répresentation'. The signifier ('Repräsentanz') is the archetype of representation. This issue of the primal repression reflects one of the most fundamental problem faced by both Freud and Lacan.

an *Urstiftung*, the act of founding a meaningful world, as its reverse side. This whole issue of 'your money or your life' and everything that goes with it was summed up effectively by Žižek (2008, 154): 'You cannot have meaning *and* enjoyment'. Or to phrase it differently: 'You cannot have your cake and eat it'. You cannot keep unconditional enjoyment intact whilst consuming it bit by bit in the world. It is one of Lacan's most fundamental figures of thought.

In retrospect, in this elaboration of the real and its relation to the symbolic we can hardly fail to notice the constellation of German Idealism in all its diversity, from Hegel to Schelling. With respect to Hegel, this influence on Lacan is admitted by himself and has been demonstrated convincingly by, among others, Žižek (1998; 2011). As for Schelling, it was Frank (1974; 1997; 2002) who established a clear link with Sartre and, in a derivative sense, Lacan as well. In both cases it is ultimately about the opposition between a primary state of unity, the immediacy of life, an unbroken indifference *and* the principle of form, of limitation, of the Spirit. However, with Lacan – and Cassirer as well, albeit in a different form – this opposition is not played out as a metaphysical struggle between two *forces*, but rather as an opposition between two *levels*: the level of the real and that of its symbolic transformation into a world, with the real being erased at the same time.

Reality is a 'mixtum compositum' of that part of the real that can be processed symbolically as well imaginarily. From this perspective, the word 'real', as it is still often used by post-Lacanians ('real time') could be considered to be redundant and sometimes even misleading. Secondly, the real is nothing like a substance that 'exists within itself', for instance a 'substance jouissante', where Lacan could be conceived as an ally of Deleuze. Lacan was never a speculative idealist, but does not appear to be a speculative realist either (of the Spinoza type). Lacan stands firmly with both feet in modernity: Man is not able to bypass the symbolic access to reality. Whatever form symbolisation may take, it will never be able to tell us anything about what the real is. And yet reality *does* exist: What appears in front of me, *is* there. In this sense, Lacan is an ontological realist, in line with Cassirer. The real exists outside, 'Jouissance' exists outside (*ek-sistance*), but does not really exist for us. *Reality* does exist for us, but once the real comes into existence, anxiety will follow, as has been shown.

3.7 The Later Lacan

The focus on the real becomes even stronger in Lacan's last period, from 1973 onwards, which is defined as the Lacan of the Real. In this period, in his explanation of his ideas he devotes a great deal of attention to the author James

Joyce. We need to consider this here, because what has been said in the foregoing does not wholly apply to the later Lacan, the Lacan of the Real. Some may argue, the later Lacan would be the true Lacan, Lacan come into his own. The idea that we here would be dealing with the true Lacan is understandable. After all, here we see a person in the last years of the adventure of his life, an autonomous thinker without any urge to prove or profile himself. He tires easily, and finds, after having always been able to rely on an amazing vitality, that his strength, his *immanence vitale*, the real inside himself, is failing him. We find him devoting him special attention to the real, which is reflected in the title of the 1974–1975 seminar: R.S.I. – first the Real, then the Symbolic and the Imaginary, all capitalised. We notice two things: the arrangement and the capitalisation. The real now comes first, rather than the symbolic, so the symbolic has lost its primacy (in relation to the imaginary and the real). And yet we must not conclude that the real has now been given primacy – it is only being put first. The three orders are put on equal footing, made equivalent, which is a new development. While the imaginary used to be subordinated to the symbolic, this difference in hierarchy is now gone. Indeed, they undergo a generalisation, with the imaginary no longer being primarily related to the mirror stage and to narcissism, but instead being put in a relationship with the Gestalt experience, that which forms and generates a whole (*consistance*). The symbolic is also generalised, to something that creates a hole (*trou*) in the imaginary and real. The real is defined as that which is placed outside (*ek-sistance*): outside the imaginary and the real, not relating to them. The upgrading of the imaginary register, which runs parallel to its being broadened, signifies a clear and significant difference compared to the classical Lacan. It is assigned a position of representation in its own right.

Raised to the second power. Within the context of this generalisation, the epistemological idealism of the Cassirer type remains in force. For example, Lacan argues that the categories in the world are introduced by the symbolic. Space is emphatically referred to as a 'verbal construct', relying as it does on language. This is hardly a new perspective, but its reaffirmation takes place in rather bold terms (Lacan 2005, 95). This should not surprise us and is even necessary to some extent, because as part of this new design it no longer gives primacy to the symbolic. The difference between reality (the world) and the real needs to be stressed once again, as well as the symbolic construction of reality (Lacan 2005, 132).

We can distinguish yet another difference, as the three registers are not only undergoing generalization, but are also made autonomous to a certain degree. We see this reflected in the capitalisation (and the use of nouns): the Real, the Symbolic, the Imaginary. Where 'imaginary' and 'symbolic' are used to take the form of adjectives and as relating to an order, the scene has changed. Lacan (1974–1975, session of 11 March 1975) now speaks of the Real as a real to the second power (*réel à la puissance deux*), thus putting more emphasis on the real. The 'Jouissance' is not merely something that is expelled dynamically, but is actually placed outside (*ek-siste*) (Lacan 2005, 125). The pre- and post-symbolic real (cut off from primordial symbolisation) is now being specified in these terms. As before, it is still referred to as impossible, but to this he adds the qualification of unthinkable (*impensable*), although it may show itself in a fragmented way (*bouts de réel*). It 'connects with nothing', it is termed an 'un-world', actively rejecting meaning (*forclôt le sens*) – a choice of terms that puts us in mind of chaos. The qualification of without-meaning is hardly surprising, because it is part of the concept of the real. What does surprise us, however, is its qualification as an activity. The *via negativa* comes into force here: the real is 'without order', 'without law', 'without space' (Lacan 2005, 137–138). Remarkably, 'time' is not mentioned. Whether this is coincidental or not, in the latter case the real would be temporarily structured (as with Bergson, or Whitehead's process metaphysics, Bloch's materialism). Whatever the case may be, the association with process metaphysics-type of the Whitehead variety, but also with Deleuze, comes to mind. These typifications ('without order', 'without law', 'without space') go well beyond that of the qualitative unknown: We only know that the real exists, but *do not* know what it is. Now we read: 'We *do* know what it is, be it in the form of a knowledge of what is not (without order, without law, etcetera)'. This may seem like a minor difference, but it is in fact fundamental. Moreover, it runs deep: without order, without law. The real is assigned a particular definiteness and autonomy (which it did not have before, at least not to such a degree). Post-Lacanians such as Žižek take these sketchy indications and prefer to give the Real (now often capitalised as Lacanian Real) a grisly interpretation.

We see this happening not only to the real but also to the two other instances. Where the imaginary and symbolic orders were closely intertwined with the classical Lacan, by virtue of their hierarchical relationship – the affirmation of the imaginary identification standing in front of the mirror ('that is me') by the big Other ('yes, that is you') – the elimination of the hierarchical link causes them to part company. This disconnection has far-reaching consequences: from now on they are strangers to each other (*si étrangères*). Obviously, they already differed (image and word), but this distinction is highlighted even more. No longer primarily related to each other, they acquire a higher level of autonomy (more than they already had). This becomes very clear from the strengthened conception of alienation that had traditionally been assigned to the symbolic (according to Lacan's views): indeed, it comes from the outside. Also this 'from the outside' becomes an outside 'to the second power'. This means we are not only in the grips of language while being involved as a subject-in-being, but in the grips of a language, which is purely external in nature. As a result, the symbolic no longer takes the form of an objective mind (the classical Lacan type), implicating alienation but allowing separation as well, but instead acquires the quality of the real. The symbolic still provides categorical structure (see before), but now has also become intrinsically traumatic. It is an act of violence being unleashed. No longer in the grips of language, we are being sucked dry by it. Thus, language is compared to a parasite or a tumour that consumes us – although the image of the parasite is not wholly absent in previous work (Lacan 1991a, 190). During these years, this image often returns. Raising the real to the second power is therefore associated with a raising to the second power of alienation in and by language.

For example, Lacan (2005, 95) wonders how it can be that a normal person does not to conceive the words on which he depends as either being imposed or being implanted (*mots imposés*). From the classical Lacan's perspective, this answer can quite easily be answered, namely by saying: for the very reason that alienation in and by language is followed or is at least accompanied by separation – withdrawal – in which the child, the subject either accepts or rejects certain qualifications it has been labelled with and thus chooses to engage in a relationship with these words (*laisse-toi nourrir*). Yet, if the power of language (and therefore also the power of the Other) is so strong, precluding any form of contribution by the subject (which in this case cannot demur), this answer is no longer valid and the Other have been made omnipotent.

The father. At any rate, the inquiry into the mode of connection, of intertwining between the three distances becomes urgent. The problem is addressed by the model of the Borromean knot. whose basic concept is simple, but its elaboration most certainly is not. It refers to three circular rings that are connected in such a way that whenever any of the rings is detached or cut, all three will fall apart. Consequently, each of the three rings passes over the second and under the third ring, respectively. Each ring represents an instance (R, S, I), while the knot as a whole (or rather, the chain) does the same. And each ring is characterised by internal closedness, by *consistance*. According to Lacan, this type of ideal intertwining hardly ever occurs, if at all: it represents an ideal case, an extreme concept. And yet he feels that also there a fourth ring is required in order to name each individual ring as being R, S, I, respectively. The normal situation, however, is that of an error occurring in the intertwined rings. The subject is faced with the task of compensating for or repairing this original mistake, this basic fault (which can occur in different forms). Again, a fourth ring is required to hold the three rings together, naming and qualifying them individually as R, S, I as well. This fourth ring, which he calls a sinthome, would be equal to the Name-of-the-Father, but here it means something different than in the classical Lacan's definition: finding its origin in the Symbolic, it functions in its own right.

While, with the classical Lacan, the Name-of-the-Father was the signifier of the Law, here it is conceived as Father as Naming (*le Père comme nommant*). This is the new element introduced in the Séminaire R.S.I. (1974–75, session of 15 April 1975). Two difference are involved. Firstly, the *range* is changed: from prohibiting to naming. Secondly, it makes Lacan refers back to another register than that of the Law, namely that of language, while reducing the role of the father to its radical function: naming, nominating, assigning (*nommer à*).

In explicit Biblical terms, Lacan refers back to a figure of thought that precedes the Law, Mozes' Law of the Mount Sinai, returning to the story described in *Genesis*, where father Adam is revealing reality by naming things and animals. The range of naming goes even further, is no longer limited to Adam, but instead is about creation itself. Indeed, creation in terms of *Fiat lux* ('There be light, and there was light') can be imagined as the outcome of a declaration about the ways of the world: 'This is real, that is imaginary and that is symbolic'. Indeed, this is *not* about a naming (*nomination*) *within* the world, but rather *unto* a world, in which the real, the imaginary and the symbolic are named and thus connected from symbolic act.[8] This also changes the *role* of the father itself – the second difference. According to the classical view, it is the Law that fulfils a key role, with the actual father being little more than a representative of the Law (in fact, he can easily be missed). The father now assumes a key role, has become an *actor*. Decisive here is not the presence of the *Law* (in the story of the mother), but the presence of the *actual father as an actor* (as an actual person, one that explains how things work). This is the new meaning of the Name-of-the-Father: the father as a direction-giving figure, as the father who 'says it'. Consequently, the Name-of-the-Father no longer occupies a privileged position and ceases to function as the constitution of human existence. Instead, the Name-of-the-Father is an example of a sinthome, of a fourth ring (naming the three other rings and thus keeping them together), bearing in mind that this 'belief in the father' is a neurotic construct, repairing a basic fault (Vanheule 2011).

---

8 Lacan 1974–1975, session of 13 May 1975; 'en tant que dans le Symbolique surgit quelque chose qui nomme, nous voyons ça dans les débuts du Bible, … le *Fiat lux*'. 'as far as within the Symbolic something comes to the fore that names, we will recognise this in the early chapters of the Bible, … le *Fiat lux*'.

Clinical issues. From there Lacan conceives his new clinical theory: the father as a naming agent. Once this act in which the real, the imaginary and the symbolic are named and thus connected, being attributed to the Name-of-the-Father, the father as the naming agent, has *not* taken place, we find ourselves outside the field of neurosis and potentially in the field of psychosis. No linkage has been established, and yet this intertwining can still be established by a sinthome, in order to repair the defect. In this way, also a variety of a mental disorders can be interpreted from a defect and repairing this defect. It makes these sinthomes highly singular in nature. This means there is a substantial difference with the classical theory. What the situation calls for here is a generalisation of the theory of the psychosis (which also brings a modification). Lacan now argues that any psychopathological alteration (not just the psychosis) may refer back to an original defect in the intertwining that is to be compensated by a symptom – this is what the generalisation is about. And yet the original defect would not be about rejecting the Name-of-the-Father (which, according to the classical theory, was the defect in the psychosis), but it can in fact point to different types of defects in the intertwining – this is the modification. Thus, in a different form, the defect model of the psychosis is applied to the mental disorder as well as to actual normality (of the neurosis). It should be borne in mind, however, that this defect is inevitable, because the right type of harmonic intertwining merely represents an ideal case, one that would not appear in reality. Moreover, by putting the father centre stage, he falls back on an environment-based explanation of the psychosis: a father falling short. In his study of Joyce, we will see how this works out. In doing so, he falls back to what Deleuze and Guattari (1972) denounced as familialism, a concept they incorrectly attributed to Lacan (although this was true for many Lacanians at the time).

Also psychoanalysis as a practice is given a different finality. No longer focused on an analysis of the basic phantasm, it now centres on the acceptance or modification of the interconnection, shifting it to the production of and an identification with a symptom (*sinthome*) as an outcome (Morel 2008, 39–54). What it actually means is being able to deal with it ('savoir y faire'), a qualification taken from traditional psychosis treatment. Its goal is not to cure the disorder, but rather to change the way it's being dealt with (*care*): a new type of interaction with it, based on accepting or modifying the symptom. Lacan *demonstrated* it as it were, manipulating his knots. Anyway, what we see reflected here is a certain degree of scepticism towards the change that can be effectuated through psychoanalysis.

The question in fact is whether this new conceptualisation leads to improvement, as is sometimes suggested. Opinions seem to differ. A lot remains either obscure or unsolved (aporetic) with the later Lacan. Although the concept of psychosis is diluted, the dichotomy between psychotic and non-psychotic remains intact, which leads the post-Lacanians to develop the concept of the 'ordinary psychosis' ('psychose ordinaire') – a concept that fails to occur with Lacan himself (Miller 2009). An example par excellence of the new conception of the psychosis is offered by the author James Joyce, which Lacan uses to explain his new, expanded theory of the psychosis. Based on this new meaning, Joyce might well be defined as psychotic, although no reference has ever been made to psychotic events. Indeed, he compensates his psychotic defect by 'making a name for himself' in order to get recognition. Besides, Lacan uses Joyce to explain his new conception of the Name-of-the-Father: highlighting the importance of the actual the father, his failing in Joyce's case ('carence paternelle', 'démission paternelle'), whereas the classical Lacan (2002, 575) would have rejected such an interpretation. In fact, Lacan's interpretation of Joyce offers an example of his new theory that cannot be mistaken.

3.8 Joyce and Lacan

In Joyce, Lacan recognises a compensated psychotic structure – with due reservation of course (although no mention is made of psychotic events in his biography). Joyce was the great literary innovator of the 20th century, and his most famous work is *Ulysses*, which appeared in 1922 (Joyce 2010). It describes the life on a single day in Dublin (16 June 1904) of Leopold Bloom, an advertising salesman. This description takes the form of a panoply of styles (including the inner monologue) and perspectives (arts and sciences, organs in the human body), summing up life in all aspects and levels, and particularly in all its mundanity. Its inspiration is Homer's *Odyssee*, but it is also a parody on Hegel's *Phenomenology of the Spirit*. It features the character of Stephen Dedalus, which is seen as (one) alter ego of Joyce, as well as Stephen's father, who may also be regarded as an a representation of his own father. Earlier, in 1916, a more or less autobiographical self-portrait, now with Stephen Dedalus, as the protagonist, is offered in *A Portrait of the Artist as a Young Man* (Joyce 1992). An earlier version appeared much later, in 1944, entitled *Stephan Hero* (Joyce 1969) A broader discussion would be in order here, because Lacan presents the case of Joyce as the casus princeps of his new theory on psychosis, which means a lot depends on it. Lacan's version has been discussed repeatedly afterwards (Morel 2008, 113–150; Soler 2015). Lacan proposes two main arguments.

First argument: the father. In support of his vision of a psychotic structure in the case of Joyce, Lacan points to the role of the father, particularly his failure ('carence paternelle'). The verdict is that Joyce-the-father never was a father to Joyce-the-son – he never taught him anything and neglected him in just about every respect (Lacan 2005, 88). Indeed, Joyce's father is a rather peculiar character, who was always heavy in debt and often drank too much, which caused a social decline of the family: Many times they had to move house and they lived through many a crisis. Stephen Dedalus (Joyce 1992, 186) offers the following description of his father, in which we will easily recognise the father of Joyce: 'A medical student, all oarsman, a tenor, an amateur actor, a shouting politician, a small landlord, a small investor, a drinker, a good fellow, a storyteller, somebody's secretary, something a distillery, a tax-gatherer, a bankrupt and present a praise of his own past'. This does in fact point towards an actual failure in terms of adding structure (as in 'going to bed in time'). He is a failure when judged in this limited, structuring context. And yet the relationship with his actual father was a complex one: Father John was a rather quaint character, and so was his son James, even as a child. They both stood out, each in their own way, Still, there was an intimate connection as well, which becomes evident from most of his writings. Unmistakably, Joyce's alter ego Stephen Dedalus speaks with sympathy and affection about his father, which is reflected in his sentiments of admiration, embarrassment as well as moments of playful irony and self-mockery. For example, a friend of Stephen Daedalus sends the latter's regards to the father: 'Greetings from a famous son of a famous father' (Joyce 2010, p. 236). Details from Joyce's personal life seem to bear this out. The many times that Joyce moved house in Paris along with his manuscripts Joyce never forgot to bring a portrait of his father. It suggests a relationship between Joyce as an author and the role of his father in his writings. By his own admission, Joyce owns one third of his body of work to his father, and apparently he learned quite a lot from him (contrary to what is argued by Lacan): The father pointed the way for the son in the complexity of life. In that sense, his work can be interpreted as an obscure tribute to his father.[9] Another issue, one that Lacan does not refer to, is that Joyce's father may have been overindulgent of the eldest son, whom he considered to be a prodigy and favoured at the cost of the other children, with all its associated advantages and drawbacks. When his father died, Joyce found that he had been appointed sole heir, excluding all other children (which ironically enough meant he inherited a small fortune). In that sense, we may speak of a lack of the actual father ('carence paternelle'), not in the structuring sense (which Lacan referred to), but rather in terms of

---

9 Meanwhile, an exhaustive biography on James Joyce's father has been published, written by Jackson and Costello (1998): *John Stanislaus Joyce: The Voluminous Life and Genius of James Joyce's Father*. From this work, a strong influence and mutual respect become apparent.

the level of intimacy and the expectations held out by the father towards the son (expectations that the son may well have lived up to, and in fact even surpassed). The emphasis that Lacan puts on the actual failure of John Joyce as a father, is in line with the new theory but not with the classical one. Based on the classical theory, an actual failure of the father would not be truly relevant in respect of the function of the Name-of-the-Father. What matters here is not the failure of the father but the lack of the signifier of the father, of the Law, of separation (Lacan 2002, 557). It is this very point that was picked up on by Joyce (maybe from his own catholic background). He describes the position of the father-function as an empty space which is to be filled by the actual fathers, as in the apostolic line of succession (Joyce 2010, 186). Consequently, Stephen Dedalus (Joyce's alter ego) calls the father (in the true Lacanian spirit) a 'necessary evil': necessary because of the universal function, and evil on account of its empirical and often oedipal substantiation. It is well in keeping with Lacan's famous saying (2005, 137) that the oedipal father can be missed, subject to the condition that he can be used. As a person, Joyce lived by this functional conception as well. A picture taken in 1939 shows James Joyce with his son Georgio and his grandson Stephen, sitting below the portrait of his father John: three successive manifestations of one and the same function and place: that of the father (Freund 1985, 65). Why is this function necessary? Again, Joyce leaves no room for ambiguity: as a counterpoint to the mother-child love. Yes: '*Amor matris*, subjective and objective, may be the only true thing in life'. Ultimately, fatherhood is nothing more than legal fiction (Joyce 2010, p. 186). Noticeably, Joyce fails to include his mother in his works – just like Lacan fails to consider her in his own interpretation – be it that motherly characters can certainly be found in Joyce's writings, such as Molly Bloom in *Ulysses* and Anna Livia Plurabella in *Finnegan's Wake*. Yet we know that Joyce's mother tended to tie her son to her apron strings, which made it difficult for him to sever the bond. It will mostly appear in disguised form, symbolised by Ireland and Irish Catholicism which he must seek to escape (and which she strongly opposes): 'When the soul of a man is born in this country there are nets flung at it to hold it back from flight […] I shall try to fly by those nets […] Ireland is the old sow that eats her farrow'. (Joyce 1992, 157). Apparently, the core of Joyce's problem is not his failing father, but the 'old sow that eats her farrow'. This iron grip, this alienation Joyce attempts to escape from by leaving home, which is in fact an escape (with all its associated feelings of guilt and fear): *non serviam*, I will not serve (Joyce 1992, 90). This refusal is expressed in the historical fact that Joyce acts against the express wish of his dying mother by not fulfilling his religious duties ('non serviam'). This disregard of his mother's wishes connects the ending of *A Portrait of the Artist as a Young Man* with the first chapter of *Ulysses*.

It signals the transition towards artistry. To achieve this, he does indeed need support from his father, represented by the portrait that he has carried with him all his life.

Second argument: the body. Supporting the psychosis notion, Lacan points out the impotence of his protagonist to transform fleeting sentiments (of resentment and anger) into the lasting passions of love or hate. As a result, these feelings cannot be sustained, but can only be discarded, almost like a shell. Joyce repeatedly returns to this theme.[10] In line with his classical psychosis conception. Lacan (2005, 150) interprets this phenomenon as a product of the incapacity to experience the body as one's own, as being connected, which incapacity would be characteristic of a psychosis, also according to the classical theory. Indeed, it deserves mention that Lacan's classical psychosis theory also serves as a backdrop to his thoughts on Joyce, next to his new conception (Miller 2005, 211). Then again, a fictional character (Stephen Dedalus) can never coincide with the author (James Joyce), never mind a highly stylised, constructing author such as Joyce. It is a leap that can never be made. Although Stephen Dedalus is his alter ego, the two are simply too different – which already becomes evident from his earlier version in *Stephen Hero* (Joyce 1969). Moreover, this type of experience does not necessarily originate from the psychotic spectrum, but rather points to a deep split (between body and mind), with the body being experienced as base and repulsive: 'He had known neither the pleasure of companionship with others nor the vigour of rude male health nor filial piety. Nothing stirred within his soul but a cold and cruel and loveless lust' (Joyce 1992, 72). For one thing, this would be in line with the gnostic brand of Catholicism in which Stephen Dedalus had been steeped, with its characteristic split between heaven and hell, between mind and body, God and Satan – with Joyce's attitude also being split: yes and no (Joyce 1992, 188).

However, it is *art* that enables this non-connection to be remedied, with the artist's personal experience – a cry, a cadence, a mood – being transformed into a flowing or rhythmic story, with experience itself being discarded, refined (Joyce 1992, 166): 'As a fruit divested of its soft ripe peel'. For this reason, it would make more sense for Joyce to attribute these early experiences to the protagonist (introducing it in a subtle way), as a kind of stepping stone or preliminary stage leading to artistry. What initially is only a lack or handicap is transformed into a bonus: Things that fail in life will bring success in authorship,

10 Joyce 1992, 62, 63, 114. Lacan (2005, 149) only refers to p. 62: 'as easily as a fruit is divested of its soft ripe peel'. A similar event he gets his wrists slapped (Joyce 1992, 40–44) unfolds in a different way and is handled adequately.

in art. This is line with the essential theme of the book: Stephan Dedalus' (alias James Joyce) life *as* an artist.

Perversion? Taken together, these elements would not specifically suggest the presence of a psychotic world. It is hard to imagine that a psychotic person, whatever his qualities may be, could have written a highly variegated and subtly composed work as *Ulysses*, a book *devoid of* orthodox rigour. So what do we have here? Particularly from Lacan's perspective, we might consider the possibility of a perverse world (not necessarily Joyce's own world, but rather the world conjured up in Joyce's works). Lacan (2005, 149) does briefly mention this option in regard of Joyce as a person, but disqualifies it. What is shown by Joyce can actually be framed in the basic classical theory of alienation and separation, in this case producing the outcome of a partial separation, in the sense of perversion (here, perversion should not be taken in its material meaning of abnormal sexual behaviour, but rather in its formal sense, as a split). Indeed, rather than being caught in the nets of the Other, as would be true for a psychotic person, the protagonist is in fact able to leave Ireland, he *can* choose to emigrate, and he *must*, because, being a pervert (in the formal sense defined by Lacan), he must debunk conventions and semblance and cannot simply join in the game: They are mere conventions. In each cultural expression, Stephen Dedalus therefore recognises a usurpation of individual thought, of personal emotions: There is always massive alienation. Culture, language is not solid, as you might think, but can in fact be unravelled, as is shown in *Ulysses*. It is therefore no coincidence that Joyce's project in *Finnegans Wake* should result in the forming of a unique Joyce-ian language idiom. The conflict arising between the subject on the one hand and culture and language on the other, which has a hold on the subject, is universal – any person will be faced with it. It is also one of the main themes, if not the main theme, of Joyce's antipode: Thomas Mann, first of all in his own version of 'Portrait of the Artist as a Young Man', entitled *Tonio Kröger*, be it in different terms (artist vs. bourgeois). Typical of Joyce is how he resolves this matter in terms of a split (which is specific but hardly unique), whereas Thomas Mann opts for a more mediating solution (in both his life and his work). Embedded in Joyce's solution – not-serving (*non serviam*), not being a slave, most certainly not of the symbolic order – is the contrary case, already sequestered: that of subjugation, of choosing to be a slave, be it at a phantasmatic level. We see this theme emerge with advertising salesman Leopold Bloom, main narrator of *Ulysses*, and *also* one of Joyce's alter egos. (Allegedly, the loquacious Bloom would resemble Joyce more than did the reticent Stephen Daedalus). Opposite Stephen Dedalus' not-serving (*non serviam*) we find Bloom's 'at your service' mentality (Joyce 2010, 395). This servility is played out in the famous masochist passages found in the

Circe episode (Joyce 2010, 388–523). Which actually includes a cameo of Stephen Dedalus with the physical abuse to which he had been exposed, now in a masochist context, in terms of the physical sensations that form the second argument with Lacan (Joyce 2010, 486).

Indeed, this split returns in the father-figure(s). They are omnipresent yet impotent and consequently violent fathers, who nonetheless find themselves protected by the mother: authority is recognised, but then again it is not. In *Dubliners,* Joyce (2000) describes, with remarkable sensitivity, a number of these impotent/violent fathers in which, with some reserve, we might recognise his own father – most notably in the stories 'A little cloud', 'Counterparts' and 'Grace'. His sensitivity should not surprise us, because children growing up with violent, alcohol-addicted parents are often highly susceptible to atmosphere, quite easily picking up on the mind-set of others ('hyper-mentalising'). In that sense, this finding of being split might also be applicable to Joyce as a person – not based on his experiences of a protagonist described by him, but rather on the grounds of his ability to describe them as such: based on the content and structure of his body of work.

We might qualify this approach as subversive. In and through his works, the author Joyce needs to break away from the conventions of the novel and later, of language, in order to shoot down the semblance of self-evidence. Where Thomas Mann turns just about anything into a parody, whilst staying with certain boundaries, Joyce chooses to overturn these. Indeed, he cannot state that they are mere conventions, everybody knows this, don't make a fuss (the things his father would say, as a true father). Instead, he is intent on not making the community forget that this is an ultimate truth – a truth that there is no truth.[11] In his final extremely cryptic work, *Finnegan's Wake*, he creates a comprehensive language, with its own voice, a true glottal language, choosing not to conform to an existing language or its conventions. Again we find: *non serviam*. His approach fails to produce a psychotic mannerism or psychotic rigour – his work is much too diverse to suggest that: his earlier work is highly nuanced and sensitive, while his later works may be considered contrived and thorough to a fault – and maybe overly witty as well (although, inevitably, not

11 Remarkably, Lacan's chief discussion partner with respect to Joyce, Aubert (2000, 69) also points to the significance of precisely this statement (unintentionally lending support to the perversion thesis with Joyce). Also without realising it, he introduces another argument, when pointing out that for Joyce the laws of society are universal and immutable (Aubert 2000, 57). This perspective lacks insight into the impotence of laws, insight into the dialectics with laws depending on individual subject to become effective. Their supposed omnipotence needs to be challenged or mocked (following a perverse strategy). In other words: we have alienation, with separation taking the form of 'yes and no'.

all will agree). This is reflected in the many homonyms and word contractions he uses, particularly in his late work *Finnegans Wake*, at which Lacan could also excel, incidentally. Joyce's work, most notably his late work, evinces a type of 'oracular speech' which was also strongly favoured by Lacan himself. A fine example is the term 'sinthome', with its many embedded cryptic references (also to Joyce!). Joyce takes this to the extreme, as was true for the later Lacan.

Whatever the case may be, when taken in this sense the case of Joyce might serve *not* to expand Lacan's psychosis concept to preserve the dichotomy, but rather to break away from this dichotomy by introducing an intermediate group halfway between psychosis and normality, elaborating it by taking perversion as a starting point: perversion and all its variations. Allowing in 'gradations of separation' would then constitute a meaningful correction to the very static scheme of psychotic *versus* non-psychotic. What Lacan refused to allow in – the field of the personality disorders or psychopathies – might now be embraced, whilst giving it a unique substantiation (in line with the current psychopathology of personality disorders). In that case, a mental disorder is still conceived as a dysfunction of separation and symbolisation, but a range of gradations have now been added. Within this new design, the Name-of-the-Father retains its general function in the case of the neurosis and essential normality (see Chapter 4). The differences between the classical Lacan and the later Lacan will summarised in more detail in the next paragraph.

3.9 Substance or Function

No less important is the fact that a substantial part of the later Lacan's views, as represented here, is in line with the classical theory in its more or less final form. Remarkably, the later Lacan chooses to qualify the role of the Name-of-the-Father as being only one of the solutions to reach intertwining. In doing so, he also abandons the fundamental notion of a father function as being detached from the father as an actual person. He now elevates the actual father to the level of the one who names things and categories, thus replacing the Name-of-the-Father with the Naming-Father. The difference may seem minor, but it is not, as was shown in the foregoing section. First of all, the range of naming is wide: giving a name to things, naming the various orders of the psychic reality – the real, the symbolic, the imaginary – as such (R, S, I). Moreover, in this condition, the father no longer functions as a mere representative but instead becomes an actor, a guarantee for validity: naming things, telling what's what. By contrast, the classical Lacan made a clear distinction between function and actor (as a specific and unique contribution, unlike Freud). This is what we might refer to as Freud's error – having function coincide with person – being repeated by the later Lacan. It will automatically cause the role of the father as a person to be upgraded. Lacan's (2005, 88) interpretation of Joyce shows exactly that: father-Joyce being blamed for not having taught son Joyce anything. In the final analysis, the later Lacan reinstates Freud's actor-father: father says. This contradicts the classical theory and can hardly be seen as an improvement, but as a drawback. Indeed, Lacan struggled in his career to distance himself from this limited, Freudian, 'paternal' meaning. However, already in the 1950s he declared the oedipal complex to be a myth, reducing its essence to the castration being involved (Lacan 2002, 820). This becomes evident once again when, in his final years, Lacan (2005, 22) refers to the oedipal complex as a symptom, a personal myth. Indeed, the classical Lacan had already transformed the oedipal complex as defined by Freud into a formal structure. Indeed, his aim has always been to formalise and functionalise relationships. When conceived formally and functionally, the Name-of-the-Father can be expressed in an empty denominator (x), with x taking a variety of forms while invariably serving the function of symbolising an empty space (Lacan 2002, 557). Its interpretation is diverse by definition, the work of the mother symbolising an empty space, gestures and decisions she makes – all of this, provided it has this separating function. This process, this function, is essential. It is *this* function that allows for a father to be present as an actual father, as a caring, giving father – on which level an actual father can fail and will fail, indeed. That is all in the game.

Substance. It seems that Lacan is neglecting the functional perspective on the relationships concerned. This would be true for the notion of the father as no longer being conceived in a formal and functional sense (as a Name, as a function), but rather as an actual, substantial person. It is also relevant for the registers of the symbolic, the imaginary and the real, insofar as what initially was called orders became rings, or things – see before. The symbolic now takes the form of sheer exteriority, associated with the image of a parasite sucking or a cancer eating away. With the later Lacan, the alienating power of the symbolic becomes an alienation to the second power, turning it into a kind of substance.

We see also the real move towards substance. In the Lacan reception, this real made autonomous gets most of the attention. Which is quite understandable, when taking into account the cultural perspective current in the 1970s and 1980s. Just like existentialism was criticised for ignoring the significance of structures, leading to the rise of structuralism, so was structuralism accused of not devoting attention to the real. This led to the theme of the real becoming dominant in Lacan reception in the 1980s. It does tickle the imagination: no law, no order, not connected with anything, an un-world. It ultimately takes the form of a destructive force, like fire (Lacan 2005, 121). This may sound like a strong statement, implying that you must be very naive to see things differently, which is definitely true for the post-Lacanians. And yet such a substance-driven conception of the real does offer a form of metaphysics, an individually biased world image, such as proposed by Deleuze (1994). Undoubtedly, Lacan is a philosopher of the difference, a representative of the French philosophy of difference – which also applies to Deleuze. And yet, in contrast to Deleuze, the difference is not there in reality as in a substance, nor is any formal unity found in reality, in the substance of reality. Indeed, this difference is being proposed in the symbolic, which is posited. This means that Lacan is *not* a Spinoza nor a Spinozist, because he has both feet in modernity: We cannot bypass the symbolic to access reality. Indeed, even Zupančič (2017, 118), while trying to ally Lacan with Deleuze, also has to recognise their fundamental divergence, which results from essentially different concepts of negativity. Following Deleuze's concept of negativity, it manifests itself in something that happens in the real, being directly productive, whereas Lacan denied such a straightforward, immediate way.[12]

Nevertheless, the later Lacan appears to move in a more speculative direction. Still, the real *is* not violence, it merely *appears* as violence, as an infringement. There is no point in speaking of violence, or of without-order, until it is put in a relationship unto an order, a law. While the classical Lacan was an ontological realist (the real is there but cannot be known as such), he now moves towards a brand of speculative metaphysics. Be that as it may, the question of the real, the real squared, as well as of the symbolic squared, is merely a derived issue. What lies at its heart is the autonomisation of the order as such.

However, we might argue that Lacan's knot theory is not a theory but a practice. In his knot practice he demonstrates the intertwined or 'knotted' quality of the conflicting tendencies associated with the psychic reality, in the dynamics of existence, and in the second chance that would be afforded by psychoanalysis. An ontological, Platonising interpretation of the knot theory would disregard this very point (Porge 2000, 244–248; Duportail 2008, 105–135). This criticism may seem valid, but it is not. Also in the performative explanation,

12 Miller (2011, 8), however, believes this to be true. As a key phrase, he quotes a fragment from *Encore* (Lacan 1975, 26), in which the terms 'substance du corps', 'substance jouissante' appear. However, its context proves beyond doubt that 'substance' is the body signified by the signifier: the body token within the *function* of the signifier. For one thing, 'substance' is not the same as 'permanence, existence'. Here (in 1972) we are probably dealing with an allusion to Deleuze (and Guattari), without him even subscribing to Deleuze's views.

the orders remain presupposed as entities, substances, in their own right, which, because of that, need to be connected: Each individually they are characterised by 'consistance', by an internal closeness. They themselves are not conceived relationally, as being mutually connected, a relationship in which the subject is also implied. Only *this* will turn the intertwining into an urgent issue, which it wasn't before. As was shown in the foregoing, this criticism does not necessarily disqualify the later Lacan entirely, but it does serve to qualify its contribution. The image of the three rings is an evocative one, it has didactic value. Yet here Wittgenstein's maxim would apply: 'an image kept us prisoner' ('ein Bild hielt uns gefangen').

Image culture. To this we should add – as an aside – that an application of Lacan's later thought, which he does not mention himself, might become quite topical in the 21st century: not the raising to the second power of the real, but that of the symbolic as well as the imaginary (without actually having to refer to substance). The all-pervasive presence of the image (in the present culture as an image culture) and of the symbolic (in the virtual world) remind us of the conception of the symbolic proposed by the later Lacan: as a hypertrophy, a growth, a huge parasite consuming everything. The symbolic has now truly become the Other, the Other with a big O; the entity that knows everything, even knowing things the subject does not know themselves – what it will do, what it suffers from, etcetera. Steven Spielberg's 2002 film 'Minority Report' was an early example, themed on an all-knowing Other that can even read minds: a not-limited, not-divided, not-crossed out Other ('Autre non barré'). Mediation has grown to such proportions and has become so all-pervasive that it can hardly be experienced as alienating *as well*. Today, all things are measured by their external appearance. This finding is not new in itself, but the sheer size, scale and uniformity are (including the marketisation and commercialisation of 'everything' contained in it). This issue might best be addressed by introducing a 'new symbolic form in being', although it is not yet clear how this social experiment would play out on a global scale. It might be close to what Heidegger qualifies as *Framework* (*Gestell*), while describing a world as being locked in modern technology and where all things have to be 'enframed' in order to exist (see Chapter 2).

The classical Lacan. Summerising, in respect of the later Lacan the key question does concern his tendency to substantivize what used to be orders in their relationship to a subject in being and 'in actu'. As a result the question of the intertwining of the three orders creates a problem, considering that these orders has been defined as existing initially in isolation, as substances (*consistance*) which have to be mutually connected in a second term. Which highlights a fundamental misconception: *proton pseudos*, in Cassirer's terminology.

The issue of the statute of the real (and the symbolic) with the later Lacan is actually only a derived issue, and therefore secondary. However, when push comes to shove, much of the classical Lacan is also retained in the later Lacan: man as being carried by a central void (*vide central*), represented by the figure of the *torus* (Lacan 1976–1977, session 14 December 1976). Also here, with the later Lacan, the drive is *not* about the real, but it is merely its effect, the echo, of speech on the body (Lacan 2005, 17). Again, Lacan's highly specific insight into the nature of the drive remains intact. Indeed, if there is any point at all in speaking of *the* imaginary, *the* symbolic and *the* real, this can only be done based on the premise that they are mutually connected and that the subject has been implied from the start, in relation to language and the real.

The classical Lacan kept emphasising the themes of relationality and functionality. For example, he repeatedly referred to the maxim 'the Other does not exist', which means that language only exist in a performative, effective manner and affect all language users, male or female. Differences and language only exist in a performative, effective manner, and affects all language users, or subjects. This would be the subject (in being): This subject in being finds its place in the intermediate zone (*entre deux*) between the signifier and the real, life itself. Thus there are *two* sides: the side of the living being *and* the side of the Other.[13]

Indeed, the life of an individual, to be male or female, unfolds halfway between the real and the symbolic, by means of its representation (*laisse-toi nourrir*). From day one the subject-in-being is part of the game, which unfolds in the field of the signifier via alienation and separation. Its classical elaboration was offered in the *graphe du désir*. Here Lacan (2002, 805–818) described in great detail the transformation of vital tension, resulting from the confrontation with language and the Other, into a desire that is underpinned by a phantasm as well as by the imaginary – excluding the ultimate real, Life, or 'Jouissance'. This non-symbolised Life would be unliveable and is therefore tantamount to Death, unless it appears in its represented, symbolised film, which effectively brings exclusion. Consequently, this representation

13 Lacan (2002, 849) summarises: 'On the side of the living being as a being that will be taken up in speech – never able in the end to come to be altogether in speech – [...] the subject seeks an object to take the place of the loss of life he has sustained [...]. On the other side, the side of the Other – the locus in which speech is verified as it encounters the exchange of the signifiers, the ideals they prop up, the elementary structures of kinship, the metaphor of the father as considered as a principle of separation, and the ever reopened division in the subject owing to his initial alienation – on this side alone and by the pathways just enumerated, order and norms must be instated which tell the subject what a man or a woman must do'.

offers a transformation that can only be accomplished performatively, 'as one goes along'. Only in this sense can we speak of the symbolic order, the symbolic forms, the real, as functionally affecting a subject (regardless of its configuration).

What about the earlier Lacan? In fact, in addition to the later Lacan (within the context of his public appearances) we also recognise an earlier Lacan next to the classical Lacan, which can roughly be dated to the period between 1953 and 1956. The basic coordinates (the symbolic, the imaginary and the real) have already been set, acknowledging the loss instituted by language – 'le symbole comme meurtre de la chose': the word as the killing of the thing, causing the thing to be lost (Lacan 2002, 319). However, ideally, this loss can be repaired in full speech, in the 'parole pleine' (Lacan 2002, 381). This last point obviously runs counter to the classical Lacan, who argues the opposite. In the background we see Hegel fulfilling a conciliatory role. However, the fact that at that particular moment he failed to fully think through the implications of the concept of the signifier, is only relevant here. This can hardly be held against him, but it is also not a reason why a separate Lacan should be introduced. He soon dropped the option himself: to speak is to create a break, one that cannot be repaired, not even ideally or in some infinitely distant future – as was believed by Hegel and, to a certain level, also by Cassirer. This would also be the right moment to take a closer look at the relationship between Lacan en Cassirer (who at times is quite close to Hegel in some way).

3.10 Lacan and Cassirer Juxtaposed

In the vision of both, symbolisation marks a shift to a different state of being, with the world becoming possible as a reality. It is a leap without continuity, owing to the fact that this shift actually amounts to making this cut – culture *is* caesura. This notion connects the two: Lacan and Cassirer. The elements that separate them in this connection will be explained and summarised in this section. Rather than making an attempt to read the one from the other, for example Cassirer reading from Lacan (Lofts 2000), the two are being juxtaposed. Considering that we have already offered a prelude to the key point, this summary can be kept brief. Indeed, it is this very concept of a caesura that both connects *and* separates them. This caesura has a dynamic *and* a static component, as was shown before. The dynamic component concerns the loss of immediacy, while the static component is about the exclusion of reality per se. It is the fact that both chose to substantiate these components in a partially different way that sets them apart. What follows here is a summary, a repeating of findings, not actually offering any new insights in that sense. And yet in the process of repeating it may in fact bring something to light: the nature of their relationship. This would offer a plea for bringing together these two figures, or figures of thought: Lacan and Cassirer.

Immediacy. Lacan (2002, 821) summarises its loss as follows: 'We must keep in mind that jouissance is prohibited [*interdite*] to whoever speaks, as such'. We have seen this before in the present chapter: Immediacy must be eliminated, as giving in to 'Jouissance' (the choice for enjoyment rather for meaning and a meaningful world), will not lead to liberation, but only to decay and ultimately to the destruction of human relationships (Widmer 2006, 131). This explains why this choice is called 'lethal'. It is the death drive, the desire for sheer destruction, in whatever form it may occur. Cassirer raises this point in almost identical words, although he obviously did not speak of 'Jouissance', but rather used the qualification of 'the paradise of pure immediacy'. We have seen this before in Chapter 2, and it actually sums up its guiding principle. Cassirer comments (PsF I, p. 49/p. 113): 'The paradise of pure immediacy is closed of'. And he continues: 'In truth, the negation of the symbolic forms would not help us to apprehend the essence of life; it would rather destroy the spiritual form with which for us this essence proves to be bound up'. He wrote these words in 1923, referring to the ultimate death drive according to Lacan and Freud (1955a) before him, who addressed this theme from 1920 onwards in 'Beyond the pleasure principle' (*Jenseits des Lustprinzips*). It is a variation on the 'your money or your life' theme. If you choose to save your own skin, you will preserve life, albeit a limited, deficient form. If, by contrast, you choose boundless enjoyment, you will lose the possibility of living in a meaningful world. This choice, however, is not for once and all, but only exists through repeating and is realised in the sum of actual, daily representations ('mediate representations').

Consequently, the death drive is not some mythical entity but instead manifests itself when we begin to flag in our daily work. Taking part in a culture, however much one may try to distance oneself from it, means working to maintain this culture on a daily basis, from which satisfaction and pleasure can actually be derived, be it only partially and in a circuitous way, through culture. The strong pull from the direct path of unfragmented enjoyment is always there, however: the death drive (immediacy, 'Jouissance'). Thomas Mann shows this in his epic 1924 novel *Der Zauberberg* ('The Magic Mountain') in a most wonderful way. The novel's protagonist, Hans Castorp, chooses to withdraw from daily life and leaves for a sanatorium high up in the mountains. Falling under the spell of this place, he finds himself unable to leave this magical place, one that symbolises sickness and death, set against the backdrop of the apocalyptic horrors of the Great War, of utter destruction. Like Cassirer and Lacan, Thomas Mann set out to prove that human life implies renunciation and can be lived only through the path of cultural labour, to quote Freud. Its immediacy is closed off or, in Lacan's words, is repressed, with life becoming liveable only in a de-lived, cultural sense. Yet, in his work Thomas Mann shows this will never be a run race. Although reputed to be a humanist author who, like Cassirer and Goethe, is also a champion of culture, his work is pervaded with death drive, and this novel is no exception. He feels that culture is the product of the tension between life and destruction as well as self-destruction: an vision on arts steeped in Romanticism, which is quite close to Lacan's own vision (Praz 1970).

According to Lacan, this repression of life is bound up with alienation within the symbolic order. Man as a subjective mind is stamped by the objective mind presented to him from the outside: It is reflected in man's helplessness, distress, his thrownness and dereliction (Lacan 2013, 27–30). The image of man as an hostage ('otage') of the signifier emerges, eventually (1991a, 323–327). Indeed, the young child, while being exposed to enigmatic signifiers, will have to conform to an external order that is alien to itself, from which as a next step it can and must free itself to a certain degree: the dialectics of alienation and separation. As a result, any form of appropriation, of internalisation of language and culture is bound to be associated with alienation. This means that Lacan is operating much more in line with Hegel, with the inevitability of conflict and inherent tragedy, however without the Hegelian possibility of a final synthesis. In this respect, he also deviates quite spectacularly from Cassirer's thesis (PsF III, p. 44/p. 39): 'The entering of the ego as a spiritual "subject" into the medium of the objective spirit constitutes not an act of alienation but an act of finding and determining itself'. Cassirer pays little heed to the tension between individual and culture, between the subjective mind and objective mind, and is therefore incapable of doing justice to the complexity of interhuman relationships in that respect – although, admittedly, Lacan tends to take this to the extreme.

Cassirer, in turn, will put Lacan in his place. Particularly in his early days, Lacan regarded the process of conforming to culture, and the 'renunciation of enjoyment', as the consequence of a *prohibition*: initially, he conceives the caesura introduced by culture as a consequence of a prohibition, an act of censure. This was likely to happen, considering that this view was in line with the ban on incest, as formulated by Freud and later by Lévi-Strauss, which ban Lacan would go on to enlarge: 'jouissance is denied to he who speaks as such'. We have seen this before, on several occasions. A conception of 'Jouissance' as being forbidden would still leave its very possibility open, indeed: In the absence of a forbidding father, it can still happen. An interpretation of an impossibility as being merely a prohibition, which would still leave a backdoor open to its possibility, turns out to be a neurotic construct, the core of any neurotic constructing. Only later did Lacan realise that this was about a structural impossibility rather than a factual, contingent prohibition (Juranville 1984, 199–207). Taking part in a culture may require abstaining from the immediacy of life, but this requirement does not constitute a moral imperative – rather, it takes the form of a 'logical' requirement or necessity. Although a Law does exist, it would be a 'fallacy' to conceive the Law of culture as a contingent ban: the Law of separation which is necessary on account of its being implied in the transition to culture. From his Neo-Kantian stance, from day one Cassirer saw this much more clearly than Lacan did initially (or Freud before him, for that matter).

The real. Here Lacan in turn corrects Cassirer. Cassirer might agree with its qualification as being impossible, because he also believes that the real per se cannot possibly be known outside the realm of symbolisation. It can, however, be known as the sum of all knowledge proven to be valid either through approximation or asymptotically. Just like the thing-as-such is the sum of all perspectives on the thing (seen, felt, weighed from all sides, and so on) – rather than something that would underlie it – so is reality-as-such the sum of all validated symbolisations, and not some other underlying entity. Reality itself is supposed to be inexhaustible. Cassirer is not the only one to support this view, as it is finds broad support with the likes of Merleau-Ponty (1962, 5–7). Merleau-Ponty opens his chef d'oeuvre with offering a paradigmatic example, namely Müller-Lyer's optical illusion, which is formed by two parallel lines that 'objectively' have the same size, but appear to have different lengths:

>—<
<—>

From the viewpoint of the Gestalt, the expression, they are different, yet they are equal when viewed from an objectifying perspective. This discord in its mode of being-given he resolves by arguing that the lines (as things-as-such, 'in the domain of being'), 'are neither equal nor unequal', which thus makes them indeterminate. This view is actually quite close to that of Cassirer. Reality per se is given, disclosed in a particular way, framed and represented. The real itself is inexhaustible, with reality offering as many views as there are viewpoints.

This is clearly different in the case of Lacan. The difference is not found in any conflicting view in terms of idealism *vs* realism, with Cassirer being the idealist and Lacan the realist. In fact, Lacan is *also* an epistemological idealist, as was show repeatedly. In 1972, Lacan (2011a, 131) even went so far as calling Plato a Lacanian. The symbolic order imposes its forms on the world: Even space is referred to as a verbal construct, also with the later Lacan. The difference is found in the type of structuring chosen. Where Cassirer defines the starting point of primitive symbolisation as a *simple line* ('Linienzug'), Lacan speaks of an identifying, an unary trait, a *single trait* ('einziger Zug'). While Cassirer chooses a meaning-giving consciousness as point of departure, Lacan proceeds from a differential type of structuring, carving up the real into a world, while cutting off the world from reality itself. This reality cannot be 'internalised' or reached, not even in the asymptotic meaning of a threshold value. Contrary to Cassirer, with Lacan the real is not a border concept, but rather a *leftover concept*. The real manifests itself in a *clash* whenever that which is excluded comes knocking: the real as a trauma, as violence. While Cassirer (and Merleau-Ponty) chooses to render the real 'harmless' by merging it into the sum of world disclosures, Lacan's notion of the real as a trauma, as an impossibility – as a *logical* consequence of his theory of the signifier and the castration it brings – actually corrects it. The concept of the signifier *implies* that of the real, as an impossibility, as that which cannot be processed from the sum of all systems of representation, and which is 'unsayable' from within. We could say that this insight constitutes Lacan's correction of Cassirer's view. And yet it may well be that Lacan eventually overshot the mark. Certainly from Cassirer's perspective, qualifying the real as such (without law, without order, as unthinkable, etcetera) would be taking things too far. Ultimately, this would lead to a pre-modern philosophy of substance and metaphysical speculation – indeed, if it has not reached that point yet.

Safeguards. There is also a third way in which Lacan's and Cassirer's path diverge. This does not concern the issue of reality, but rather that of truth. In doing so, we are dealing with the reverse side of the inquiry into the real. Cassirer presupposes a relationship within a single world, and eventually a mutual relationship between the whole range of worlds – safeguarded by categorical forms (space, time, causality, etcetera). This would be an underpinning field of unity of meaning, which safeguards the mutual relationships and coherence within and among worlds – with the various worlds fundamentally representing variations on a single categorical scheme. This serves as a guarantee that truth is in fact attainable, be it in an infinite future. The ultimate aim of classical (transcendental) philosophy – including its modern-day, qualifying variants, including Cassirer's – is to offer such a guarantee or safeguard. Truth, true reality, reality within truth, is the sum of all world disclosures. Consequently, *truth* and *method* are not in conflict with each other. Following his teacher Cohen, Cassirer could say: truth *is* method, truth is the sum all insights that can be attained through method. Not so with Lacan, for he argues that this guarantee can never be supplied. There is no Other of the Other, no meta system validating a particular system, and so there is no ultimate foundation. This ultimate foundation is the very object of the search on which the philosophy of ultimate grounds focuses.

Solid ground is not only lacking in the final analysis, but actually from the very start, in the daily experience of things. Indeed, signifiers will never generate a stable 'unity of meaning'. Its indeterminate quality resonates in the field of 'things' that are subject to it: The indeterminate quality of the concept turns its scope, its reference, into an indeterminate thing itself.[14] What Cassirer can do – generalise from thing to world, and next to it, from the sum of worlds to reality per se – is precisely what Lacan *cannot* do. No such addition would be feasible. With Cassirer, perspectives are centred, like slices from a cake adding up to a whole cake (the cake is sliced homogenously after all). With Lacan, there is no such convergence between the various type of reality disclosure. It is, however, not necessarily impossible: the concept itself, the intension may actually come into contact with the real, provided it is a true intension (*le vrai intensionnel*), but that would happen by coincidence at best, rather being embedded in a more or less rational development, as was argued by Cassirer (Lacan 2005, 152; Miller 2005, 217, 238). Together, the range of perspectives form a quilt, a collection of bits and pieces in which 'little pieces of the real' ('bouts de réel') may emerge With both, truth is only partial, but with Lacan's the carved-up condition does not allow for synthesis.

3.11 Lacan and Cassirer Put into a Mutual Relationship

This would enable Lacan and Cassirer to be juxtaposed as well as to be put into a mutual relationship. While Cassirer interprets 'being' from meaning ('No being is tangible or accessible except through meaning'), Lacan chooses to interpret 'being' in the first place and at a deeper level, from the empty signifier, with a variation on Cassirer: No being is tangible or accessible except through empty signifiers. The difference goes back to a difference in level, while the

14 Lacan, 1975, 23: 'Ce qui caractérise, au niveau de la distinction signifiant/signifié à ce qui est la comme tiers indispensable, à savoir le référent, c' est proprement que le signifé le rate. Le collimateur ne fonctionne pas'. (Which, at the level of the distinction between signifier/signified, typifies the relationship of the signified up to what is present as a necessary third, i.e. the referent, that is exactly what is not accomplished by the signified. The scope simply fails to work'.) In other words: it is the very distinction (in the sense of Lacan) between signifier and signification that incapacitates the referring function of the signification.

nature of this difference also qualifies its significance. Indeed, the fact that we are dealing with a difference in level makes that these differences 'might be overcome', allowing for a synthesis in which Lacan and Cassirer take turns correcting each other. It actually seems that, on closer inspection, both models are not incompatible – at least from the perspectives of signification and the signifier – complementing and correcting each other. This would not be just to keep the peace, but because they engage in a dialectical relationship, implying whilst opposing each other mutually, as figures of thought. Three issues require attention – see also the final paragraph of Chapter 2. *Firstly*: Cassirer's philosophy is incapable of taking account of the meaningless, in language (*non-sense*) and the real (*ab-sense*), while Lacan focuses on the meaningless, in language and in the real, to the point where he approaches signification merely in derogatory terms. Neither the one, nor the other, is plausible, the more so because both categories imply each other in their opposition. The signifier also can only function in a field of meaning and, for lack of any reference to it, will lose its signification (Jakobson 1987, 7–18). A signifier may be characterised by a semantic void, but also brings a field of possible meanings into being. To make a case against *Lacan*, at least the category of meaning, either in the sense of Cassirer or taken more broadly, will have to be maintained and to be freed from any devaluation. But this highlights only one aspect of the matter. *Secondly*: This opposition is also echoed in their cultural concepts, with Cassirer underplaying the tension between individual and culture, whereas Lacan overstates the preponderance of culture, while exaggerating man's initial state of helplessness and dereliction. As a result, to make a case against *Cassirer*, much more emphasis will have to be put on the complexity inherent in this relationship. Mutual correction is therefore required, while additions are possible. *Thirdly*: This opposition returns in their respective concepts of the real, reality. Against *both* can be maintained that both their concepts of the real have to be qualified. Essentially, however, they both contribute to a philosophy of culture, a transcendental philosophy of culture: How is culture be made possible, and what are the implications of a cultural mode of existence for man?

Putting Lacan and Cassirer in a dialectical relationship brings a modification of a philosophy of symbolic forms, enriched with a contribution from the Lacanian perspective: a third concept of symbolisation, as an outcome of this virtual dialogue. Obviously it is still grounded in the notion of symbolisation conceived as creative representation, in which we find ourselves cut off from immediacy. Symbolisation *through* the subjective mind can occur only *from* the objective mind, with each form of symbolisation being maintained performatively, as lacking ground. It is here that we find ourselves cut off from immediacy. The term symbolisation effectively expresses this event-characterised quality: It is an event in which I and others are involved and for which responsibility can be taken – it is not some anonymous process taking place outside ourselves. Secondly, the dialectics of alienation and appropriation, of self-loss and identification, of dividedness and unification come into play, which is a result of entering the symbolic forms, in line with Lacan. And finally there is the meaningless-ness, the relationless-ness of being, the as-such. This as-such is certainly not an empty notion because, given that symbolisation is supposed to mediate, there must be something that is to be mediated, even though this something is given only within the context of mediation, not outside. And yet this as-such cannot be imagined as a substance, as an entity in its own right. What we see here is an object-pool that continues to elude (or breaks through) reality, which means that speaking of being, of the real, may be inevitable but misleading as well. Indeed, when being manifests itself traumatically, this trauma will be related to a subjectivity and thus acquires the quality of a trauma – also in line with both.

Phenomenology of symbolisation. This third form of representation thought, which incorporates the mutual corrections resulting from the Lacan Cassirer dialogue, is formulated in an open manner and can thus be specified further. More specifically, what should be added is the notion of a three-level structure of any symbolic form: the level of the image and the myth, the level of objectification in language and the level of formal principles. These three levels actually correspond to the three forms of symbolisation maintained by man as an individual, as a subjective mind – as a result, they also function as characteristics of the human condition at its various levels, as its existentials. With Cassirer, the explorative power of this distinction is particularly visible. To this can be added the concept of the Name-of-the-Father as the signifier of delimitation, of the caesura, where the dialectics of desire find their anchoring point – at the level of the individual as well as at a cultural level (in line with Lacan). After all, culture, any culture, implicitly brings delimitation: culture *is* caesura. Thus, the concept of a fundamental or primordial symbolisation, in which being, the real, is represented, is indispensable, which leads to the notion of the three domains of symbolisation: one's own body, external reality, the Other. Through this fundamental symbolisation, each undergoes a mutation – a transition to a different state of being, a transfer to a symbolic universe. Indeed, the result of this transformation is on a par with the basis phenomena, in Cassirer's sense: fundamental perspectives on the world (See Chapter 4).

Together, this open scheme leads to what might be termed a phenomenology of symbolisation. This choice for the term 'phenomenology' points to Cassirer, who uses it in the subtitles of the various sections of his chef d'oeuvre, in reference to Hegel: a phenomenology of knowledge, of the language form. Cassirer

(1996, xvii) even considered including it in the general title of his key work, namely 'Phenomenology of Knowledge' instead of 'The Philosophy of symbolic Forms'. To be sure, the term of phenomenology would nicely fit its ambition: a description of the Spirit in its various concrete, empirical manifestations, on the level of the subjective and objective mind (Cassirer GW 23/2006b, 58). Although it may have been a better choice, he decided at the last minute to drop this option – possibly on account of is associations with Hegel. Next, the term 'symbolisation' would be more appropriate than symbolic form, because the latter would have too strong connotations with static, delimited and delimitable fields of culture of the past. It underlines the dynamics of symbolisation as being a process of symbolisation and re-symbolisation.

Thus formulated, this concept points to another branch of phenomenology, namely that of Husserl and Heidegger, in their common focus on the possibility of disclosure of reality. The *as* figure, inherent to symbolisation, offers common ground here, whilst being the key figure of intentionality as well. With respect to classical phenomenology, Waldenfels (2006, 34) summarises it well: 'Succinctly said, intentionality means that something shows itself as something (*etwas als etwas*)'. And Heidegger's (1962, 149; Bremmers 2000) core message reads equally that meaningful appearance of beings invariably involves an event in which an entity is taken *as* being that entity: *something as something.* The *as* structure is decisive, while being the key figure of human experience – indeed for Cassirer and Heidegger as well. However, Cassirer adds an important qualification. He introduces plurality, a plurality of perspectives of meaning: Something is only given as something, whilst being something *else* as well. Thus, plurality is born: While being apprehended as a man (*ens qua ens*), a man could simultaneously be perceived as a fellow citizen, or as a stranger, or as an animal or slave, and so on. To see is to see *as:* x *as* x, x *as* y, *as* z ... and so on. There is a plurality of appearing, with a *simple line* appearing in multiple ways, as Cassirer's favourite example. There is not only one, exclusive way of representing the real, transforming it into true reality, nor is there only one way of recovery of true meaning. Moreover, all depends upon difference. And that is precisely where Lacan enters the stage, it is his decisive contribution. Something, a *single treat*, a mark, can only appear as such, while being different from what is not-marked. A meaningless caesura or gap has to be introduced before meaningfulness can emerge. Ultimately, we see Heidegger's fundamental question resonate here: Why is there something, rather than nothing? The answer could be: *There is something rather than nothing, because there is something as something* (*ens qua ens, etwas als etwas*)*, which differs from something else as well, allowing for new meanings to emerge.* The *as* figure, while being conceived in terms of difference and plurality, introduces a gap into the real, opening up a space in which the real can appear as meaningful reality and where a multitude of meanings can be recovered – either through a simple line *or* through a single trait, a dash. Then again, as opposed to Heidegger's views (1962, 212), Reality (not the Real) is seen as being dependent on signification as well as on the signifier (but not just on 'care'). It is the ongoing process of symbolisation and re-symbolisation that allows the world to be, whilst not being part of the world itself.

This general scheme has to be put in practice, albeit in the most modest way. It calls for empirical specification and concretisation, which is of course true for any scheme. This requires us to first return to the human condition itself, as outlined in Chapter 1. Can the three different levels of the human condition distinguished there be re-interpreted from a phenomenology of symbolisation? Is man actually an *animal symbolicum*, can he be defined as such? This sums up the theme for the next and final chapter, in which the outcome of Chapter 2 on Cassirer and Chapter 3 on Lacan, summarised here, will be brought to bear on the nature of man. The three levels of the human condition and the three domains (of life, of external nature and the Other) will be put in mutual relationships. Next, different fields of application will have to be discussed, namely: the phenomenology of perception, the genealogy of language and the *homo symbolicus*, the political and legal domains, including representative democracy and the constitutional state, the core of morality and human rights. And we most certainly cannot leave out the field that reflects any possibly failure or modification of fundamental symbolisation, leading to the emergence of disparate types of worlds: the mental disorder in all its forms. These topics will be touched upon briefly in the next chapter. This may bring to light if a perspective of symbolisation would actually be productive and provide more insight into the present.

CHAPTER 4

Variations on the Theme of Symbolisation

The purpose of this chapter is to explore a number of questions associated with the concept of symbolisation which results from the comparison between the philosophies of Lacan and Cassirer, put in a dialectical relationship. This involves at least three types of questions, three problem areas. First of all there is the fundamental, conceptual issue concerning the validity of the idea of symbolic mediation itself. This issue, which has been addressed by Cassirer and Lacan in their time, is still as topical as ever – certainly today, in the early decades of the 21st century, with realism including naturalism being the dominant type of philosophy. Secondly, there are also questions of a factual, empirical rather than a conceptual nature. Is the empirical material underlying Cassirer's and also Lacan's theses maybe outdated, and is the resulting concept sufficiently open to new empirical developments? Is the idea itself still viable today? Scientists, often of a positivist persuasion, are likely to frown upon Cassirer's ambition to effectuate integration of findings from a range of scientific disciplines within a particular philosophical concept, and may consider this endeavour to be inept. Within philosophy as well this idea will hardly find a warm welcome, as philosophy, in its scientific form, tends to stay within the remit of addressing technical and historical questions. Which of course is perfectly acceptable, except that traditionally it has been more than just a set of specialised fields, also having a more generic quality. Such a generic project would therefore retain some degree of validity. However, this requires embracing experience, taking facts as the point of departure: the fact of language, the fact of myth, of science. And yet over time any fact will be viewed from different perspectives. By its nature, Cassirer's project is a 'work in progress' that by definition needs to be updated (as has already been done partially in the explanation itself). This leads us to the empirical material which he (and Lacan) took as a basis: Lacan's debt to structural linguistics and Cassirer's evolutionary perspective of his time. In view of this, recent developments in the fields of linguistics and evolutionary science – the origin of man, of language – should be given due attention.

Thirdly, we have the field of normative questions. Clearly, the concept of a symbolic form as well as a symbolic order includes a normative component – as has been discussed in the foregoing. But what exactly is its scope? Lacan did write about ethics, but it remains to be seen if he was actually referring to ethics in an accepted sense. Cassirer did not explicitly address this topic, but in his

 | DOI:10.1163/9789004373662_006

case the question has been raised repeatedly whether ethics could be deemed part of his project, and if he would therefore have been capable of writing an ethics. This matter will be discussed in a section dealing with politics, law and morality. The normative question also plays out at an even more fundamental level, with respect to the possibility of failure of the symbolic function as such. This disruption, the pathology of the symbolic function, is not considered to be of secondary order by Lacan, nor by Cassirer.

Consequently, the range of themes addressed in this chapter is substantial, whereas the extent of the discussion is limited. This limitation is justified by the fact that use is made of what has been discussed in Chapters 1, 2 and 3 already, while succinctness is called for on account of the limited scope of this closing chapter. It will be made up of little more than fragments, initial steps. As a result, this final chapter consists of a number of mini-essays, which may be read in isolation rather than sequentially. Obviously, their tentative quality only adds to their being subject to debate. This, however, is inevitable and is not really a problem within this set-up, actually being part of its design. Its ambition does not reach beyond offering suggestions, which sets this chapter apart from the chapters dealing with Cassirer and Lacan, which represent the very heart of this work. They are nothing more than variations on a common theme, one that refers back to a scheme, namely that of symbolisation, as will be outlined briefly in the section below (see Annex).

For a proper understanding, this will be preceded by a brief summary of the concept of symbolisation, that evolved from the comparison between Lacan and Cassirer, referring back to the final paragraph of Chapter 3: a philosophy of symbolic forms, conceived as a phenomenology of symbolisation. This concept therefore does *not* coincide with Cassirer's nor with Lacan's views, but is rather based on putting them in a mutual relationship. Here, the central theme is outlined once again, while referring back to the hermeneutical image of man, the model of the human condition as outlined in Chapter 1. This may or may not bring to light whether the symbolic function might underpin it, effectively serving as its foundation.

4.1 The Human Condition and the Symbolic Function

The fundamental thesis of the philosophy under discussion is that there is no access to reality other than through representations or symbolisations – which is the guiding point of view. Symbolising means conceiving 'something' *as* something different, which creates presence that will always be mediated presence: to see is to see *as:* x *as* x, and *as* y, or *as* z. Through this mediated presence, something appears by referring to what it is not itself, using 'three modes' (of image, word, formula). Within it, that which existed 'before', which is being, becomes inaccessible, is crossed out. Thus, this state of being, the real, is conceived 'as being …'. The three dots, the 'empty space', would then represent the core of symbolisation-in-its-strictest-sense: as a void. However, this void does not exist as-such, but is introduced by the symbolic system, as an external order, rather than being part of the real itself. From this order, these symbolic forms, the fabric of world relationships is woven. More specifically, what should be added is the notion of a three-tiered structure of any symbolic form, the levels of which actually correspond to the three modes of symbolisation maintained by man as an individual, as a subjective mind. Therein, the real is represented, which leads to the distinction between three domains of the real: one's own body, external reality, the Other. – It effectively summarises the three fundamental themes of the process of symbolisation: (1) the three *modes* of symbolisation, relying on an order with an equal three-modal structure (2) the *three domains* of the real to which fundamental symbolisation refers, (3) being transformed into the *three levels* of the human condition. For an explanation see also the Annex.

Three domains. These domains turn out to be: (1) the real of life and the body, (2) the external real, and (3) the primordial Other. Through this fundamental symbolisation, each undergoes a mutation – a transition to a different state of being, a transfer to a symbolic universe. Firstly: life, the immediacy of life (*immanence vitale, Unmittelbarkeit des Lebens*). The vital tension inside the body is represented, and through representation is transformed into a subjective body, which enables the experience of the body as one's own body ('I am thirsty', 'I am hungry', 'my ear aches'), thus replacing the condition of physical tension. Outwardly, the own body will function as a cradle of intentional relationships, enabling a representative connection with that which exists out-there, adopting form as intentional phenomena (bread, water). The real of vital life is transformed into an intentional experience, effectively pushing out (Lacan) or denying access to (Cassirer) the immediacy of life itself. As life is turned into an experience, life as-such must give way. Secondly: the external real (the static real). Along this path, the real is disclosed as a 'world', as a range of different situations. In this case, the external real is presented as a world of space, of time, causality and interaction, with the external real being tamed, hemmed in. Thirdly: Here, this curbing, limitation or 'castration' focuses on the primordial Other and its boundless pleasure, thus enabling desire, social life, and language. In fact, we recognise the three levels of the human condition, as outlined in Chapter 1 and elaborated in Chapters 2 and 3: *intentionality, being in the world, dependence on language and the Other*, but reinterpreted as being underpinned by the symbolic function, while being the result of a symbolic transformation. It marks the transition to another state of being, with the body being transformed into bodily intentionality, the external real into the world of space and time, and the primordial Other into the Other and Otherness (culture).

Three levels, sources. It can be seen as 'labour of culture' ('Kulturarbeit'), to quote Freud, which might be compared to reclaiming the Dutch Zuiderzee from the sea: 'Wo Es war, soll Ich werden', which Lacan (2002, 524) translated as: 'Where It was, I must come into being'. This transition should be interpreted as a leap, which is primarily conceptual rather than empirically tangible in nature, as a thing that eludes any empirical explanation. It marks the 'transition to another genus', another state of being, in Cassirer's words. Indeed, it can be conceived as an original phenomenon (*Urphänomen*) in Goethe's sense, a phenomenon that cannot be explained empirically: e.g. the transition from nature to culture, from nature to a perspective *on* nature. Moreover, the outcome of this transformation, the range of perspectives themselves, is on a par with the *basis phenomena* in Cassirer's sense: the basic perspectives of the human mind, its *sources* of knowledge, the windows on the world, the ways of disclosing of reality (1996, 115–190). Within this framework, he distinguishes three basis phenomena, three perspectives – no more, no less. Firstly, the sphere of life, the I-phenomenon; secondly, the sphere of Action (action-reaction, interaction), the You-phenomenon; and thirdly the sphere of the Work, the It-phenomenon, the spirit of objectivity (see Chapter 2). Each of these effectuates a disclosure of reality on its own: from the I-perspective via the intentionality, from the You-perspective via interaction within a given situation, and from the It-perspective, via the objective mind of culture (1996, 180–183). Obviously, the *three basis phenomena*, the three perspectives of the human mind, run parallel to the *three levels* of the human condition mentioned above (and discussed in detail in Chapter 1): intentionality, worldly situation, and structure. The similarity between the basis phenomena of the human mind in Cassirer's sense and the three levels within the human condition, originating in hermeneutics, at the very least provides an argument in favour of the validity, the usefulness of this distinction between three levels of the human condition: three, precisely three – but *now* being conceived as expressing the symbolic function. Indeed, they should be imagined functionally, each fulfilling the function of disclosing the real at their particular level of cohesion: first as a phenomenon, then as a world, and finally as being nameable or unsayable, as a lack. And this outcome is achieved from three *sources*, along three paths, each of which is characterised by an *as* structure: along the path of intentionality ('seeing' is 'seeing as'), along the path of categorical structuring of the world (as being spatial, causally structured), and along the path of language (reality as being nameable or unsayable). This reflects its symbolic, representative function: unlocking he real as 'being…' (See also: Mooij 2018).

Obviously, the distinctions introduced between the three levels of the human condition by no means represent watersheds. They are mutually related, because representations in one field will support those in another field, but also because whenever failure happens, they may well drag each other down in their fall. Moreover, they are not stable intrinsically, for the mere fact that the real is involved. Any symbolisation, while being partial, will leave the real partially unaddressed, which causes the return of what was left out (as an infringement): from the immediacy of life, the external real, the primordial Other. Indeed, the obvious applicability of the threefold distinction within the human condition, the human mind, provides an additional argument in favour of the threefold distinction between domains of the real, as has been proposed, while running parallel with it.

Three modes. And yet the symbolic function is not undivided, but is actually made up of three modes: expressive, objectifying and formalising (or phrased in an equivalent terminology). Indeed, these three modes of the symbolic function may play out at any of the three levels of the human condition. Firstly, intentionality has three ways of symbolising – expressive, objectifying, formalising; or imaginary, symbolic, formalising. Secondly, also at the level of the world, the world manifests itself according to these three modes – mimicked in myth, objectified in language, formalised in science. Thirdly, the three modes of the symbolic function are also reflected in the objective mind, in a cultural domain, i.e., in the three-tiered structure found in any symbolic form (as was shown by Cassirer, and will be explained in the following).

Conclusion. The symbolic functions transforms the three domains of the real into the three levels of the human condition (as well as into the three basis phenomena of the human mind). At each of the three levels, the symbolic function can play out in three modes. *The three levels of the human condition, the three sources of the human mind, are underpinned by the symbolic function in its three modes, in relationship to the three domains of its effectiveness.* Summarizing: the human condition is made possible by the symbolic function. A schematic overview is included in the Annex.

4.2 The Medial Turn in Philosophy

Obviously, the above conclusion is speculative, a first attempt at best, and its schematic character may look somewhat contrived. Admittedly, it is only a schematic representation, intended to be instructive and add some level of organisation. And yet such a schematic overview may also give the wrong impression. It is important to realise that the distinctions made here are no substantial but functional ones, which makes that any item categorised may well fall into another category as well. Moreover, the conclusion is only a particular elaboration, a specification of a more fundamental thesis: the medial turn in philosophy. Cassirer (2005, 260) had already explained the fundamental thesis very clearly: 'Man can never understand reality, he can not even think if it, without wrapping it in certain signs and symbols, in the words of language, in mythical tales, in artistic or religious images. That is the magic circle in which the whole life of man seems to be included [...] He does not have an immediate but a mediate access to reality, and this mediation is the very principle of his life'. Indeed, any access to reality will proceed based on interpretation and is therefore mediated. The very notion of 'the given' itself is therefore a myth: 'the Myth of the Given' (Sellars 1997). This fundamental notion is aptly reflected in the term 'medial turn' (Lenk 1993). Above, this term also expresses the fact that, in its turn, mediation through interpretations or symbolisation relies on external media of symbolisation. This means mediality is therefore *two-fold*. The symbolic function enables a symbolically mediated, medial access to reality, but is operative only within autonomous media, or medial structures (the objective mind).

This does make the concept of the 'medial turn' with its implicit fundamental thesis current, but it will obviously also be met with criticism. As mentioned before, contemporary philosophy is witnessing something that might be called a 'realistic turn' (in the wake of a current naturalistic trend). Of course, we cannot discuss each of these forms within the present context. There is no need to either, because the type of arguments put forward in this discussion is not essentially different from arguments holding sway in the days of Cassirer. Although the examples may be different, the reasoning often is not. And yet this realism does have an unmistakable appeal. Remarkably, criticism of the medial line of thought should also come from phenomenology, a brand of philosophy that traditionally has paid a great deal of attention to the notion of mediation (intentionality and its intentions of meaning). This type of criticism will be discussed below, touching as it does upon the very heart of the matter (more so than in in the naturalist debate). The dispute is about the idea that perception is always and partially determined by context (or meaning, as Cassirer would put it). This point is being argued and obviously affects the very heart of medial thought. It can therefore hardly be dismissed as a minor issue, because it is highly relevant to today's realism debate: We are able to know reality as it is, directly, without circumvention. This also highlights its significance.

That is why, despite its rather abstract character, a discussion would be warranted here.

First point of criticism. This concerns – and this is essential – the very thesis of mediality itself. It is argued that the proponents of the medial turn themselves are caught up in myth: not the myth of the given, but the myth of mediality. Man is supposed to be not separated from reality only to find some form of access again through interpretative means. Indeed, man is part of it, which means that any terminology referring to 'access to reality' would be inappropriate. So how should this relationship be imagined in this case? For the very reason that the underlying opposition between mediality and direct givenness is not based in truth, there is no referring back to the notion of direct givenness (which is in fact part of the opposition). Instead, the point of departure is shifted from 'the given' to 'giving' itself. This leads to the primacy of perception: Perception itself creates presence. It is not 'I' who has a perception, no, perception has 'me' ('das Mich der Wahrnehmung'). Following this thesis, the subject becomes subordinate to perception rather than to interpretations. Perception brings a direct presence into being from which the perceiver cannot escape. This thesis is anathema to Cassirer's beliefs (or to hermeneutical phenomenology and general hermeneutics, for that matter), according to which any experience is deemed interpretative. This thesis can only be maintained if perception has an interpretation-free core or, indeed, if it *is* the interpretation-free core of experience (Wiesing 2009, 131–148; Benoist 2011, 88–118). From this perspective, perception would therefore produce neither knowledge nor truth – indeed, this would again constitute a form of interpretation and symbolisation. It merely serves the function of experiencing presence, of experiencing reality: being part of reality as a human and that is *there* for you. The function of perception would then be to feel, to smell, to see that there is *something*, regardless of the question *what* exactly. This does not call the existence and function of interpretations into question, but it does limit their scope: They do not play a part in the experience of reality. The question if this is a feasible road to follow.

Reply. Is the description of perception as experience of a presence that takes hold of the subject, actually an adequate phenomenological description? First: would it be justified to narrow down our scope to the subject as a sole individual? Shouldn't we rather conceive perception as *also* being done by the other, obviously only potentially so – 'can you see it too', 'did you hear that'? If there is any point at all-in speaking of a 'me', would it not be preferable to speak of an '*us*' rather than a 'me' in perception? Perception will always be co-mediated by a reference to the other (the Other). Secondly: is this 'I' really as passive as is being argued ('das *Mich* der Wahrnehmung'). This is true at least partly: perception grabs you in a certain way and may not let go, but this will only be true up to a point, considering that you can also escape it by averting your gaze. This sheer passiveness does apply to pain, however, because there is no escaping from it, it will cling to you, drag you along. However, what could be said about the perception of pain – pain has me – fails to apply phenomenologically to intentional perception. Thirdly: the separation between a contentless and contextless *that* and a *what* with a specific content and context is merely artificial and has no phenomenological basis either. There is not 'this-there' experience ('Diesda') to which an interpretation is added ('a house'). Consequently, experience never has the quality of a this-there or a pure being-itself ('ipseity'), but instead will exist in relationship to 'something else'. An undefined perception is already a perception of 'something *as being* undefined' ('vague'). This is the key argument Cassirer put forward in the paradigmatic example of the drawn line ('Linienzug'), the line that will always carry some degree of meaning. This explains why perception is never about sheer presence, but instead about a presence that is run through with absence. This does not put reality at a distance, far from it. And yet reality is not experienced either as a naked 'that' of perception ('materia nuda'), detached from 'how and what' – it merely becomes a 'pool of presence', which cannot exist without referring to 'something else' (image, concept, formula). Added to this, and this is the final criticism, is the fact that experience of reality is established through a specific interaction between the organism and its environment, between the body and the world. The experience is organ-specific, with those organs partially fulfilling a role in the survival of the organism, and partially being included in the symbolic structure of the 'own body', as well as fulfilling a role in pleasure mechanisms. The faculty of hearing produces sound that 'exists' (to me and others) and that offers pleasure ('do you like this as much as I do?'), but that does not 'exist' outside hearing, which is true for all sensory qualities. Consequently, the experience of reality is also mediated at a bodily level, namely by the body. This makes the body also 'a gateway to the world', providing access to the things ('accès aux choses') according to De Waelhens (1961, 59–70).

Second point of criticism. The criticism of medial thought from phenomenological quarters discussed here does not challenge the role of interpretations as such, but only limits its scope, as was mentioned before: they are supposed not to play a part in the *experience* of reality. Nor does this criticism challenge the role of mediating interpretative systems, of symbolic forms. Once again, however, it plays the card of reality. Also in the field of symbolic forms, medial thought would not attribute reality to these forms, instead relegating these to the position of mere 'transcendental' structures (Benoist 2011, 139–168). This second point of criticism thus becomes relevant to the second main thesis of the 'medial turn', namely that interpretations in their turn are mediated by representative systems. This criticism also fails to hit the mark, however, because, particularly in the case of Lacan and the French sociological tradition, strong emphasis has been put on its reality aspect: the exteriority of the symbolic order, its empirical reality, which is expressed in social coercion, in social institutions. Subjective intentions and societal values meet in a 'social fact'. Social reality is reflected in the psychic reality: outside=inside. Then again, the empirical reality of the symbolic order would not detract from any transcendental function it might have, because this function suggests that empirically 'there is no escaping it'. In the final reckoning, this second point of criticism therefore does not constitute a real critique of medial thought, but actually confirms it here.

Experience of reality. As was shown before, the heart of the criticism of medial thought is assuming a *non*-medial experience of reality, as being determined non-intersubjectively, without context or meaning ('Diesda', 'ipseity'), as something from which the perceiver cannot escape. As argued above, any criticism offered does not necessarily mean that this phenomenon could not occur as such. It most certainly can, but *not* in the context of ordinary perception of reality. Indeed, this is known particularly from *psychosis*: the 'elementary phenomena', the experiences that the person involved may have in the very first stages of a psychosis. They are defined as 'elementary' because the experiences themselves are quite autonomous, characterised by a selfness ('ipseity') without being connected to other phenomena and lacking all meaning; they are being experienced as pure presence, and because they are coming 'from the outside' the person involved finds itself unable to escape it physically. It is precisely this pure 'being-that without any meaning' that defines its psychotic nucleus. Only as a second step will this person be able to attribute meaning to these initially meaningless ('Diesda') phenomena, through sensorily mediated hallucinations (auditory hallucinations, optical hallucinations), and to rationally frame these experiences in the form of delusional thoughts. Lacan would formulate his own psychosis concept on the foundations of the concept of the 'elementary phenomena': that which was rejected from the symbolic now returns from the real. That which was excluded from a representative referential structure, now returns as pure presence, as that which had in fact been determined by the absence of a representative referential structure: the real.

This is an essential finding, because reality as defined by medial thought as outlined, is not found in the reality within perception or as reality of the symbolic systems. It cannot be found in the 'internal concept' of reality: the reality embedded as a core *in* perception or *in* social structuring. Instead, it is found in its 'external concept': reality as being inexhaustible, as excessive (Cassirer), or traumatic (Lacan): the real. This concept of reality (as the real) remains within the context of medial thought as outlined, fully intact. The conclusion would therefore be that it is still appropriate to speak of 'access to reality' which is medial in a twofold sense: access is mediated by representations, which in their turn are part of mediating representative systems or symbolic forms – the symbolic order. Perception relates to 'reality', while being rooted in a 'mentality', and anchored in a symbolically structured 'own body' that is shaped culturally. A rose is a rose, and yet a rose can be viewed, as painted in a still-life, in an infinite number of ways. It is the same rose, but always different, while the same-rose (as a selfness or 'ipseity') is not given outside. The rich quality of, and surplus within, human perception is not found in the identical 'Dingsda', but rather in the wide range of conceptions. Concrete phenomena, such as a rose, thus represent reality (with its inexhaustible and traumatic qualities) *as well as* its conception. They represent both matter *and* mind, finding themselves at the crossroads of both. Could this point perhaps be made more concrete?

4.3 Symbolisation in Perception

The foregoing paragraph served to reconfirm the representative quality of perception, which can briefly be summarised as: to see is to see *as*. The implicit conception might be elaborated further.

Perception. Perception is interpretative in nature and establishes a relationship with the real, which is experienced as reality. According to Cassirer's fundamental thesis, this is reflected accruing three modes, three levels. There is the objectifying perception: a rose in a garden which is red and has five petals. Furthermore, it is a dicotyledon plant of the Rosaceae family, which includes 91 genera and 4828 species. This turns the objectifying perception into a formalising perception. Below these two levels, we find the pre-objectifying Gestalt perception. This actually works around our backs, at a preconscious level, without any active involvement from an I. And, as opposed to the slow-acting objectifying, attentive perception, it acts very fast indeed, creating the familiar world we have learned to accept as our own. The fundamental distinction between these two types of perception and of intentionality have already been discussed in depth, in Chapters 1 and 2.

The slow form of perception has meanwhile become the theme of much research into the psychology of perception (as well as the psychology of thought and memory). This resulted in a distinction between two systems (of perception, thought and memory). The first system is intuitive, emotional and preconscious, while the second system's orientation is conscious, more cognitive and logical. The conceptual distinction of two forms of intentionality was thus given empirical hands and feet. In the process, the preconscious form of perception turned out to be highly significant: quite often, the preconscious form of perception proves to be decisive in most decision-making processes that take place intuitively, in a split second, in daily life, in constructing one's own world image, in a professional context, in science, economy, etcetera (Kahneman 2012, 19–108, 377–407). Thus, preconscious perception arranges things, much like a shadow cabinet, outside the rational, objectifying self. There is a parallel with the optical illusion of two lines that are objectively of the same length, but which at first glance will be perceived as being of different length: the Müller-Lyer experiment – to which Merleau-Ponty also referred (see previous chapter). This first impression is decisive.

This Gestalt perception tells us: *this is* how it is, that's how things work. But, in a second movement, it also says: this is how it *is*, emphasising *is*. It offers a sense of reality, as we realise that there *is* such a thing as reality (the point made by Cassirer). Thus, the Gestalt experience also implicitly carries the rationale for the experience of being. Then again, objective and experimental perception each contribute to its further structuring (which makes it essentially three-tiered). Indeed, indexical perception, perception with an index of reality, is a complex process of interpretation that cannot be reduced to a single isolated element. And yet its basis is formed by the preconscious sphere. If this is absent or inactive, the experience of *un*reality or *de*realisation will result, with the world being experienced as unreal, as being part of a film (including the experience of alienation towards the person himself: depersonalisation). But when it is effective, the Gestalt experience will produce the experience of familiarity and self-evidence, which could be summed up as the human aspect of the cosmos – with things having an individual face, 'looking at us'. This might explain why so many painters speak of things looking at them (Merleau-Ponty 1964, 31), which in the first instance turns us into beings that are looked at, subjected to a gaze that circumscribes us (Lacan 1986, 75). The Gestalt experience, mythical experience, the experience of the self-evident, lays the foundation for the experience of being, or the experience of reality. The objective, active experience does not.

Here, the Gestalt experience is passive in nature. It unfolds at a preconscious level, behind our backs (without any active I-involvement), *and* it grabs you, holds you in its grip, making it inescapable. You *will be* touched by what you see, what you hear – but not by anything or anyone, regardless. This is where the own contribution comes into play (to see is to see *as*). Thus, an activity or accomplishment lies embedded in the passive quality of the Gestalt experience. It may be a passive accomplishment, taking place behind our backs, but it is an execution just the same – a synthesis, a symbolisation. Perception needs to be 'executed', not only in conscious but also in preconscious life. This accomplishment will decide whether or not an affective bond will be forged with what is seen, heard or palpated.

And yet this preconscious execution does not have the last word, being founded itself in the deeper layers of the psychic reality. They are more difficult to grasp, particularly for scientific research, for the very reason that they are highly singular. That does not make them any less important, though. Indeed, perception does not only reflect the preconscious, imaginary manifestations, but also the unconscious symbolic ideals. To some extent, these will determine what a person loves or does not love, what they find repulsive or not. Ultimately, deep down, it is delimited by a phantasmatic framework, which defines the level of appeal of what or who is being perceived. This framework cares little about what 'reality' has to offer (because: to see is to see *as*). One person will see something in another person, where the other will be struck by something completely different. As a result, that which moves and fascinates one person, will leave the other quite untouched, or may even fill them with revulsion. This phantasmatic basis or libidinous foundation of a person's life reaches much deeper than the Gestalt experience that underlies natural self-evidence. Indeed, the phantasm is *not* self-evident. Although it is highly personal and, to quote Freud, it constitutes the very essence of a person, it is also alien to the self-image and to the person's higher ambitions. Structurally determined in part, they hover around structural details: Freud's primal fantasies or scenes, with gender and generation differences lying at the heart. By definition, their range is limited, and they are perversely tinged (Laplanche and Pontalis 1985). As the leading example of Freud (1955c) suggests (referring back to his daughter Anna): 'A child is being beaten'. Likewise, they are culturally defined, with the physical pleasure system being shaped through the life history, the 'castration history', in their confrontation with the Other – in this example, through the confrontation with father-Freud. In that sense, they come from the outside.

And the Other is also watching, even if only peeping around the corner, without being seen. To see is *to be* seen, *to be* addressed. This external and later interiorised gaze and voice also holds the ideals and precepts of the environment, which the person will have to live by in order to be valued and accepted (without actually knowing it). This external determinedness also resonates in the imaginary manifestations of how a person is supposed to be (in terms of mirror image and exemplary behaviour). Combined, these phantasms, symbolic ideals and imaginary reflections, shaped in the interaction with their environment, colour the perception of what a person is and does.

Mental representation. So far, we have only discussed perception insofar as it can be reconstructed as a function offering itself 'from perception itself' (and which has often been specified further in empirical research, as we have seen). In addition, in the domain of the cognitive neurosciences much attention has been devoted to the cognitive-neural principles underlying perception. A short comment might be in order here. Short, because this field is simply too vast and complex to be discussed in any detail. And yet a comment is warranted, for the very reason that the commonly used fundamental concept of the cognitive neurosciences is at odds with the medial line of thinking. Indeed, these tend to reject the interpretative quality of perception. Current here is the terminology of representations which (as a replication of reality) are processed as next step: 'These representations are then shuttled to the surrounding cortical regions which send further processed representations to the hippocampus' (LeDoux 1996, 193). Therefore, it is dominated by a specific theory of representation, taking the form of 'representationalism', with a representation being conceived as an image of reality. Indeed. the mirror theory of knowledge is in fact *the very* antithesis of medial thinking (see Cassirer).

Although this is the dominant theory in the field, it did meet with some criticism, namely in the form of the theory of the *embodied cognition.* This was developed by those who criticised the representationalism of current cognitive neuroscience. It rejects the concept of representation (in this sense), instead conceiving the being bodily-in-the-world (being-to-the-world) as primary, a conception in which this type of mental representation would not play a part. And yet, from the perspective of medial thought objections could also be raised against this viewpoint. Although the theory of embodied cognition rightfully rejects the concept of representation as duplication, it also rejects – without justification, this time – the concept of representation as such (Dreyfus 2002, 372–374). Thus, both apply a limited conception of representation – the cognitive approach when subscribing to it, the theory of embodied cognition in its rejection. As a result, the theory of the embodied cognition throws away the child with the bath water. After all, representation cannot be conceived as the duplication of a content in another medium, but instead is the medium itself, effectuating the transition to another state of being. Rather than being given as a mental representation within the mind, the thing is produced *by* the mind: the 'thing there' is the representation of reality from within the mind. What is suggested by Dreyfus (2002, 373) is quite a good approximation: 'The best representation of the world is the world itself'.

This means that mental representations can continue to play a role – as opposed to what the theory of the embodied cognition proposes. In the presented conception, the mind is conceived as an extremely complex system, with complexity at least being raised to the power of two: internally and externally. 'Seeing a tree' is not an isolated 'mental event', but is actually part of complex self-referential system, with terms mutually referring to each other: 'a tree perception' refers to the concept of a 'tree per se', to the range of numbers (one), to the specification of a location, of time, etcetera. Consequently, consciousness appears to have an 'internal' referring quality, the quality of a system, which would render a one-on-one relationship problematic, even in a sophisticated form. Secondly, perception refers to what 'is': the tree, the street, the ditch, with the articulation of consciousness data taking place from the external intersubjective situation as well from the structure of language and culture. Here, the term 'external' is not quite appropriate, considering that the intersubjective situation (the Other) and language (culture) are also *part of* individual consciousness itself. In the final reckoning, the inside-outside opposition fails to work. Consciousness is structured intrinsically intersubjective and lingual, while its consequences – dividedness and reflection – also need to be taken into account. Thus, the sphere of the mental, is determined not only by subjective intention, but is also determined intersubjectively (by the situation) and structurally (through language and culture). Consequently, the 'inner world' (of man) is fundamentally co-defined by the 'outer world' of culture, of the symbolic order. We could actually speak of an embodied symbolic order. The individual representation, the subjective mind, also reflects the objective mind, which means that the subjective mind, 'the mental', is determined not only by the condition of the brain but is also nurtured by culture. Just like the subjective mind is *inside* the body, in the fingers, so does the objective mind reside in the body: the voice, the look, the posture – the culturally defined mimics and pantomimics, the regionally determined vocalisation and inflection. Thus, the bodily phenomena represent both the subjective and the objective mind. The mind is tied to a medium – not a mental space with shifting representations inside it, but, being both a subjective and an objective mind, as the medium of representation *itself*, with a range of refractive indexes.

This human capacity of symbolising or representing in the field of perception and action did not appear out of the blue, without any previous history. As was discussed in Chapter 2, Cassirer did in fact comment on its genesis. Lacan did not, but he did refer to a similar type of data. The inquiry into the origin or genesis of the symbolic function and of language today is a highly topical issue that has the interest of a wide range of disciplines, whereas before it attracted little attention (as being too speculative to merit a scientific effort). The question could therefore be formulated alternatively as: could the symbol-theoretical interpretation add meaning to the inquiry into the origin of man and language?

4.4 Homo Symbolicus: An Evolutionary Perspective

It is important to stress that any difference between man and animal cannot be studied in a straightforward, empirical way. Each concept is theoretically charged, and this most certainly applies to 'man'. Any type of inquiry into such a difference will presuppose a particular *concept* of man, one that has ontological and maybe even metaphysical implications. The biological anthropology of the first half of the 20th century, to which both Lacan and Cassirer referred, would be a case in point. Compare the typification of man based on its ex-centric position as proposed by Plessner (1975) with that of the biological defect ('Mängelwesen') put forward by Gehlen (1966), as described in Chapters 2 and 3. Moreover, it is made to function as part of a specific strategy (for example to accentuate the distinction, or to tone it down). Moreover, a great deal of empirical material has meanwhile been gathered from prehistorical archaeology, palaeo-anthropology, evolutionary biology, genetics, ornithology, and cultural anthropology and, since recently, also neurosciences. The amount is so overwhelming that anyone is certain to find something to their liking. Since specialists disagree more often than not, the specialist critique is not necessarily fatal, the more so because this matter is and will remain highly speculative in nature. Then again, the majority of contributions in this field were developed from a naturalistic viewpoint, emphasising continuity between man and the animal world. With this type of approach running in the blood of many evolutionary researchers, it will inform their thoughts on this matter to a high extent. Obviously, this is not the place to discuss this matter at any length, and it will therefore only be touched upon briefly in the closing section of this paragraph. Indeed, the aim of this paragraph is to briefly outline an alternative to the mainstream.

Thus, based on medial thought a hypothesis might be advanced that obviously can never aspire to be more than just that (occasionally using the same data, but adding a different kind of interpretation). It would therefore be in line with the paradigm that dominated the 20th century, which highlighted the difference, the discontinuity between man and the animal kingdom. It would be a logical choice to embrace the concept of man as a 'homo symbolicus', a concept that has also been proposed within the present context (Corbey 2005, 121–134). But now an extra dimension is added. After all, it would be compatible with the line of thought developed here to enhance this symbolic quality by endowing it with the quality to acknowledge and produce 'negativity'. This negativity becomes evident from the presence of oppositions at a Gestalt level (open/closed, proximity/distance) and of differentials (+/–) at a more objectifying level. It appears that higher animal species are often particularly adept at identifying natural patterns (like changes in the wind) and signal-meanings (of sound, colour and smell) – as is known from biosemantics – but actually lack *this* capacity. A primate or bird may be able to respond to the fifth or fourth beat on a gong recognising it as a particular sound sequence, but probably not to the fourth *as* being the fourth, or the fifth *as* being the fifth of a series with its implicit distinction between 'unit' and 'sequence'. Brandon (2000, 17) writes: 'Merely reliable responding differently to red things, is not yet being *aware* of them *as* red. Discriminating by producing repeatable responses (as a machine or a pigeon might do)...is not yet *conceptual* classification'. It may be able to recognise a pattern, but not *as being* a pattern, in the sense of 'that is the same one', or 'that is another one'. In the latter case, what matters is the role of identity and distinction, the role of 'the not'. Whether this difference is considered to be big or small is a matter of appreciation: continuity (in biosemantics), or alternatively discontinuity may be elected to prevail (theory of symbol). Either viewpoint could be defended. However, what can never be a matter of appreciation is its *consequence*, which is in fact quite spectacular. After all, the act of counting, breaking continuity and combining the elements thus produced will enable the creation of a cultural order, one that is posited and 'made'.

This means that man is not just a 'homo symbolicus' but, insofar as being a 'homo symbolicus', also becomes a 'homo faber'. Indeed, a specific form of tool use is implied in the ability to symbolise. This 'symbolic tool' is not a stick that extends the body or a rock thrown into a pool to raise the water level. Nor is it a stick that is finely poised for throwing. Rather, it would be a stick used to create something of a different order than the stick itself and which has become part of common usage: thus, we will use an x number of sticks to build a fence or to separate 'the inside from the outside'. The fence and the spatial order thus created would be of a different nature than defining one's territory through body odour or more sophisticated methods. In this case, the spatial order would be an 'order' that is posited.

Besides, he who creates an order will also introduce a concept, and who introduces a concept creates order: this is the central point raised by Cassirer. Man creates a world by means of symbolising or conceptualising: making for the world ('Gestaltung zur Welt'). Beyond forming his world, men forms himself, by making a concept or representation of himself. When conceiving 'the idea' of the symbolic, at the same time man produces an 'idea of himself', obviously not as a conscious idea, but in an operative, effective sense, for example 'as being different from the animal'. This distinction is therefore not purely descriptive, merely offering a state of affairs, but is in fact performative: it is instituted, posited, effectuated. Thus, man *exists* as the concept he has formed of himself, or as the representation of that which he identified with. Consequently, man-as-such does not exist – 'man' exists only in a particular form or guise (identity), trying out this concept of this representation as a project within a community, until he decides to develop another concept or other representation, etcetera.

The question 'when' this fundamental possibility of transformation actually came into being is of a different, empirical nature. An answer to the question, if any, should therefore be provided by the empirical disciplines. Then again, conceptually it is not likely that such a transition would occur overnight, considering that for symbolisations to be effective they need to be embedded in symbolic forms which are outwardly consolidated while having a solid social infrastructure. Then again, in light of the current state of knowledge, chances are that this process unfolded in the early stages following the emergence of Homo Sapiens sapiens. Indeed, although the capabilities of Neanderthal man has been valued more highly in the last decades compared to before (Roebroeks 2000), we may not want to attribute this type of symbolic capability (of language and counting) to them, for want of material relics. However, the material relics of unmistakable symbolic nature of the Cro-Magnon man offer direct evidence to support this contention: the linear patterns in cave drawings and the notches made in bones (Cassirer's simple line and Lacan's single trait). Together they constitute the very foundation of symbolisation (through signification and signifier), be it at a nucleic level. Their elaboration may lead to a development or genealogy of the symbolic forms (as well as a development within each form). It is therefore a long road from the mythical form of symbolisation in terms of inside/outside, gods/men, to today's analytical, formal type of symbolisation. And maybe yet other forms of symbolisation are awaiting. Indeed, man will never show himself as a 'nude' man (or 'materia nuda'), but always in a particular form, cover or guise, in a variety of forms. Thus, prehistory and history jointly give us an overview of the ranges of man's metamorphoses, of his transformation. If there is one thing history teaches us, it is the amazing versatility present in the life form of the biological species called 'man'.

Cultural diversity is more than just a factual, empirical matter. Factual cultural diversity is rooted in fundamental diversity as its logical necessity. Indeed, it is the corollary of man's symbolic state of being, based on which he can only exist in a represented form, and consequently in essential diversity. Each specific form, each single specification is posited, and in that sense becomes a 'pose'. This diversity resonates down to the level of the individual, as each man is also the principle of his own concept or identity. This own, unique identity is therefore always posited, likewise qualifying as a 'pose'. This type of identity is associated with unicity, or singularity. Thus, each man becomes part of culture in all its variety, while *also* remaining quite unique – a perspective that is also relevant within the ethical domain (see below). Man is the only species that is made up of individuals that do not represent an instance of its species. Just as, following Hegel, single man is the sum of his deeds (held together by a virtual unity), so is man as the sum of his empirical guises or representations (only bound together by a virtual unity, which will not become evident until post-factum). Man is what he will have turned out to be at the end of his life's adventure. Its strength lies in his symbolic diversity, but this is also his weakness. Maybe it will show that his symbolic way of life is too unbalanced to survive from an evolutionary perspective. Whatever the case may be, symbolic variety is only one aspect of the matter. We see variety within an invariant infrastructure of constants. This relates to the presence of an order, a symbolic form or order per se. Its primary component is language, but also language has its own field of experience and most likely also its own genesis. Obviously, its exploration and research have moved on since the days of Lacan and Cassirer.

Language. Language offers a wealth of possibilities for research, for sound physiology, with disciplines ranging from historical and comparative linguistics and structural linguistics to generative grammar and social-pragmatic approaches (see Chapter 2). In addition, since Plato, philosophy of language has produced a spate of theories on 'what language actually is'. This variety becomes evident, for one thing, from the fact that the outcome of the research into whether (some) animal species would or would not have linguistic capabilities depends on the concept of language was chosen as a starting point. Would the capability to create a specific form of syntax be a prerequisite, or maybe the presence of phonematic structure, or should we assume that language is essentially a specification of the capability to recognise signals and natural patterns, which each single animal organism possesses to a greater or lesser extent? The concept will determine the empirical outcome. Maybe, following the outlined symbol theory, we will be able to determine what the conceptual contribution might be – which will of course be speculative, just like any theory proposed in this field would be.

Language, above all, is made up of sounds. Why did the voice, its sound, turn out to be so well-suited to its purpose, why is that the 'language of sound' went on to fulfil such a central role? In order to communicate, the organism has to rely on what it can produce: sound, the look (mimics), movement (pantomimics), stool and sweat, saliva. For the production of signal meaning, all excrements can play a role to delimit territories (saliva or urine) or either to attract or to repel (smells and pantomimics). Certainly with orthostatic man, sound offers advantages for always being available as well as being controllable. It is a product of respiration that, depending as it does on the autonomic nervous system, occurs automatically while also being controlled by the somatic nervous system (thorax, throat, mouth, and tongue, in conjunction with the specially shaped hyoid bone). It offers the possibility to break the natural rhythm of the life flow of tension and relaxation, of breathing and out, of homeostasis and continuity, allowing bits of sound to be produced that can be combined and recombined. A specific type of sound production (using palate, tongue and hyoid bone) is a precondition for language to exist, but is not an adequate condition in itself. What lacks here is structure. Then again, this natural basis might be used to develop an artificial structure, with the artifice only being reflected in the structure itself, not in the matter: natural continuity is crossed out, with a different type of structure being superimposed. Building on Cassirer's and Lacan's philosophy, this idea of language could be conceived as follows, bearing in mind that this merely a mental exercise.

Language is not only made up of the level of sound and the voice, but also the level of the signifier and the word, and the level of the sentence. Phrasing it differently: its structure would consist of three *levels*: (1) the sound image, (2) the word, and (3) the complex sentence. The sound image itself has already been removed from its natural context, as we have seen, thus becoming artificial and different from a signal-meaning (such as the call or threatening mimics), although conceptually it is quite close. And yet it is a meaningless sound, a signifier, that can be repeated as sound (if only for the pleasure offered by repeating): *iteration*. Thus, different meaningless sounds can be identified as being the 'same'. This leads to the uncoupling of direct expression or direct appeal, freeing up the way for the function of reference. A second step would be joining sounds together to form words, and words to form word clusters: *combination*. This also constitutes a major step, because here we are witnessing the genesis of the word and word clusters. The word might thus be seen as the basic building block of language. A third level would involve the development of complex syntax, or *recursion*. This is sometimes referred to as the 'Droste effect' or 'nesting doll effect', the effect of infinity: a box within a box, an image within an image. In this case: 'a sentence within a sentence within a sentence', the process in which a sentence has one or more sentences embedded in it: 'I believe that Peter hopes that John will come, but John is asleep. Here we are dealing with four sentences ('I believe', 'Peter hopes', 'John will come', 'John is asleep') rolled into a single sentence. According to Chomsky (1965), this capability, this competence of *recursion*, is essential within human language production, and is therefore innate. With Chomsky, recursion is the 'principle of all principles'. Alternatively, we might define it as being the third stage in an ongoing process, the steps within this process being: iteration, combination and recursion. Here we find ourselves at the level of the signifier, of words, and sentences: imaginary iteration, symbolic combination and formal hierarchy. This means that language function cannot be reduced to any of the three: either (1), recursion (with Chomsky), or (2) the combination of phonematic differences into words and sentence parts, or (3) iteration. All three would be 'required'.

If these are or might be the general characteristics of language, then the next question would have to inquire into its origin, into its evolution, or rather: its evolution *into* language. For a long time, this question was not considered relevant because it could not be answered scientifically. However, from the second half of the 20th century onwards it has become the object of a general and heated debate (Kuckenburg 2016). It is believed that language that (more or less) meets the three aforementioned criteria was born roughly between 100,000 and 50,000 BC. Consequently, a commonly raised question is how it was possible for language to develop (from an evolutionary perspective) in such a short period of time. Maybe language emerged out of nothing (a position adopted by Chomsky), for example through genetic mutation. From an evolutionary perspective, however, this is most unlikely. It would be more likely that its layered structured developed in stages: first mimetic representation, then the forming of words or a primitive way of word clustering, and finally syntax.

This view is in line with the evolutionary perspective embraced by Cassirer, but also with current ideas with regard to the evolution of language (Hombert and Lenclud 2014). This warrants a brief comment. This view is based on the belief in the presence of universal language characteristics features, when compared with animal communication systems (ACS). Human language would then differ in three ways, in addition to the fact of its cultural state of being (Hockett 1960; Hombert and Leclud 2014, 403). The sign (1) is detached from the 'here and now', a shift occurs allowing something to be represented as being present whilst being out of view (*displacement*). It is characterised (2) by double articulation, in the sense that something meaningless (such as a phoneme) may produce a meaning-carrying entity (such as a word) when combined with other phonemes (*duality of patterning*). Finally (3), there is the capacity to produce an infinite number of sentences (*productivity*). The three layers described above are clearly distinguishable here. The first characteristic or layer refers to the birth of a symbolic system, of representation as such through the introduction of a triadic sign concept (sign-referent-meaning); the second characteristic refers to the birth of the word to be combined with other words (the word as a meaning-carrying entity); the third refers to its complex syntactic, hierarchic structuring.

The line of thought advanced from an evolutionary orientation is that there may be preliminary stages of language in which the first and maybe even the second step were taken. We have the stage of displacement, next to that of primitive word clustering, and finally the syntax stage. In the displacement stage, sound and gestures are used, mimetic means, to convey knowledge about a situation that is out of sight: the sign used as a signal. Here we see a return of the old idea of gesture as being the cradle of language. In the second stage, we see something like a protolanguage emerge, with these primitive signs being merged or structured holistically, like in the holophrase, the interjection, the call (Bickerton 2014, 73–108). The third step of course is the big leap: the inventions of syntax, of hierarchy, of a system of rules. This is where Chomsky puts the caesura. In this context, we speak of 'merging', of connecting differential elements to produce a phrase and its recursive structure. We might assume that the third step, the invention of the formal structure, will have a strong retrograde effect on two competencies acquired earlier: mimesis becomes iteration, clustering leads to the forming of series. Invariably, they include the standards upheld by a community (this is correct, that is not).[1]

In this way, it can be made hypothetically feasible that language and culture, when conceived as a system, are essentially different from anything that lacks a concept of system, enabling a new, non-duplicating form of representation to come into existence. Which leads to something completely new: man as *homo symbolicus*, bringing a spate of symbolic activity, including all its associated normative practices supported by the community. Most likely, this step had a very long preparatory phase leading up to it (even though it may have come about quite randomly). This may also explain the speed of it all. Indeed, it is very well possible that this relies on the capacity to recognise and form patterns as well to recognise and form signs, essential for animal organisms and developed to a highly sophisticated level in higher primates, whilst also being differentiated within the hominids (see above). However, after the 'invention' of the possibility of caesura and the combination of elements in an iterative, serial *and* recursive manner, this readily available capability was put to use in a different way than before, based on the age-old physiological notion of function creating the organ ('la fonction crée l'organe'). Now that 'man' himself had upset the species-specific natural alignment (of food provision), the productive tools were already in place to take on the new challenge. Which explains why language, so it seems, developed over a relatively short period, but also

1 Bickerton 2014, 73–108. Hombert and Lenclud (2014, 420–428) attribute the first step to Homo Erectus, a million years ago, the second step (2014, 459–460) to the (common) ancestor of the Homo Sapiens (and Neanderthal man) and the third step (2014, 396/7) to Homo Sapiens sapiens.

why pattern recognition and vocality continued to play a key role in language development. This vocality is what Cassirer defines as language in its sensory expression, what Lacan calls tongue language, or 'lalangue', and what James Joyce introduces in *Finnegans Wake* as the language of sounds – sonority, rhythmicity, the voice timbre, the melody – which is why language is bound to be mimetic and therefore interactive and collective, also because of its higgledy-piggledy nature (which is exactly what Joyce demonstrates). These considerations are obviously speculative of nature, and quite unavoidably so. They build on the dominant line of thought of the 20th century, as an update of Cassirer's brand of philosophy (the 20th-century model of which Chomsky is also a representative, in his own particular way).

Later, a *naturalistic paradigm* would rise to prominence, interpreting changes in terms of supposed evolutionary advantages, as well as in terms biology and neurobiology. As mentioned before, this discourse is naturalistic in nature, while its knowledge pretension is realistic: this is how it happened. Any attempt at an in-depth discussion would fall outside the scope of this paragraph. Notwithstanding, interesting perspectives have been developed. Again, we see recognition of man as a symbolising creature or symbolic species (a name that definitely resonates with naturalism) (Deacon, 1997). Interesting here is that the symbolising capacity and language are considered in terms of their mutual differences *and* similarities. Conceptually, the similarity would be that the use of a cognitive symbol by man is first and foremost deemed to take place within the context of a social system of symbols (with language as a prime example); on the side of language, it implies that the emphasis is not on syntax, but rather on its cognitive content, and therefore on semantics (as opposed to Chomsky). The difference lies in the finding that with language the emphasis is on the social context of the system, and with symbolic cognition the emphasis is on the cerebral basis in which it is produced (viz., the prefrontal cortex). Language thus becomes a virtual system existing outside the organism, while cognition exists as a real cerebral system within the organism. Here we recognise the image of language as a parasite (an analogy also used by Lacan in a different, more negative sense). The comparison here would be that the language might be compared to an external parasite engaging in a symbiotic relationship with its host (the brain), mutually reinforcing each other in the course of evolutionary development (producing an evolutionary benefit). This process is reflected in the term co-evolution.

Points of similarity and difference between this model of the 'symbolic species' and the model of 'homo symbolicus' as outlined in this paragraph now come to mind. A point of agreement would be its basic conception, while the difference would lie in its realistic (evolutionary and neurological) elaboration. It is this realistic basis that causes problems in the process of elaboration, as it brings the assumption of a well-defined boundary ('symbolic threshold') marking the transition from a pre-symbolic stage to a symbolic stage. This sharp boundary, however, cannot really be reconciled with the key role of the brain in this transitional process, seeing that the development of the neocortex is a long-term process. Its concrete elaboration will also lead to a very early location of this transition (well before Homo Erectus), which is not plausible either. It seem that the weakness of this model is actually situated in its realistic elaboration, because of its 'high ambitions'. This may actually be the general flaw in many realistic, naturalistic explanations: their ambitions are simply too high. A toned-down form of idealism might provide the solution here (for example following Dennett (1996), using the method of instances being attributed), which would ultimately pave the way for a more reconstructive and therefore constructive approach. There is yet another point, namely that besides having too much ambition there is also the belief that one knows more than one actually does. In the field of evolution there may be a lot more imponderables than is taken account of, while more knowledge remains unchallenged than is justified. Maybe evolution proceeded in a much more contingent fashion than is commonly believed, involving species whose traces have been erased for good (Gee 2013). A more qualifying view of evolution might come to the aid of the traditional, more constructive scheme. Particularly here, realistic knowledge may well continue to remain beyond our grasp (which obviously does not detract from the great value of traditional and contemporary palaeo-anthropology).

Whatever the case may be, this would certainly not warrant discarding a more constructive and speculative model such as that of *homo symbolicus* as outlined in this paragraph. In support of the model of the homo symbolicus presented here would plead its alignment with the three-tiered structure of language. This is also a construct, but one that is not highly speculative and can actually be made plausible (see above). It also reflects the three-way split that characterises or ought to characterise any symbolic form as a structuring figure, as it was modalised here for language. Its high level of applicability would certainly support this. Its applicability is also reflected elsewhere, namely in the political arena. This may seem like a giant leap, but it is not actually, considering that language and politics, language and the community, are also intimately related. Having said that, its execution would take us to quite a different world of concepts and experiences than the one under discussion, requiring a serious mental shift. Such shifts, however, are part of the design of this chapter, which is made up of mini-essays succinctly addressing a wide range of major themes, their common denominator being a single theme on which a variation is offered: representation or symbolisation.

4.5 The Symbolic Order from a Normative Perspective: Politics, Law, Ethics

Political order and representative democracy. Language cannot exist without a community, a social structure or social institutions – as was already observed in the evolutionary considerations discussed in the foregoing. Aristotle described man as possessing language *and* as being a community creature living in the polis. The first political philosopher of modernity, Hobbes (1996, 12) was equally adamant in asserting that no society or state can exist without language; 'Speech, consisting of *names* or *appellations*, and their connexion … without which, there had been amongst men, neither commonwealth, nor society, nor contract, nor peace, no more than amongst lions, bears, and wolves'. The question would arise whether the three modes of representation with their associated layered structure, applicable to language, might also be identified here: imaginary, objectifying, formal layers within a political order. And if so, how exactly? Moreover, the normative quality which is inherent to each domain of the symbolic form, of the symbolic order as a whole, gets full emphasis here. Symbolisation implies the inevitable relinquishing of immediacy, creating a void, a central void. That is why the void creating as well as safeguarding the symbolic system will be central to the discussion of this particular theme. Both questions will be discussed in their interrelationship.

This makes the design of this paragraph different from that of the previous one, in which we attempted to integrate empirical material into a more comprehensive vision. Here, by contrast, the ambition is to specify a conceptual framework in an empirical way – top-down rather than bottom-up. The role of the historical experience has thus become secondary, merely serving to clarify the scheme. The reference is not empirical politicology, but the political theory (and, by extension, the theory of law and ethics). This a priori approach, also because of this strongly succinct character, may come across as somewhat apodictic, but that is not the intention – this is merely a proposition, a suggestion, nothing more.

From the current perspective, rather than just one political order there are of course many – although their number is limited – because they can be made subject to structuring. What results is a ranges of structures that differ among each other depending on the choice to highlight one or more of the layers mentioned. First of all, we have the premodern feudal system (where no historical divergences are introduced). A dominant trait here, if we could speak in such general terms, is the mythical form of representation. The king rules by the grace of God, representing society as a whole and its natural hierarchy in a top-down fashion. This representation is embodied through the body of the king, for which reason the body itself is essential, as is evidenced by the significance of his birth and death. This body is twofold in nature (Kantorowitcz 1957). In part, it is the natural body that every human possesses, but it is also the head of the Crown (keeping the social fabric together). These two bodies of the King can be distinguished from each other, but are in fact inseparable. This relative state of un-separation aptly defines the specific mythical form of representation. The Eucharist in the Roman Catholic tradition is also a fine example. Here the bread is just bread, the wine is just wine, but at the same time the bread *is* the body of Christ, and the wine his blood. They are not 'just' representatives or symbols of Christ residing elsewhere. Rather, they coincide to create a mythical mode of experience: 'God is in our midst', with the 'is' being a far cry from the 'is' in 'it is cold here'. The same mythical mode of experience can therefore be found in feudal systems, finding an essential apotheosis in its final stages: the absolutist rule of the monarch – 'I am the state', 'l'état c'est moi'.

Breaking away from this state of cohesion therefore constituted a major step, with this caesura marking the transition to modernity, in which a new form of representation of a political order would hold sway. In some cases it was associated with a lot of bloodshed – think of the French Revolution. The sovereign power of the monarch was replaced by the power of the people. And yet it would be a fallacy to think that this put paid to the role of the myth. Also the modern system cannot do without a mythical foundation (Gauchet 2005). Indeed, what underpins the system is an imaginary foundation myth that provides basic unity: the foundation myth of man as an empowered creature, of 'freedom, equality and fraternity' as the new tenet of faith. As a next step, modernity is presented as a closed entity while being contrasted with anything that went before and would be referred to as 'pre-modernity'– which might be called a strongly simplified representation of the facts, to say the least. And yet this new construction did turn out to be effective, while based on the myth of self-determination the process of political decision-making is moulded according to the mode of representative democracy. What lies at its heart – not as a 'nucleus-as-such' but conceived from a representational line of thought – is the introduction of an external difference between the representative (of the people) and those represented (the people) *and* of an internal difference between the representatives ('the political parties'). Instead of, or rather on top of, the foundation myth, comes the structuring principle of 'the difference', which generates identities (parties) and their mutual differences ('the opposition'). It is important to acknowledge *that* there is a formal difference, which becomes evident from the fact that the semantic or substantial differences between the parties often seem to be minor (to the outside world at least). Within this context, however, effective government is possible, with the process of elections guaranteeing a change of power and instituting a void within the system that cannot be filled permanently – which sets it apart from any form of totalitarianism (Lefort 1989).

Thus, *representative democracy* creates a void that did not exist before, like a vase creating a void that did not exist before. The people's representative represents the people, the vox populi, but in such a way that on the one hand it creates the direct will of the people as a mythical entity, while on the other it is erased. That is the void it creates, replacing the mythical will of the people, the 'will of all' ('volonté de tous'), with the construct of a generic will ('volonté générale'), which is constructed on the basis of a variety in partial perspectives. This variety represents the will of the people through political parties, which at the same time is crossed out as a whole. This produces a gap or gulf between the representatives and the people, which must not be eliminated but should be retained in some form or other (in a functional sense). A great politician is someone who can relate to prevailing sentiments in large groups of people and rather than just echo opinions he transforms and interprets (represents) these in a way that is still recognisable, thus embedding his actual discourse, integrating it into a discourse that goes much further (reflecting the contours of a desired world). While bridging the gap caused by representation, it also causes the gap to be retained. Many do not quite succeed in combining the two efforts, these two accomplishments. And yet the loss of this gap would effectively mean the end of representative democracy, which could then be transformed into a direct form of government that by definition is totalitarian, with diversity no longer being safeguarded.

Here may well lie a challenge for the representative democracy of the future, the reason being that the notion of representation itself, with its implicit distance, has become less self-evident in recent years. The demand for full transparency and the suggestion of immediacy imposed by modern media (which are both illusions) do in fact undermine the 'credibility' of thinking in terms of representation. The traditional constellation creates distance, a gap between government and citizen. In turn, citizens relinquish any direct influence through the delegation of decision-making authority to the political system (which only then transforms them into citizens, into a person with a right to vote). In the guise of a citizen rather than of man of flesh and blood, man becomes part of this political system of representation. What required here is trust on the part of the citizen as well as being prepared to bestow authority on authorities.

Here, in *authority*, lies a problem. Hardly a new one, because the theme of authority and authority loss have been experienced for over a century, since Durkheim, on account of the fraying of social structures as such. The decline and associated dwindling of the father function were already discussed by Durkheim as well, whose theses about this supposed decline have influenced Lacan's conception of fatherhood strongly (Lacan 2001, 23–84; Zafiropoulos 2001). Obviously, we have witnessed an acceleration since. This does not mean that the universal father function, the Name-of-the-Father in the sense of Lacan has been dismantled, but its empirical substantiation has become rather feeble (compared to before). The later Lacan did try to come up with an answer, but his answer fails to satisfy. And yet the fact remains that the word of the expert has now become 'only an opinion', with the associated loss of authority resonating in the political arena. Only in representation can something exist as something else, which reflects the very core of the theory of symbolisation presented here. This is also true for the field of political representation: Only in representation there *is* such a thing as an authority that has power and gives direction. This is where the rub lies, with the increasing loss of instances being endowed with some level of authority. Authority needs to be earned at a personal level and can also be lost just as easily (for want of underpinning by an institution). This does not mean that the need for authority has been lost, for this is where the human condition makes itself felt: man as a creature of the lack that drives him to look outside for guidance. Any human society could not possibly function without authority: someone who 'tells them what is what'. We want the powerful Other to tell us what to do, somehow we need to be facing in the same direction. Once, religion fulfilled this role, and Durkheim believes this social role constitutes the very core of religion as such. Today, we tend to look to science to fulfil this direction-giving and binding role, and without the shift becoming truly manifest, it has come to fulfil the role that religion once had. Alternatively, we may look for and find authority ourselves (using Google), its postings being accepted as a source of truth. Or maybe still: public figures, politicians, authors, moralists, scientists who, based on their merits, we are keen to give authority. So yes, there is a need, but also a deep-felt urge, for authority.

This is a real problem for representative democracy. It requires trust and willingness to give authority. It needs broad popular support, with the result that the elaboration will be tied to place and time and will be in line with the prevailing culture. Consequently, representative democracy is not suited for export, because it cannot be realised unless taking account of internal and external power structures. It is based on the principle of self-determination of a people, which is a commendable principle in itself, but not a right that can be enforced. The more so because formal democracy (the right to vote) has only limited value when failing to be embedded in matching institutions, without material democracy. It is also vulnerable, because it has no natural structuring modalities to fall back on: it is intrinsically fragile and still developing. It will function as long as broad popular support is there, which is until that time when 'the people' no longer feel represented and rise up, possibly leading to adaptation or revolution. And yet revolutions and their integration have their own kind of logic. The internal logical of modern political system must be fulfilled, at least from a representational perspective.

This is where the formal aspect of representation comes into play, because a new configuration must be made to fit within the formal boundaries or principles of this system of political representation – unless the system itself crumbles. These principles may be open in nature, but are not unlimited, defining as they do the boundaries of admissibility of political decisions. The principles return recursively at the level of actual government, where they find elaboration through objectification in the form of laws. Thus, the level of actual government represents an intermediate layer, situated between the mythical basis and the principles at the top.

Rule of law and the judicial system. The political order is only one pillar of the social structure, because right next to it we find the pillar of law, of the rule of law. Just like we could say that in premodern time politics and law are highly intertwined, we could argue that in modernity, since the Age of Enlightenment and the French Revolution, their mutual relationship has been thought through and that both have gone their separate ways to some extent (ideal-typically of course) – bearing in mind that one order implies the other, be it as a separate entity. The concept of the modern democratic rule of law reflects both this separation and connection. First of all the separation: power is exercised, but law prevails. Its validity is not unlimited, however, because a rule of law will only apply to the extent that it is actually accepted, which means it has no guarantee outside itself. And just like the political order creates a void (in crossing out the will of the people), so does it the legal system create its own, intrinsic type of void. The void that accomplishes law as a system of representation involves the evacuation of power in order for the legal system to be divested of political power within the context of separation of power and law. Here we see the separation of 'powers' at the time-honoured 'trias politica', which is still functional at least as a fiction. Around this void, a system of legal terms and concepts is built, partly supported by new constructs or fictions (like the fictitious assumption that all are deemed to know the law, etcetera), but on which an entire judicial world is formed. It opens up positions between what become legal subjects, whose mutual positions are determined in relationship to legal standards and procedures. This proves that law and power are not merely separate systems, but that they actually engage with each other. The law imposes standards on power, a process that unfolds through the introduction of legal principles based on which the wielding of power, also though discursive practices, can be judged in terms of legitimacy. And then it turns out that there is yet another aspect to the relationship between law and power. This relationship is ambiguous, as power also supports the legal system.

Intrinsically powerless, in order to perform the task of controlling political power, the legal system operates within the sphere of power. Thus, as a secondary step, the law is vested with power ('the power of law'), which means that any court sentence will be binding or enforceable. In that sense, the law, although essentially powerless, has been 'infected' with power. It needs to have this power, because it is the task of the law to offer protection from fellow-citizens with bad intentions as well as from institutions or the state itself that might resort to abuse of power. – the small other and the big Other – and must therefore have the power to enforce this protection. Finally: from day one, the law has been tied to power, as at any given time it will add legal stature to factual balances of power. In that sense, the actual law will always be 'solidified power'. Indeed, the path leading to the legal system was paved by power, with the establishment of an order – any order – being preceded by a struggle of power for this new order. The 20th century, with its two world wars, is a point in case, while the 21st century bears testimony to this through its many regional conflicts. That is why any reference to self-constitution (of a legislative assembly, at any level), or even the notion of one, is based on a 'fiction', a symbolic construct or imaginary myth. Even a rule of law may have a shady past. It often asserts its power in a way that does not shy away from unnecessary violence (like in the prosecution and execution of punishment in the prison system). Most certainly not everything is coming up roses here.

With modern political order, the rule of law shares *three levels* (which are potentially available to any system of representation). At the top we find the principles, the ideal outlines, the ideal fictions which – impotent in themselves – are made concrete in laws that need to be explained and implemented on the level of objectification and enforcement, with its associated 'technique' and practised violence. Below it, at the bottom level, we find the mythical level of law, its archetypal images. Indeed, the law has a mythical level as well, with its most significant myth being, quite remarkably, the notion *that* justice is meted out: that reasonable trust and authority are bestowed on those who serve the law, that a court of law sentence truthfully reflects the course of events, that those guilty are duly punished and that those who are innocent are acquitted, that the sentence leads to ill-deeds being requited, with balance restored and future danger averted. Obviously, such notions are valid, but inevitably there will be a gap between myth and practice. Juridical evidence can be tenuous by necessity – it is not related to the life world, but rather to a world constructed by law itself (which, at some later or earlier point in time, might be constructed differently), with retribution essentially taking the form of a more mimetic retaliation than is believed or hoped, and where the law is certainly unable to provide complete safety (although efforts are made to accomplish this). Having trust in the legal system and the legitimacy of its practice is not without ground, but means that trust is also based on a fiction, a mythical fiction, which still needs to be maintained somehow. It explains why miscarriages of justice often cause a shock in society. More often than not they will be the outcome of a dysfunctional legal practice. And yet they are inevitable, from a fundamental, structural perspective. Their inevitability is determined by the fact that the legal system is an autonomous system of representation that sets its own rules of evidence, and in that respect the bar cannot be raised too high. Thus, the law has its own system of representation, while the requirements imposed on evidence are not those of the scientific world.

Finally: *jurisdiction*. The judge administers law within a legal system, which means he does not judge based on what actually happened. Such as ambition would be unrealistic. Instead, in the case of criminal law, for example, his ruling will be informed by the fact whether the charges brought are related to a fact punishable by law, and whether the course of events can be proved legally and convincingly, after which an appropriate punishment (and/or corrective measure) will be imposed. This implies that jurisdiction carries its own language, vocabulary and range of doctrinal concepts. As a result, jurisdiction is based on its own system of representation. It may still draw on the language of the life world and its concepts, but these undergo judicial transformation and refinement. They are always on a semantic remove from their terminological equivalents in colloquial language and are to be considered counterfactual in relation to the facts of the life world (De Jong 2016, 26). In doing so, the mode of attribution are often objectified to some degree, indeed just like in the life world. A person may claim to have sincere intentions ('I acted prudently and conscientiously, believe me'), but ultimately it will be its environment, the Other, who will judge the nature of the action – just like the audience decides whether something is funny or not. In that sense, man is not the sum of his intentions but, to quote Hegel (once again), he is the 'sum of his deeds' (which express his actual intentions and through which they can be known, and be known only). In jurisdiction, however, which operates within its own remit, its own order, this role becomes even more poignantly evident. At this level, most likely there is no fundamental difference between common law and continental law systems. After all, the judge or the jury, respectively (both representing the legal community) will both attribute actorship ('you did it'), while also determining, based on rules of experience applying normatively, the manner of intentional involvement – sometimes in spite of what the accused stated ('you did it purposefully, accepting the risk that this might happen'). Indeed: it is the judge who establishes the rules of experience which the average person (normatively, not statistically) is supposed to abide by, specifying how the average person can reasonably expect others to react. What the judge does – normatively establishing rules of experience – asserts the role of the Other through the establishment of rules and expectations. But the judge will also modify, transform these into a different medium, namely that of the system of law.

Also within jurisdiction, the three levels distinguished within the system of law return. After all, in jurisdiction three paths of legal disclosure (in an broad sense) may be distinguished: (1) legism, (2) interpretative case law, and finally a (3) law based on principles. They correspond exactly to the 'three levels' reflected in each representative system. Here, we find these three levels – mimetic, objectifying and finally formalising – once again, now within jurisdiction rather than within the system of law. From this perspective, legism is defined by mimetic representation, because it argues that legal reality reflects the life world in an unfragmented way – a notion that is embraced mythically. A case law puts paid to this pretence and the presupposed isomorphism, recognising that the juridification of the life world by necessity brings a transformation. Indeed, the formal truth of the law is fundamentally different from the material truth of the life world. Finally, there is a brand of jurisdiction that deals with principles, that reflects on the principles of law itself, underpinning its justification in order to construct the applicability of legal provisions. Because of the primacy of principles this brand of law is very open. From the perspective of such law of principles, humanity could be an example of an end term of a jurisdiction founded in human rights (leaving aside its scope). Humanity would thus become its unifying trait and it would offer a type of formal representation, in the sense of Lacan or in that of Cassirer. It is a either a virtually empty term which nonetheless drives this range $S_1(S_2)$; or it offers a more concrete addition at a semantic level ι $(\varepsilon_1, \varepsilon_2, \varepsilon_n)$, with in both cases the principle being removed from the range of legal provisions, while still driving it. However, there is nothing or no one to guarantee its effectivity, seeing that it only applies to the extent that it is actually accepted by citizens, themselves, or by the legal community. Even the presence of a rule of law within a constitutional state would offer no guarantee against excesses, nor does it represent some form of endpoint of political history. Nor would this be likely from a symbol-theoretical perspective, considering that the three-level structure of the political order and legal order potentially accommodates a multitude of substantiations, but not necessarily a teleology in the sense of an endpoint of history, in whatever form. The cycle does not have to end somewhere.

This qualification does nothing to detract from the ethical significance of the legal system, but this is a different matter altogether, and can certainly never be a run race. Here, the law primarily has an inward focus, because it strives to institute and safeguard boundaries, responding with retribution in cases of transgression (be it to a limited extent) or with attempts at prevention (to a limited extent): this is mine, that is yours, this is my body, you have no right to touch it. Setting and guarding boundaries thus becomes a fundamental function, if not the very source of law and criminal law in particular. In a way, this applies to any system of representation: it both introduces and guards boundaries.

Morality: two moral cores. What is the ultimate foundation of penalisation? This would be the fact that human beings are deserving of protection – with the extent of protection and the range of what is deserving of protection differing among the various cultures and legal systems. Despite variations in their elaboration, the moral core will be the same: the fact that man is deserving of protection, as a living being expressing itself and being capable of self-determination through this expression. This may be interpreted as a variation on Kant. The path chosen by Kant to establish the moral status of man as being worthy of protection a priori, however, would not be compatible with a brand of philosophy such as that of the symbolic forms. Rather than depart from an a priori, it chooses a 'primitive fact' as its point of departure: the factuality of the order of culture. Morality is part of this, and actually shows a development or genealogy (which obviously only involves ideal types). Morality starts with that of a closed group (with the fixed codes of prevailing morality), developing into that of a local community or national state, with objectifiable civic virtues, finding its intermediate 'endpoint' in an open, universal and principle-driven form of ethics, which is deemed to apply to every person. This genealogy does not merely concern 'the past', but is also reflected in the 'three levels' of a moral order: the group-specific codes of prevailing morality, of virtues that can be practised in a variety of ways, and the general moral principles that need to made concrete in manners that may differ strongly, depending on location and time.

This still leaves the inquiry into the assumption that man is worthy of protection as a person unaddressed. It cannot be based on any of the three levels, but only on their common trait, namely that of 'man' as carrier of the symbolic function, man as a symbolising creature. And because each human being expresses this universal in their own unique way, this means that *each single* human being is worthy of protection. Man is not worthy of protection as a species (as opposed to the panda), but as an individual, because each human being, more than being an abstract carrier of the symbolic function, realizes the symbolic function in their own unique way. Where Kant departs from the axiom of man as a rational creature, a philosophy of symbolic forms, of medial thought, takes the fact of culture as its starting point, ultimately arriving at the fact that man is deserving of protection as the carrier of unicity – 'I am one too' – based on the principle of culture.

Man being deserving of protection is not a normative addition to the fact of man's cultural mode of existence. In fact, it is equal to, has similar roots as man's cultural mode of existence. The entrance into culture marks the transition to a different, normatively charged state of being, which elevates man from the order of nature into culture: at birth, man is given a name, and when he dies he will be buried. This name implies rights as well as duties, however primitive they may be (in respect of parents or ancestors). After his death, the grave, as a material memento of the unicity of his symbolic life, must not be desecrated and deserves protection. Man's life being worthy of protection and its memory is therefore *not* founded in life itself, which is supposed to be sacred, but rather in man's cultural mode of existence. Death leaves a gap in the community structure, general though it may be, leading to a ban on manslaughter. This does not necessarily imply that no man will ever be killed accidentally or deliberately, nor that killing is not allowed, but first and foremost it implies that man occupies a different position in the natural order than does the animal (which is also included in it, for example as 'can be hunted/cannot be hunted', as 'possession'). Through the embodiment of a general principle, each man also becomes his own principle, which in that sense renders him unique. In that sense, each man, regardless of his good or bad deeds, represents a unique value. This reflects one of the two cores of Lacan's interpretation of Sophocles' 'Antigone' (Lacan 1992, 344): the unique value of each man, whichever. The other core refers to the unique value of individual desire. Universality and unicity thus coincide.

So what is the foundation of this unicity or singularity? It is the fact that entrance into culture is followed by (or is associated with) an partial exit. Man relies on the cultural domains offered (of law, of politics, of language), but may also choose to relate to them. Using Lacan's terminology: Alienation is followed by separation – there is a second round after the first. Man finds himself in the grip of culture, of language, but only partly so. As was repeatedly shown before, this is down to the nature of language itself. Being in the grip of *language*, man is able to escape the *grip* of language. Indeed, language has an open character, enabling man to add his individual interpretation and signature to what he finds there. The choice for an individual signature represents a response to what the Other asks from me, desires from me, tells me to be: a singular relationship towards the family (or families) of origin, towards its ideals, towards the extended family, group structures, tribal forms, etcetera. Which also implies that each human being has the option to make a singular choice, which is not limited to modern culture and its autonomy-thinking. This is also true for members of premodern or tribal societies, at least from this perspective.

Thomas Mann's ambitious and grand novel *Joseph and His Brothers*, which was based on the eponymous story from the book of Genesis, aims to demonstrate precisely *that* – with the universal scope of the mythical experience being glimpsed between the lines. Here, Joseph is the deeply spoiled preferred son – a typical Thomas Mann character – while each of his brothers engages in a unique relationship within this family dynamics: each brother is different from the other, but is also part of the set of (twelve) brothers, born from different marriages, each a patriarch of one of the twelve tribes. This may show that, also in a tribal society, ideals and their derived preferences may be important, but do not necessarily cast the response from later generations in stone. Again they have the option or even find themselves compelled to take up a position that obviously is not a conscious choice informed by explicit reasons, but does in fact represent the 'order of a choice'. Although the outcome is uncertain, we know that a choice *must* be made, The outcome leads to a recognisable choice: This is typical of Joseph, that is typical of Ruben and there is Benjamin again, with his quintessential traits.

The yardstick for a successful singularity is therefore not found in authenticity related to an inner self, but is about recognisability, the way a particular person lives his life, shapes his existence. Singularity becomes evident from what a person does or does not: it expresses itself through the sum of a person's deeds. It shows what the person *is*, turns out to be, or has been. For the very reason that a singularity is about making a 'choice', it also includes the notion of responsibility. This singularity is hardly a secondary matter, but is in fact part of the concept of becoming-a-subject within a symbolic order: It shows its moral component. Each person will make the universal symbolic function concrete in their own individual way, which results in a specific subjective position from which each person shapes his world, for which he is responsible: 'One is always responsible for one's position as a subject' (Lacan 2002, 858). This responsibility goes far, as it affects not only the deeds, but the very character, a person's unique features. Indeed, this has far-reaching consequences and may therefore lead to excess tension, bringing the need for this responsibility to be limited to what falls within a person's capacity, to what can still be done: *savoir-faire* (Lacan 2005, p. 61). In the practical domain, no one is deemed to deliver the impossible, most certainly not. But it does imply that man can to some degree be held responsible for the way he shapes his world, and consequently also for the contours of his own desire, a field in which he ought not to make concessions.

Lacan considers Antigone from the eponymous tragedy to be the archetype. In his interpretation, she is faced with the choice of following her desire, indeed, her duty, and bury her brother, who died in battle, *or* to quell that desire and obey her uncle, who represents the governing law, the ruling: This reflects the second core of Lacan's interpretation of 'Antigone': the singularity of one's own desire (Lacan 1992, 392). This yielding to pressure will bring into being a sense of guilt or remorse: if only I had followed my own desire. Antigone being a classical, premodern character, bears testimony to the fact that this morality is of all times, then as well as today. This moral assignment obviously does not tell us that we should live according to our own desire, without compromise, a thought that ran through some post-Lacanian circles. Attractive though this may sound, it would essentially mean that it is okay to kill a person for the fun of it. This would be a self-centred, criminogenic interpretation, as well as being untenable for the fact that a person's own desire is inevitably entwined with that of others. It does mean, however, that we should investigate our own desire, also in the way it is entwined with the desires of others: To what extent can I fulfil my desire, and the way I want to approach life, 'my own' desire, or in fact that 'of the Other'? It admonishes us to stay in touch with the complexity of desire, to live by it (and ultimately not be guided by what is opportune or by what life throws at us): In the end, it is nothing more than 'do your duty'.

The morality that is inherent in man's cultural mode of existence – at least according to a type of philosophy such as that based on symbolic forms or a symbolic order – is made up of two cores. Here, the term 'morality' does not specifically refer to individual morality, in the sense of Kant, as opposed to morality as a group phenomenon (an opposition formulated by Hegel), but rather to a proto-moral or moral nucleus. The former proceeds from the fact of culture, of the cultural order, leading, once elaborated to a morality of Kantian flavour centred around legitimate mutual expectations and duties, aimed at providing mutual protection ('thou shalt not kill, shalt not steal'). The second moral nucleus is congruent with the first, but primarily refers to the manner in which an individual life ought to be lived from this order, revolving around the question: 'What do I really desire?' This second moral nucleus can be situated within the other major orientation of contemporary ethics: the ethics of a good life. This is also about the recognition of the divided state of desire. It is this very dividedness and the fact that desire is not massive that accommodates freedom: 'What will I do, what will I not, what is it that I desire myself?' Indeed, the choice for a particular desire will not be made after ample contemplation and deliberation, but will instead take shape in the course of a lifetime.

We cannot say 'this is how I am', because this is precisely the question, and not the answer. It also enables the requirement to stay in touch with the desire, to reflect on it. A conception of man as a symbolising creature, will there connect both *moral* nuclei: an order that asserts man's being worthy of protection as a symbolising creature, and the resulting task of man to take responsibility for one's own life-based-on-desire.

This morality, with its two moral nuclei, does not necessarily contain a detailed brand of morality, never mind a normative ethical theory, but such an elaboration might be founded in an ontology of being a man, as outlined here: The fact that man has no choice but to *be* his particular view as a symbolising being. A functional ontology of man also brings a deontology: Man's 'state of being' implies a particular type of 'duty'. This may seem more dramatic than it actually is, seeing that this moral nucleus manifests itself in daily life, with proto-ethics taking shape initially in etiquette. This concerns the symbolism of society and how it shapes the salute, the handshake or refraining from a handshake, the welcoming words, which together form the basic layer of the symbolic order, but which also and invariably have a moral quality. As part of the texture of mini-meetings and mini-separations they therefore express the respect for the person of the other (in whatever form or degree). This should also become evident from more primary forms of confrontation: the violence with which it may be associated therefore need to be tempered by some form of respect for the other's perspective, which may lead to a restriction of violence and engaging in a dialogue. Essentially, this is about taking part in culture, which from a certain point onwards will always be a culture of dialogue.

The process of entering the culture, of taking part in the practice of symbolisation, however, is not massive and is therefore at risk of (partial) 'failure'. This failure may occur during the period of upbringing, if the child fails to be recognised as a potential subject with its own desire or, alternatively, if the recognition of an objective world, the order within, fails to occur. This possibility of failure of the symbolic function may carry a person beyond the limits of normality, or what is accepted as such. This possibility leads us to the final field of application to be discussed: psychopathology, the domain of the psychic disorder. It signifies the final transition within this chapter. But once again, at its heart lies the possible significance of symbol-theoretical interpretation.

4.6 Shades of Symbolisation: The Psychic Disorder

To this end, we refer back to the outline of psychopathology in Chapter 1, giving it a different substantiation. The various types of psychic disorder are regarded as an expression of a partially defective symbolisation and separation. This functional failure may manifest itself in any of the 'three domains of the real' to which symbolisation refers (see the first paragraph in this chapter). *This* paragraph thus focuses on those *three domains*, similar to the 'three level' structure being the central point of reference in the paragraphs on the symbolic order. This shift in the conceptual set of tools is a logical one. A psychic disorder is not an 'order' in itself, nor is it a component of the symbolic order. What applies, is the concept of the real and of the 'three domains' within it: that is exactly where fundamental symbolisation, through its failure, becomes relevant. Bringing out this coherence is the central objective of this paragraph As a result, more than just highlighting another empirical field – that of the psychic disorder – from the present symbol-theory, it puts another dimension of this symbol-theory centre stage, making it concrete: the inquiry into the fundamental, radical symbolisation.

Fundamental idea. At first glance, the idea to look at fundamental symbolisation from the point of view of psychopathology may seem odd, bizarre even. And yet this is precisely what Cassirer did, proceeding from the notion that what a function accomplishes behind our backs can be identified at the point where this function fails, or partly fails. Through this deficiency, the mechanisms of the symbolic function will show themselves. This notion is less outlandish than one might think, because it is in line with the fundamental Neo-Kantian concept that the workings of the mind cannot be identified directly or through introspection (as opposed to what transcendental phenomenology believes to make possible). It can merely be reconstructed, namely on the basis of what mental functions accomplish, based on their outcome ('Ergebnis'). Cassirer himself applied this insight to the field of neuropsychology, or neurology, by drawing on data supplied by neurologist (and cousin) Goldstein: the well-known case of Schneider (Cassirer 2002c, 257–268; Merleau-Ponty 1962, 103–116). Drawing on neurology should not surprise us either, seeing that the basic notion is not just Neo-Kantian, but is actually derived from the medical field: Dysfunction shows the function. This proved to be a fertile point of departure, reconstructing as it did the traditional neurology based on clinical picture and the pathological-anatomical substrate, the post-mortem establishment of the various brain part functions, to construct a 'map of the mind' – a detailed image of the brain that may have been refined by modern neurosciences, but has not been changed fundamentally (See also: Mooij 2018).

Not just in neurology, but also in psychiatry and psychopathology, this idea took hold. Goldstein (1964, 23–34) was the first to apply it here, namely in the field of psychosis, of schizophrenia. Such an approach casts a whole new light on psychic disorder, but also on the mechanisms of the mind, of the symbolic function which shows a defect here. The field of psychopathology, particularly psychosis, would be more enlightening than that of neuropsychology, because the disruption in the field of psychosis has a deeper impact and therefore provides more insight into the workings of the symbolic function (which obviously does nothing to lessen the devastating effects of neuropsychological disorders). It is not surprising, therefore, that the fields of phenomenology and hermeneutics (of the situation) have often drawn on psychopathology in order to clarify their ideas (Tatossian 1997). Consequently, psychopathology can hardly be regarded as a foreign body once fundamental questions about man need to be asked. And yet: more often than not, the elaboration tends to limit itself to the psychosis, the most fundamental form of psychic disorder. This is quite understandable, as psychoses do tickle the imagination. And yet there is no reason for limitation, because a modification of the representation can essentially be constructed in all types of psychic disorder. And then it turns out that these non-psychotic varieties, such as personality disorders, can in fact be quite instructive in this context. And so a broader discussion of this field would certainly be warranted here. Just like we may be dealing with uncharted territory for many a general reader, so may it represent a whole new approach for the psychiatrist and psychologist of today. It may therefore serve to broaden their horizons.

This paragraph merely aims to offer a first attempt. Lacan, in his psychopathology, has made a similar attempt, which means that a symbol-theoretical interpretation could certainly be in line with his philosophy. Lacan's scheme, however, is rather limited, certainly in comparison with those of current psychopathological views. He only recognises the categories of neurosis, perversion and psychosis (as a 'unitary psychosis'). This limitation may be overcome by introducing the category of the personality disorder, of which perversion is part (see the discussion of Joyce with the later Lacan). The result is a trichotomy: neurosis, personality disorders and psychosis. This trichotomy would moreover be in accordance with current trends in psychodiagnostics, be that the term 'neurosis' has fallen into disuse. Obviously, such a description of the psychic disorder in terms of failing, deficient symbolisation is not intended to explain this condition (as is done for instance by biological psychopathology). What it sets out to do is deepen the descriptive psychopathology, with a contribution from Lacan, as well as from phenomenology and hermeneutics (Mooij 2012, 123–234). After all, it is a first attempt, a proposition with a speculative quality.

Three levels of symbolisation: psychosis, personality disorder, neurosis. The hypothesis would then be that the psychosis is characterised by a failure of the fundamental symbolisation, and the personality disorder by a partial failure, whereas it is essentially intact with the neurosis and normality. Because at least three levels are distinguished, we might also avoid the rather massive term of 'failure' and rather speak of 'shades of symbolisation' or the even more neutral option of speaking of 'variations in symbolisation'. This hierarchy does enable us to identify the coherence within each type, as well as the difference among them (see also Chapter 1). First of all there is the psychosis, a concept that carries two meanings here. First of all, a psychosis can be conceived as a condition of failing reality-testing, characterised by the presence of certain symptoms, namely hallucinations and/or delusions. Here, the term also refers to a psychic structure, namely the fragile psychic structure underlying such a psychotic condition, whose fragility can still be compensated by a particular behaviour ('sinthome') that safeguard the person involved from a manifest psychotic image. In this context, the psychosis fulfils a key role, because it functions as a prime example, a 'casus princeps', based on which a failing symbolisation may be clarified as a fundamental principle of the psychic disorder. Indeed, the psychotic condition, observing something that is not there and harbouring thoughts that have no basis in reality without being able to correct them, show this failure to great effect, with the boundaries between inner and outer worlds becoming blurred. The psychosis as a structure shows that the separation between the inner and outer worlds, between the self and the Other is fundamentally fragile. This becomes evident, for example, from living a particularly one-sided life (as in the case of a schizoid personality disorder) that is supposed to offer protection against stimuli from the outside and from the Other, as well as from the significance of protecting against stimuli in general (sheltered housing). And, in Lacan's terminology, this would mean that the signifier of the separation has not been installed (which pinpoints the psychotic vulnerability, the psychotic fracture).

On the opposite side of the spectrum we find the neurosis, which may or may not be associated with neurotic symptoms (including anxiety and compulsion), but which has a psychic structure that is solid in itself and would not predispose towards psychotic disturbance. Here, the symbolic function does what it is supposed to do, preventing fundamental disruption: There are no serious issues with delimitation in respect of the outside world and the Other. And above: the signifier of the separation (the Name-of-the-Father, the empty space) has been installed, often in the form of a forbidding entity telling you 'this is allowed, this is not, else you will no longer be loved, appreciated by me, by us' (see the paragraph on the later Lacan). We could speak of 'over-representation', in the sense of an excess, which functions as a protective construct. This overprotection would then represent the neurotic or pathological factor.

The personality disorder takes up a midway position between the psychosis and neurosis, with disruption of the fundamental symbolisation which is however partial, being split. Entering the symbolic has been achieved, but there is a problem with the symbolic itself, with the empty space introduced by the symbolic, the signifier of the separation (the Name-of-the-Father). There may be a reference to a law, to a lawful authority, but is validity is denied simultaneously – Joyce's *non serviam*: I won't do it, no way. Symbolisation takes the form of a 'vertical split', with two worlds of experience co-existing, but not interacting: 'I know there is a law, there is a difference, but still…'. Thus, the personality disorder leads to a whole gamut of complex life forms, some creative, some highly destructive, within which the person will have to find a way to deal with this split state. Succinctly though it may be formulated, the hypothesis that the fundamental symbolisation will be intact in the case of the neurosis, while being partially operative in the case of the personality disorder and inoperative in the case of the psychosis, certainly has its merits. With the important criticism that the symbolic function will be effective only when occurring in relationship to the external symbolic order: Its effectiveness (accomplishing separation) becomes apparent from the internalisation of one or more external elements.

Three domains. In order to introduce the issue of fundamental, radical symbolisation, yet another approach would be imaginable: based on the *what* of symbolisation rather than the *how* (defective or not). Inquiring into the *how* and *what* thus becomes part and parcel of this paragraph's content. This 'what' concerns the three domains of the real to which symbolisation refers – at least according to the present scheme. To recap, these three domains are, respectively: the immanence of life as it is transformed into an experiencing body that, once included into the symbolic order, is either male or female; next, the brutal state of being that is transformed into a temporally and spatially structured world; finally, the transformation of the primordial Other into a field of intersubjective relationships driven by demands and desires. From this, three problem areas emerge (if this transformation becomes defective).

Three problem areas: (1) *the body and sexual differentiation*, (2) *spatial and temporal structuring, and* (3) *the relationship towards others, the Other*. What is the point of this? Where the psychic disorder, from a functional perspective, had been characterised by a certain degree of failing symbolisation – psychosis, personality disorder and neurosis – we now see a material aspect being added. This means we can establish whether these material problem areas can be identified in the various forms of psychic disorder. Important here is the subdivision into the three forms of psychic disorder. Based on the more or less traditional classification, each type (psychosis, neurosis and personality disorder) has three subtypes. This leads to *nine* subtypes (3x3). And what do we see? That, with all three subtypes, one of the three problem areas keeps returning, in different ways obviously. We will briefly discuss each of these subtypes, with the caveat that we are only dealing with 'Idealtypen', which does not necessarily have to appear empirically in this particular form (see also Chapter 1).

Psychosis. Traditionally, the field of psychosis is subdivided into three forms of disorder: *schizophrenia, melancholia, and delusional disorder* (*paranoia*). The question would then be in which field symbolisation has specifically failed, and where the psychotic person finds himself particularly stumped, without an answer. In schizophrenia, the *body* turns out to be the big stumbling block, in melancholy it is *time*, and in paranoia it is the *Other*.

Let's start with schizophrenia. In this context, the focus is no longer on the silent form discussed in Chapter 1, which was characterised by a gradual loss of social competencies and a decay of pre-predicative intentionality, where alerting symptoms such as hallucinations and delusions are initially missing. In the type of schizophrenia to be discussed here, however, hallucinations and delusions feature prominently. At the heart of the hallucinatory experience lies the *body*. Lying wide open, it is being irradiated, manipulated. In schizophrenia, the failure of the fundamental symbolisation would therefore express itself through the ineffective transformation of a vital immanence into an 'own body', a 'corps sujet'. The non-symbolised real aspect of life manifests itself, returning as an invasion of the non-symbolised body into the subjective experience.

The second type of psychosis is melancholia, or the psychotic depression. Here the emphasis is on the failure of the categorical structuring of *time* and also space. Traditionally, depression has been regarded as a disorder of time, with the future being cut off in the temporal experience: there is complete hopelessness, with the future being cast in stone, while the person keeps thinking back to the past: – 'if only I had…'. – as though the past could be changed in retrospect. What we see is therefore a reversal, with the past acquiring the characteristics of an open future, whereas the future has taken on the characteristics of an immutable past. How can this be interpreted? We could say that in normality, symbolisation of the external real leads to a world that contains external time (clock time), as well to an awareness of this time, the inner temporal consciousness, in which is held on to the present, the future is pre-empted and the past is remembered, and is preserved as a result (see Chapter 1). We might therefore assume that this temporalisation becomes faulty in melancholy, with a misalignment of internal and external time. This leads to the subject falling prey to a purely external time or pseudo-time, in which only loss occurs and nothing is retained in a represented form. This explains the symptom of experiencing continued loss, of time decaying, in turn bringing the consequence of experiencing decay, decomposition of the body (which is different from its open state seen in schizophrenia). A similar detachment as with time is also seen with space. Here we see an implosion of the spatial categorical structuring of the world, a detachment from the external, physical space and its subjective experience. As a result, the person involved is at the mercy of an overwhelming pseudo-space, in which he appears as bottomless and puny, incapable of pleasure (anhedonia), leaving the subject in much torment. Again, in the psychotic phenomena we recognise a specific field in which fundamental symbolisation fails, with the subject being left 'defenceless', unable to respond.

A third issue is found in the relationship towards the *Other* (the sum of all others), or intersubjectivity. This leads up to the delusion, the paranoia, where the relationship with the Other is no longer symbolised, raised to the level of representation, as a result of which the subject feels haunted by this non-represented primordial Other, who is threatening by definition and is therefore experienced as evil, as having bad intent. Again, we see a return of and invasion from this non-symbolised, non-represented domain.

The problem areas in these three traditional forms of psychosis are, from the symbol-theoretical perspective: the body and the sexual difference (in the case of schizophrenia), time and death (melancholia), and the desire of the Other (paranoia). Although fundamental symbolisation fails in each of these disorders in a particular domain, this does not imply that other domains would remain unaffected. After all, specific is not the same as exclusive. The disorder in the field of corporeality may be characteristic (pathognomic) of schizophrenia, but might be also associated with a disruption of the two other domains (of time/spatial structuring and relationship towards the Other). To put it differently: the domain-specific disruption of the fundamental symbolisation is accompanied by a general disruption. This would make sense, after all, seeing that the distinction between the three domains is not watertight. Rather than referring to an ontological category, it distinguishes in relationship to a function. This explains why 'mixed types' often occur – such as the schizo-affective disorder, found in the intermediate area between schizophrenia and mania, or the paranoid type of schizophrenia, which has features in common with the delusional disorder, etcetera.

Regardless of the specific domains, each psychosis will therefore show what happens during fundamental symbolisation: the design of a world, of a type of social bond, of a relationship unto one's own body. The psychosis rejects the common world, either temporarily in a psychotic episode or more permanently from a psychotic structure. This is obviously true only if and to the extent that the psychosis reaches, which usually does not encompass an entire lifetime, which means the person is able to reflect on the psychosis, potentially leading to a sense of wonder, anxiety or productivity. The psychotic person will therefore examine, in his experience and his quintessential reflection on it, what 'possible worlds' there are, testing each of these possibilities. This can actually be tested in practice, seeing that this process is often associated with intense fear and other types of suffering. And yet: to the extent that the psychotic person rejects the defining frameworks of space, time and social bonds, while designing fundamentally different modalities within their psychosis, they will engage in an *ontological experiment*, which may or may not be liveable. The psychotic person designs a new ontology, not in theory but in their own experience, in that sense becoming an ontologist. It is hardly surprising, therefore, that the psychotic experiences, the experiments that make up a psychosis, can seem very close to the thought experiment that play such a major role in thought experiments. Examples include the extreme thought experiment of world annihilation which were central to Husserl's philosophy, with the empirical world being 'thought away' while leaving consciousness intact, leading to the assumption of the primacy of consciousness. But also the alleged level-headed analytical philosophy, with its particular penchant for bizarre thought experiments, likes to take things to the extreme (such as putting a brain on a vessel). Whatever the case may be, what is considered to be a harmless thought experiment in philosophy can actually become a real experience in psychosis, in the experience experiment that psychosis has turned into (Kusters 2014). It makes the psychosis not just an experiment of nature, but also of the mind: exploring alternative possibilities of symbolisation within a person's own existence.

Neurosis. Here again the three domains present themselves, bearing in mind that fundamental symbolisation does not actually fail but is rather present in excess. This makes the neurosis a form of hyper-normality, an excessive form. Traditionally, the field of the neurosis is divided into that of *hysteria, compulsive neurosis* and *phobia and dependence*, with each of the field being characterised by overrating. A few key terms should suffice here. In hysteria, it is the own *body* with male/female difference. It is represented excessively, put at the centre and thus put forward, including the male/female difference: It is played out as well being played with. How do I show myself, either as a man or a woman, how do I relate to those who show themselves in the same way, or as part of the opposite sex? A lifetime of anxiety and uncertainty often plays a part here, particularly in terms of 'security'. The hysterical strategy is that of temptation, and therefore primarily takes place through exposure of the body, exhibitionism, showing one's most intimate details. Also in the social field, the strategy of temptation (of revolt, rebellion) virtually always finds a hysterical leader figure (tempting and temporarily binding the people), whose physicality and sexuality are significant, both to the person himself, who flaunts it, and to the people, who find themselves attracted to it.

Compulsion represents the opposite side of the spectrum. The body serves mostly as an instrument ('the body does not exist'), while the life ambition is that of bloodless control. Here, it is not the body but *time* that is central, in the sense that the future must be planned and controlled. The body is not cast aside but, following on from the fundamental ambition, is controlled, like others are being controlled. And yet the ambition is the control itself, prevention is a temporal category: prevention of anxiety to avert future danger. Again, anxiety takes the form of anticipation anxiety. Excessive control brings the need for more compulsion, which may lead to manifest compulsive phenomena: Prevention leads to more prevention, compulsion to more compulsion. Compulsion has a significant social impact as well. In the social rotation, it often takes over from hysteria, which is unable to create order after all, putting on yet another layer of compulsion. Ultimately, compulsion is of all times (governance is needed, the cows need milking, the trains must run on time).

In phobia and dependence, the relationship with the *Other* is the key: Should I be afraid of him or her, or can I rely on him or her. Here, anxiety often takes the form of social fears, such as avoidance behaviour and claiming behaviour both of them having a shared root, even if it is part of a person's structure. Consequently, dependence and (this type of) anxiety often go together or are playing leap-frog. Spatially, it often involves people who gravitate towards the margins and find it hard to be at the centre of attention. They also tend to marginalise themselves or, counterphobically, inflate themselves (also physically). This pattern has a social correlate as well: The state of dependence can be kindled by the provisions of the welfare state, or discouraged in a free-for-all society of the neoliberal type.

In all three forms, fundamental symbolisation remains intact, but one domain will invariably be overrepresented: the own body, the control of time and situation, the relationship with the Other. But just like with psychosis, 'specific' should not be interpreted as 'exclusive'. With each variety of the neurosis (hysteria, compulsion, phobia) not only the specific domain but also other domains are affected – to use Cassirer's terminology, they have been 'modalised'. We have seen this before, and an elaboration would not be in place in the present context, nor is it required for its objective: to pinpoint the specific domains in which fundamental symbolisation becomes defective. Once again we find that the distinction between the three is not substantive or ontological, but rather stands in relation to a function: the symbolic function.

Personality disorder. The group of personality disorders takes up a halfway position between neurotic and psychotic functioning and, by virtue of this position, is characterised by partial failure of the symbolic function. Indeed, entering the symbolic has been achieved, but there is a problem with the symbolic itself, with the empty space introduced by the symbolic, the signifier of the separation (the Name-of-the-Father). The partial effectiveness of the symbolic function is expressed in a process of splitting, with mutually conflicting worlds of experience co-existing, and are actually experienced as such without the experience of conflict: 'I am aware of it, but still'. This splitting is therefore a different process compared to the 'dividedness' experienced in the case of normality and the neurosis, with integration taking place between the conscious and unconscious, a dialectic. Once again, we recognise the 'three domains' in the three subtypes: *perversion, narcissistic personality disorder, and the borderline type*. These may therefore be described in terms of disruption of the relationship with one's own body, with time, and with the Other. These subtypes will be addressed in slightly more detail than those of the neurosis, considering that the relative normality of the neurosis makes it less productive or compelling. Another reason is that the personality disorder represents an increasingly important group socially, which may be caused by changing societal patterns, with the symbolic order becoming less static.

First of all perversion. To prevent any misunderstanding: the term 'perversion' should not be confused with 'general perversion', which characterises the human condition as such as being artificial (according to Lacan). Nor does it relate specifically to 'perverse' traits (some degree of masochism, voyeurism) with which any neurotic condition usually is accompanied. It seems appropriate to reserve the term of perversion, in the neurotic domain, for 'focal perversions', being formed by sexual fantasies of a perverse nature that if enacted actually fulfil a stabilising role. Focal perversion's core might be defined as utter devotion to the pleasure of the Other, with an excessive ban on one's own pleasure, resulting in rage. The neurotic, focal type of perversion would then provide a way out: having to do what is not allowed, which makes it right (because no guilt is involved); you are not allowed to be, and yet, in this very ban on existing, the state of being – I do exist – is experienced. The focal perversion is supposed to remedy this paradox, sometimes to amazing effect.

If this pattern is not merely focally sexual but also has a pervasive character, we could speak of a 'perverse position', analogous to Lacan's perverse structure: pervasive perversion. It extends beyond the neurotic spectre. Its background is therefore a different one: partial separation rather than a ban on pleasure. It relates to a specific structure of personality, characterised by a split which affects symbolisation of the *body*. In the resulting split, the body is represented as belonging to the own gender on the one hand, but also to the unseparated body. This means the own body will be exposed to an impending invasion of this unseparated, anonymous body, bringing the threat of being overwhelmed. This threat can be countered by looking for it actively, with the subject arranging his own submission to or coinciding with the other, effectively containing the threat (enabling lust still to be found): a do-or-die, life-or-death threat, it is either you or me. It makes that sexuality and death, the sexual experience and the death experience, pervade each other, with the sexual experience becoming highly intense and existentially significant. Then again, it is also difficult to frame or integrate psychically. Where psychic integration becomes problematic, the proven remedy to deal with such conflicts is splitting.

Moreover, this attitude is not limited to the psychic domain, but can actually be carried over into the social field. We could therefore speak of an 'ordinary perversion' ('perversion ordinaire'), with the social integration rather than psychic integration being a taboo – as a variation on the term of ordinary psychosis. This means the own body, 'the self', is under threat of the bodies of anonymous others, because of their colour, smell, eating habits, with the threat taking the form of an invasion or 'tsunami'. The advocates of segregation therefore often have a preference for a perverse strategy, with feelings of anxiety being fanned and the source of anxiety being exported and localised in the threatening body of the other. It is this very form that society is unable to address, constantly falling prey to disruption, with impotence being a dominant factor. That does not necessarily mean this would be the one and only – never mind the only current – social attitude available. The resistance against the general order and the pleasure in its disruption can also take other forms, as was demonstrated by J. Joyce en V. Nabokov and many other intriguing characters in this configuration.

There is yet another form of ordinary perversion. Here, the emphasis is not on social splitting but on maintaining the split and inner state of dividedness, leading to a 'split life'. This may be needed, but it can also be cultivated socially: not in the shape of pretending of the as-if-personality (as a form of psychosis), but in feigning that can be elevated to a true art form, such as in the extreme forms of irony, of never saying what you think, and in cultivating a world of semblance, with all the secrecy surrounding it. Films about the French upper classes often show fine examples of this current form of perversion, with all its associated villainy (compared to which the sexual variety of perversion looks almost tender). Obviously, this life attitude is not limited to high circles. On the contrary, in fact, it is part of the general social repertoire.

Psychopathy conceived as the personality disorder with strong narcissistic traits, has a different structure altogether, with the split relating to one's own grandeur *and* insignificance, as distinct worlds of experience. Also the artist, at least a particular type of artist, may carry some explicitly psychopathic traits. All must yield to build his own life's work, with the artist literally using his contacts,. Thomas Mann shows this in his novel *Doktor Faustus,* in which he outlines the life of composer Adrian Leverkühn, artist par excellence as well as his alter ego. The life motto of this composer, who fully devotes himself to his art, is therefore: 'Thou shalt not love'. This seals a devil's pact, enables greatness to be brought out. And yet this greatness is achieved by denying his own puniness, which is the essence of the devil's pact he seals. In that sense, all Faustic characters, bent on achieving their ambition at all cost, are likely to have psychopathic traits. This is probably true for Thomas Mann as well. Of course, it does nothing to detract from their greatness, and may even be a prerequisite. (At best, it may raise the question about the nature of the relationship between morality and great art or literature.)

The structure of psychopathy would then be as follows, and this is not about psychopathic traits that may be seen in great people, but we are talking about a full-blown psychopathy. Here, the weak point lies in the symbolisation of *time*, namely the representation of the future. Where in compulsion everything revolves around the future, the need to avert future danger, in psychopathy the future is actually denied: instead of the overrepresentation of compulsion we see underrepresentation. This makes that, from the perspective of grandeur, the future is imagined to be far too bright, resulting in crucial actions not being thought through and carried out in a thoughtless and impulsive manner – regardless of whether the outcome may be a crime or policy decisions. Here, the social component is evident whenever a robust performance is appreciated or sangfroid or a callous approach is required ('the psychopathic management style').

In borderline cases, finally, symbolisation of primary dependence on the *Other* fails, at least partly, in the figure of the partner. The partner is supposed to nourish the subject while threatening to suffocate him or her through 'surfeit', with proximity and intimacy becoming a real problem (as intimacy triggers fear of suffocation). The distance is controlled by an alternation of attraction and repulsion, where genuine tenderness becomes intolerable. A lasting relationship is possible, but it is this unstable form that provides stability. This pattern is also often seen in literature or film. Lars von Trier's oeuvre offers some good, though excessive examples, centred on the theme of addiction, in terms of being addicted to the Other. Also the borderline position with its specific relational form is easily recognisable in the public domain, particularly with the 'village idiot' characters, titillating and intriguing but also repelling and provoking emotions without ever engaging in bonding. This bond will only be established after their death, when they are no longer there to throw a spanner in the works.

Significance. The elaboration offered here is intended to support the concept of the psychic disorder as a result of a disruption, or more neutral, a modification of fundamental symbolisation (a type of disruption that, according to this symbol-theory, is also effective in the public domain). In doing so, it produces its ow norm concept. This norm is not external, in the sense of a burden experienced by the person involved or their social environment. Instead, the norm is internal and relates to symbolisation itself, with a particular variation being designated as deficient. With respect to the psychosis, even through sympathetic eyes, such a designation will be inevitable. It also has existential significance. From this perspective, a psychic disorder is not just a deficiency, but actually reflects core problems of existence, serving as a 'reminder': of the relationship unto one's own body and gender, until finiteness and temporality, and to the Other and his desire, which everyone will have to deal with. In that sense, the psychic disorder is partially of a different order than if it were caused by a deficit. It is a type of symbolisation in its own right, and is more or less intrinsically linked to a societal role. Thus, the existential signification stresses also the relevance of the symbol-theoretical perspective of this paragraph, and actually reflects its ambition: to explain the psychic disorder as a modification or a form of deficiency of the symbolic function, in all its various degrees. The psychic disorder, particularly the psychosis, demonstrates that the transformation of the real to an own body subject, to a world of space and time, and to the capacity to engage in relationships with other, with the Other, can in fact fail or occur in a variety of degrees. The validity of this tripartite structure cannot be assessed a priori, but its feasibility may increase based on application a posteriori. It thus offers both an explanation and support of the theory of the 'three domains' to which fundamental symbolisation refers: life, external reality and the primordial Other. Evidently, this concept of fundamental, radical symbolisation remains abstract and speculative – this is quite inevitable with such thought concepts. However, its potential applicability makes it less speculative and even concrete, with the application itself adding flesh to the theoretical bone structure.

4.7 One and the Same Theme?

In this chapter, the inquiry into representation, our core theme, has been discussed from three different perspectives. First of all, the validity of the concept itself was made concrete, in the context of a discussion of a criticism of medial thought. Secondly, attention shifted to the symbolic order, within which symbolisation occurs. Attention was devoted to the structure of a system of representation, potentially in three layers, which derives strongly from Cassirer: mythical, objectifying and formal. An explanation was offered based on language, politics and the law, emphasising that no guarantee for the validity or sustainability of any symbolic system can be provided. The same would be true for the political order and legal order. For example, representative democracy may not be an endpoint and final developmental stage, as was believed by Cassirer, and perhaps it is nothing more than an interlude in the carrousel. The normative component was also addressed (which is intrinsic to the notion of 'order'), as well as the issue of morality, considering both Cassirer's and Lacan's viewpoints. Thirdly, the issue of symbolisation in the sense of fundamental symbolisation of the real was discussed. Three domains of the real were highlighted in which fundamental symbolisation may fail or vary. Here, the order is not side-lined because a symbolisation always unfolds as part of it, even if the order's development is only in an elementary state. Psychopathology showed the possibility of failing or being modified, thus bringing out the degrees of fundamental symbolisation. Here, Lacan is the point of orientation, while the concept itself was developed by Cassirer. Thus, three aspects of the theme were elaborated: the concept of symbolisation itself, the symbolic order and fundamental symbolisation (in their mutual involvement). Far from being arbitrary, these elaborations represent the three core aspects of the theme. Each elaboration is a variation in which the theme is addressed integrally, although from changing perspectives. The essence of this theme, in a final repeat, is the symbolising capacity of man, based on which the real, the anonymous being, appears in a represented form, while also man himself is given through a range of representations: to see is to see as...', to be is to be as...'. This does not alter the fact that, despite the presence of an internal system, the elaborations offered are merely suggestions. As was said before, they are nothing more than mini-essays. Alternatives are possible and may be even close at hand, depending on where the emphasis is put. This relativity is part of the concept itself: an image of man, a model, is not a duplication of a concept, one on one. After all, an area can be highlighted in different ways, while also other areas than those discussed here may be given a symbol-theoretical elaboration, such as religion or art (Chapters 2 and 3 already offered a prelude to this), or education and pedagogy (which is eminently suited to this end). Thus, Cassirer's view of modern science can be revitalised in order to criticise the current 'big data vision' on science and to replace this inductive approach by a deductive approach, with the primacy of concept and theory, giving it prominence once again (in line with K.R. Popper's views). In the background the naturalism debate is played out ('man is his brain, his natural equipment, full stop'). The philosophies of Cassirer and Lacan, as well as the present symbol theory as a whole, oppose such views. This allows the fundamental theme of representation to be further refined, leading to an open project and, because of that, to a universal scope (at least in principle). This is given with the signature: the hermeneutical and Neo-Kantian context. This also introduces tension, as both take facts and a status quo in science and culture as a point of departure, while those facts are not universal but contingent. This tension has been mentioned before, but it would still be apposite to highlight this point once again, also in respect of Cassirer and Lacan, the two godfathers of the project, in order to further clarify its status.

Cassirer's universality is of a distinct type. After all, his point of departure was the factuality: the fact of language, of myth, of science, etcetera, and his ambition was to identify the invariant infrastructure of all these types of experience, of reality disclosure, by means of a categorical analysis of its variations. The universality he found was therefore not one of uniformity, of similarity, of being one, of an all-encompassing unity. Rather, he looked for a different type of unity: of an identity repeating itself in various ways, thus generating a unity in diversity. Heidegger (1978b, 9–13) coined the following terms to describe this terminological difference: 'das Gleiche' and 'das Selbe'. Cassirer's quest, however, is *not* for 'das Gleiche', what is identical to itself and wat makes the other identical to itself, but for 'das Selbe', for the same thing repeating itself in different ways. The unity, the universality expressed by the symbolic function is symbolic in itself. With one limitation, however: We repeatedly found that at the core of the strategy lies the process of modalisation of fundamental categories, leaving the assumed invariant basis of experience intact. Thus, process and conclusion are rooted in a semantic theory of experience, with experience contents being structured through meanings, concepts and categories (semantically therefore). The leitmotif is conceiving 'being' based on 'meaning': 'being *as* meaning'. This also offers a kind of guarantee of validity, a progression of insight and a sum of valid insight leading to the truth.

Lacan's contribution qualifies this outcome. Firstly, such a guarantee cannot be given, with the real showing itself merely in a random and fragmentary manner. Secondly, that which has not been symbolised fundamentally and thus falls outside the symbolic scope will sooner or later return in the form of an invasion of the real (in hallucinations and/or delusions). What cannot be processed as a result of temporary failure of the symbolic function will manifest itself as trauma or anxiety. The reason for this difference in conception is that Lacan does not take the unity of meaning as a point of departure, but rather meaningless terms, which can acquire meaning only in due course, and so this meaning will always be contextual and therefore undetermined. As a result, the real can never be consumed, a fish bone will always stick in the throat, it causes trauma. Secondly, the truth is partial, in a more radical way than with Cassirer. With Lacan, there is no such thing as 'growing insight' or progression. This point inexorably towards relativity, contingency and finiteness. Nonetheless, Lacan is a universalist. There is a universal law, the Law of Culture, which all and sundry must obey and which can be conceived as the start and principle of separation, of the human condition itself. Its substantiation may be either collective or highly private, but the principle itself is not. This type of existence is possible only when cut off from the immediacy of life – to which it will still remain connected (n the sense of the death wish). After all, the caesura was not made for all times in a kind of primeval time of a person's own life, but needs to be repeated constantly in various ways, by means of an empty signifier. This typifies Cassirer's core figure as well: the same ('das Selbe'), only repeated in historically and culturally different ways. The difference is that with Cassirer, 'being' is taken from meaning, and with Lacan from 'non-meaning': 'being as non-meaning', as the real, as a trauma as absence of meaning. This briefly sums up their difference as well what binds them through their mutual difference.

What binds them is the need to break away from immediacy: to speak is to break, and the resulting rift leads to the introduction of differences (at least of plus/minus, yes/no). And yet it is those very differences that make it possible to tolerate the contrasts within the other and within oneself rather than stop and worry about them, overcoming digitality (plus/minus, yes/no). This capacity enables us to engage in amazingly complex and differentiated relationships, which are never unequivocal and invariably require nuanced interpretation: She is saying this, but maybe she means that? In the latter case, the difference is accepted, ambivalence tolerated. It adequately sums up the hermeneutical approach: the capacity to which symbolisation leads and also lies embedded in it. This capacity needs to be acquired, but often turns out to be underdeveloped in the worlds of science and politics and in daily life. Which is inevitable, because in politics, science and in every day life people are expected to toe the line, which encourages uniformity, the digital quality of either/or. Initially, the Other will call the shots, and we are primarily in the grip of the Other and his language. Yet there is a way out, which is offered by the gaps left by discourse, any discourse. That is the orientation, not that of perspicacity but of nuance. It is a conception, which therefore has nothing more than the status of a conception, a symbolisation, and ultimately is merely a suggestion to conceive the relationship between man and reality *in this way*. This proposition provides the framework, the theme. Yet the ultimate test lies in its applicability and usefulness. They become apparent from the variations on the theme (which of course resonate in the outline of the theme itself). The theme must and can therefore be elaborated, deepened and refined in various ways. Thus, Lacan's and Cassirer philosophies may be used, processed productively, also for the interpretation of situations and development they did not or could not foresee.

Anyone who feels attracted to this type of philosophy, in line with Cassirer and Lacan, may choose to delve deeper, in their own individual way, drawing on their particular expertise or experience. Alternatively, one might choose to integrate this notion into their lives in order to establish if it helps or is conducive to understanding one's own life and place in society, in culture. In fact, that is what this effort is all about. After all, this is supposed to be nothing more than a proposition to see or conceive this relationship between man and reality in a particular way: the way of representation.

Bibliography

Adams, S. 2015. On Ricœur's shift from a hermeneutics of culture to a cultural hermeneutics. *Études Ricœuriennes/Ricœur Studies*, 6, 130–153.

American Psychiatric Association. 2013. *Diagnostic and Statistical Manuel of Mental Disorders. Fifth Edition*. Washington: American Psychiatric Association.

Anonymus. 1976. La raison avant Freud. Compte rendu de la *Philosophie des formes symboliques* de Cassirer. *Scilicet. Revue paraissant au Champ freudien*, collection dirigée par Jacques Lacan, no. 6/7, 295–325.

Assoun, P.-L. 2003. *Lacan*. Paris: Presses Universitaires de France.

Aubert, J. 2000. D'un Joyce à l'autre. In *Lacan, l'écrit, l'image*, École de la Cause freudienne, (Ed.), 55–77. Paris: Flammarion.

Augustinus, M.A. 2014. *Confessions*, Vol. I (C.J.-B. Hammond Trans. and Ed.). Cambridge (Mass): Harvard University Press.

Badiou, A. 2012. In *Jacques Lacan, passé présent – dialogue*, A. Badiou and E. Rodinesco (Eds.). Paris: Seuil.

Badiou, A. 2013. *Le Séminaire*: Lacan. L'antiphilosophie 3, 1994–1995. Paris: Fayard.

Balmès, F. 1999. *Ce que Lacan dit de l'être (1953–1960)*. Paris: Presses Universitaires de France.

Barash, J.F. (Ed). 2008. *The Symbolic Construction of Reality. The Legacy of Ernst Cassirer*. Chicago/Londen: Chicago University Press.

Barth, K. 2010. *Römerbrief*, C. van der Kooi and K. Tolstaja (Eds.). Zürich: Theologischer Verlag. (Original work published 1922, zweiter Auflage).

Bataille, G. 1986. *Erotism. Death and Sexuality* (M. Dalwood, Trans.). San Francisco: City Light Books. (Original work published 1957).

Benoist, J. 2011. *Éléments de philosophie réaliste*. Paris: Vrin.

Beirnaert, L. 1985. *Aux frontières de l'acte psychanalytique. La Bible, saint Ignace, Freud et Lacan*. Paris: Seuil.

Bernet, R. 1994. *La vie du sujet. Recherches sur l' interprétation de Husserl dans la phénoménologie*. Paris: Presses Universitaires de France.

Bernet, R. 2004. Husserl's transcendentalism revisited. *New Yearbook for Phenomenology and Phenomenological Philosophy 4*, 1–20.

Bickerton, D. 2014. *More than Nature Needs. Language, Mind and Evolution*. Cambridge (Mass.)/London: Harvard University Press.

Binswanger, L. 1957. *Schizophrenie*. Pfullingen: Neske.

Binswanger, L. 1960. *Melancholie und Manie. Phänomenologische Studien*. Pfullingen: Neske.

Blankenburg, W. 1971. *Der Verlust der natürlichen Selbstverständlichkeit. Ein Beitrag zur Psychopathologie symptomarmer Schizophrenien*. Stuttgart: Enke.

Boer, Th. de. 1978. *The Development of Husserl's Thought*. The Hague: Nijhoff. (Original work published 1966).

Bolk, L. 1918. *Hersenen en cultuur*. Amsterdam: Scheltema & Holkema.

Bourdieu, P. 1970. *Zur Soziologie der symbolischen Formen* (W. Fietkau, Trans.). Frankfurt a.M.: Suhrkamp.

Bouveresse, J. 1998. *Le philosophe et le réel*. Paris: Hachette.

Brandon, R.B. 2000. *Articulating Reasons. An Introduction to Inferentialism*. Cambridge (Mass.)/London: Harvard University Press.

Braun, H.-J., H. Holzhey and E.W. Ort (Eds.). 1988. *Über Ernst Cassirers Philosophie der symbolischen Formen*. Frankfurt a.M.: Suhrkamp.

Braunstein, N. 2013. Desire and jouissance in the teachings of Lacan. In *The Cambridge Companion to Lacan*, J.-M. Rabaté (Ed.), 102–115. Cambridge: Cambridge University Press.

Bremmers, C. 2000. *Overgankelijkheid. Heideggers ontwerp van een fundamentele ontologie en de kwestie van de ethiek*. Budel: Damon.

Bricmont, J. and A. Sokal. 1997. *Impostures intellectuelles*. Paris: Odile Jacob.

Bühler, K. 1934. *Sprachtheorie*: die Darstellungsfunktion der Sprache. Jena: Fischer.

Bultmann, R. 1964. *Glauben und Verstehen. Gesammelte Aufsätze*. Tübingen: Mohr. Teil I–IV.

Capeillères, F. 2003. „Geist“ und „Leben“: Au mitant de la métaphysique des XIXe et XXe sciècles. In *Ernst Cassirer. Geist und Leben*, F. Lartillot (Ed.), 235–259. Paris: Harmattan.

Casssirer, E. 1946. *Language and Myth* (S.K. Langer, Trans.). New York: Dover. (Original work published 1925).

Cassirer, E. 1955a. *The Philosophy of Symbolic Forms*, Volume 1: Language (R. Manheim. Trans). New Haven: Yale University Press. (Original work published 1923).

Cassirer, E. 1955b. *The Philosophy of Symbolic Forms*, Volume 2: Mythical Thought (R. Manheim, Trans). New Haven: Yale University Press. (Original work published 1925).

Cassirer, E. 1957. *The Philosophy of Symbolic Forms*, Volume 3: The Phenomenology of Knowledge (R. Manheim, Trans). New Haven: Yale University Press. (Original work published 1929).

Cassirer, E. 1972. *La Philosophie des Formes Symboliques*, Tomes 1–3 (J. Lacoste et al., Trans.), Paris: Du Minuit.

Cassirer, E. 1988 –. *Oeuvres*, F. Capeillères and H. Wisman (Eds.). Paris: Édition du Cerf.

Cassirer, E. 1995–2017. *Ernst Cassirer. Nachgelassene Manuskripte und Texte*, Chr. Moeckel (Ed.). Hamburg: Felix Meiner Verlag, Vol. 1–18.

Cassirer, E. 1996. *The Philosophy of Symbolic Forms*. Volume 4: The Metaphysics of Symbolic Forms, J.M. Krois & D.P. Verene (Eds.) and J.M. Krois, Trans. New Haven/London: Yale University Press.

Cassirer, E. et al. 1998. *Cassirer, Cohen, Natorp. l'École de Marburg* (F. Capeillères et al. Trans.). *Oeuvres,* F. Capeillères and H. Wisman (Eds.), volume XLVIII. Paris: Éditions du Cerf.

Casssirer, E. 1998–2008. *Gesammelte Werke,* B. Recki (Ed.). Hamburg: Felix Meiner Verlag; Darmstadt: Wissenschaftliche Buchgesellschaft, Vol. 1–25.

Cassirer, E. 1999. *Das Erkenntnisproblem in der Philosophie und Wissenschaft der neueren Zeit. Erster Band.* In *Gesammelte Werke: Hamburger Ausgabe,* B. Recki (Ed.), Volume 2. Darmstadt: Wissenschaftliche Buchgesellschaft. (Original work published 1905).

Cassirer, E. 2000a. *Substanzbegriff und Funktionsbegriff. Untersuchungen über die Grundfragen der Erkenntniskritik.* In *Gesammelte Werke: Hamburger Ausgabe,* B. Recki (Ed.), Volume 6. Darmstadt: Wissenschaftliche Buchgesellschaft. (Original work published 1910).

Cassirer, E. 2000b. *Das Erkenntnisproblem in der Philosophie und Wissenschaft der neueren Zeit. Vierter Band: Von Hegels Tod bis zur Gegenwart (1832–1932).* In *Gesammelte Werke: Hamburger Ausgabe,* B. Recki (Ed.). Volume 5, Darmstadt: Wissenschaftliche Buchgesellschaft. (Original work published 1950).

Cassirer, E. 2001. *Kants Leben und Lehre.* In *Gesammelte Werke: Hamburger Ausgabe,* B. Recki (Ed.), Volume 8. Darmstadt: Wissenschaftliche Buchgesellschaft. (Original work published 1918).

Cassirer, E. 2002a. *Philosophie der symbolischen Formen, Erster Teil: Die Sprache.* In *Gesammelte Werke: Hamburger Ausgabe,* B. Recki (Ed.), Volume 11. Darmstadt: Wissenschaftliche Buchgesellschaft. (Original work published 1923).

Cassirer, E. 2002b. *Philosophie der symbolischen Formen, Zweiter Teil: Das mythische Denken.* In *Gesammelte Werke: Hamburger Ausgabe,* B. Recki (Ed.), Volume 12, Darmstadt: Wissenschaftliche Buchgesellschaft. (Original work published 1925).

Cassirer, E. 2002c. *Philosophie der symbolischen Formen, Dritter Teil: Phänomenologie der Erkenntnis.* In *Gesammelte Werke: Hamburger Ausgabe,* B. Recki (Ed.), Volume 13. Darmstadt: Wissenschaftliche Buchgesellschaft. (Original work published 1929).

Cassirer, E. 2002d. *Idee und Gestalt. Goethe, Schiller, Hölderlin, Kleist.* In *Gesammelte Werke: Hamburger Ausgabe,* B. Recki (Ed.), Volume 9, 243–438. Darmstadt: Wissenschaftliche Buchgesellschaft. (Original work published 1921).

Cassirer, E. 2003a. Die Begriffsform im mythischen Denken. In *Gesammelte Werke: Hamburger Ausgabe,* B. Recki (Ed.), Volume 16, 3–74. Darmstadt: Wissenschaftliche Buchgesellschaft. (Original work published 1922).

Cassirer, E. 2003b. Der Begriff der symbolischen Form im Aufbau der Geisteswissenschaften. In *Gesammelte Werke: Hamburger Ausgabe,* B. Recki (Ed.), Volume 16. Darmstadt: Wissenschaftliche Buchgesellschaft, pp. 75–104. (Original work published 1923).

Cassirer, E. 2003c. Sprache und Mythos. Ein Beitrag zum Problem der Götternamen. In *Gesammelte Werke: Hamburger Ausgabe*, B. Recki (Ed.), Volume 16, 227–312. Darmstadt: Wissenschaftliche Buchgesellschaft. (Original work published 1925).

Cassirer, E. 2003d. Von Herman Cohens geistigen Erbe. In *Gesammelte Werke: Hamburger Ausgabe*, B. Recki (Ed.), Volume 16, 480–486. Darmstadt: Wissenschaftliche Buchgesellschaft. (Original work published 1926).

Cassirer, E. 2003e. *Philosophie der Aufklärung*, In *Gesammelte Werke: Hamburger Ausgabe*, B. Recki (Ed.), Volume 15, Darmstadt: Wissenschaftliche Buchgesellschaft. (Original work published 1932).

Cassirer, E. 2004a. Form und Technik. In *Gesammelte Werke: Hamburger Ausgabe*, B. Recki (Ed.), Volume 17, 139–183. Darmstadt: Wissenschaftliche Buchgesellschaft. (Original work published 1930).

Cassirer, E. 2004b. „Geist" und „Leben" in der Philosophie der Gegenwart. In *Gesammelte Werke: Hamburger Ausgabe*, B. Recki (Ed.), Volume 17, 185–207. Darmstadt: Wissenschaftliche Buchgesellschaft. (Original work published 1930).

Cassirer, E. 2005, *Vorlesungen und Studien zur Philosophischen Anthropologie*. In *Nachgelassene Manuskripte und Texte*, Chr. Möckel (Ed.), Volume 6. Hamburg: Felix Meiner Verlag.

Cassirer, E. 2006a. Zur Logik des Symbolbegriffs. In *Gesammelte Werke: Hamburger Ausgabe*, B. Recki (Ed.), Volume 22, 112–140. Darmstadt: Wissenschaftliche Buchgesellschaft. (Original work published 1938).

Cassirer, E. 2006b. *An Essay on Man: An Introduction to a Philosophy of Human Culture*. In *Gesammelte Werke: Hamburger Ausgabe*, B. Recki (Ed.), Volume 23. Darmstadt: Wissenschaftliche Buchgesellschaft. (Original work published 1944).

Cassirer, E. 2007a. *Zur Logik der Kulturwissenschaften. Fünf Studien*. In *Gesammelte Werke: Hamburger Ausgabe*, uitgegeven door B. Recki, Volume 24, 357–490. Darmstadt: Wissenschaftliche Buchgesellschaft. (Original work published 1942).

Casssirer, E. 2007b. The Concept of Group and the Theory of Perception. In *Gesammelte Werke: Hamburger Ausgabe*, B. Recki (Ed.), Volume 24, 209–250 Darmstadt: Wissenschaftliche Buchgesellschaft. (Original work published 1944).

Cassirer, E. 2007c. Structuralism in modern linguistics. In *Gesammelte Werke: Hamburger Ausgabe*, B. Recki (Ed.), Volume 24, 299–320. Darmstadt: Wissenschaftliche Buchgesellschaft. (Original work published 1945).

Cassirer, E. 2007d. Thomas Manns Goethe-Bild. Eine Studie über 'Lotte im Weimar'. In *Gesammelte Werke: Hamburger Ausgabe*, B. Recki (Ed.), Volume 24, 267–298. Darmstadt: Wissenschaftliche Buchgesellschaft. (Original work published 1945).

Cassirer, E. 2007e. *The Myth of the State*. In *Gesammelte Werke: Hamburger Ausgabe*, B. Recki (Ed.), Volume 25, Darmstadt: Wissenschaftliche Buchgesellschaft. (Original work published 1946).

Cassirer, E. 2014. *Davoser Vorträge. Vorträge über Hermann Cohen. Nachgelassene Manuskripte und Texte*, C. Möckel, (Ed.), Volume 17. Hamburg: Felix Meiner Verlag.

Cassirer, E. 2015. *Substance and Function, and Einstein's Theory of Relativity*. (W.C. & M.C. Swabey, Trans.) London: FB7c Lmt. (Original works published 1910 and 1921).

Cassirer, T. 2003. *Mein Leben mit Ernst Cassirer*. Hamburg: Meiner Verlag. (Original work published 1981).

Chomsky, N. 1965. *Aspects of the Theory of Syntax*. Cambridge (MA): MIT Press.

Clavreul, J. 1978. *L'orde médical*. Paris: Seuil.

Cohen, H. 1917. *Kommentar zu Immanuel Kants Kritik der reinen Vernunft*. Leipzig: Meiner, zweite Auflage.

Cohen, H. 1987. *Kant's Theorie der Erfahrung*. In *Werke*, H. Holzhey (Ed.), Volume 1/1–3. Hildesheim: Olms. (Original work published 1871).

Corbey, R. 2005. *The Metaphysics of Apes. Negotiating the Animal-Human Boundary*. Cambridge: Cambridge University Press.

Danto, A.C. 2013. *What art is?* New Haven/London: Yale University Press.

Deacon, T.W. 1997. *The Symbolic Species. The Co-evolution of Language and the Brain*. London/New York: Norton & Company.

Deleuze, G. and F. Guattari. 1972. *L'Anti-Oedipe. Capitalisme et schizophrénie*. Paris: Minuit.

Deleuze, G. 1998. *Difference and repetition* (P. Patton, Trans.). London: Athlone Press (Original work published 1967).

Dennett, D.C. 1996. *Kinds of Minds. Towards an Understanding of Consciousness*. New York: Basic Books.

Derrida, J. 1972. *Marges de la philosophie*. Paris: Minuit.

Dilthey, W. 1961. *Der Aufbau der geschichtlichen Welt in den Geisteswissenschaften*. In *Die Philosophie des Lebens. Eine Auswahl aus seinen Schriften*, H. Nohl (Ed.), 230–339. Stuttgart/Göttingen: Teubner/Vandenhoeck & Ruprecht. (Original work published 1910).

Dretske, F. 1995. *Naturalizing the Mind*. Cambridge (Mass.): MIT Press.

Dreyfus, H. 1991. *Being-in-the-World. A Commentary on Heidegger's Being and Time. Divison 1*. Cambridge (Mass.): MIT Press.

Dreyfus, H. 2002. Intelligence without representation – Merleau-Ponty's critique of mental representation. *Phenomenology and the Cognitive Sciences* 1, 367–383.

Duportail, G.-F. 2008. *Les institutions du monde de la vie*. Grenoble: Millon.

Durkheim, E. 1947. *Les règles de la méthode sociologique*. Paris. (Work original published 1895).

Endres, T., P. Favuzzi, T. Klattenhoff (Eds.), 2016. *Philosophie der Kultur- und Wissensformen. Ernst Cassirer neu lesen*. Frankfurt a.M.: Peter Lang.

Eggers, D. 2013. *The Circle*. New York: Random House.

Ferrari, M. 2003. *Ernst Cassirer. Stadien einer philosophischen Biographie*. Hamburg: Felix Meiner Verlag.

Feron, O. 2009. Mein Leib als „Integral der Erfahrung". Das vorprädikative bei Merleau-Ponty und das Ausdrucksphänomen bei Cassirer. *Zeitschrift f. Kulturphilosophie, 3*, Heft 2, 231–240.

Fink, B. 1995. *The Lacanian Subject. Between Language and Jouissance*. Princeton (NJ): Princeton University Press.

Foucault, M. 1966. Une histoire restée muette. *La quinzaine littéraire* 8, 3–4.

Foucault, M. 1970. *The Order of Things. An Archeology of the Human Sciences*. New York: Random House. (Original work published 1966).

Frank, M. 1974. *Der unendliche Mangel am Sein*. München: Fink Verlag.

Frank, M. 1997. *The Subject and the Text: Essays on Literary Theory and Philosophy*, A. Bowie (Ed.), 97–122: The "true subject" and its double: Jacques Lacan's hermeneutics. Cambridge: Cambridge University Press. (Work original published 1980).

Frank, M. 2002. *Selbstgefühl. Eine Historische-systematische Einleitung*. Frankfurt a.M.: Suhrkamp.

Frank, M. 2010. „Der schwere Schritt in die Wirklichkeit". Über das Werden eines Frühromantischen Realismus, *Athenaeum, 17*, 13–31.

Freud, S. 1957. Repression. In: *The Standard Edition of the Complete Psychological Works of Sigmund Freud*, J. Strachey (Ed.), Volume 14, 141, 146–158. London: The Hogarth Press & The Institute of Psycho-Analysis. (Original work published 1915).

Freud, S. 1955a. Beyond the pleasure principle. In: *The Standard Edition of the Complete Psychological Works of Sigmund Freud*, J. Strachey (Ed.), Volume 18, 1, 7–64. London: The Hogarth Press & The Institute of Psycho-Analysis. (Original work published 1920).

Freud, S. 1955b. Group psychology and the analysis of the ego. In *The Standard Edition of the Complete Psychological Works of Sigmund Freud*, J. Strachey (Ed.), Volume 18, 69–143. London: The Hogarth Press & The Institute of Psycho-Analysis. (Original work published 1921).

Freud, S. 1955c. 'A child is being beaten'. In *The Standard Edition of the Complete Psychological Works of Sigmund Freud*, J. Strachey (Ed.), Volume 17, 179–204. London: The Hogarth Press & The Institute of Psycho-Analysis. (Original work published 1921).

Freud, S. 1959. Inhibition, symptom and anxiety. In *The Standard Edition of the Complete Psychological Works of Sigmund Freud*, J. Strachey (Ed.), Volume 20, 87–174. London: The Hogarth Press & The Institute of Psycho-Analysis. (Original work published 1926).

Freud, S. 1961. Negation. In *The Standard Edition of the Complete Psychological Works of Sigmund Freud*, J. Strachey (Ed.), Volume 19, 235–239. London: The Hogarth Press & The Institute of Psycho-Analysis. (Original work published 1925).

Freund, G. 1985. *Three Days with Joyce*. New York: Persea Books.

Friedman, J.T. and S. Luft (Eds.). 2015. *The Philosophy of Ernst Cassirer. A Novel Assessment*, Berlin/Boston: De Gruyter.

Friedman, M. 2000. *Carnap, Cassirer, and Heidegger. A Parting of the Ways.* Chicago (Ill.): Open Court.

Gadamer, H.-G. 1985. *Truth and Method* (G. Barden and J. Cumming Trans.). New York: Cross Road. (Original work published 1965, 2th edition).

Gallagher, S. 2005. *How the Body Shapes the Mind.* Oxford: Clarendon Press.

Gauchet, M. 2005. *La condition politique.* Paris: Gallimard.

Gee, H. 2013. *The Accidental Species. Misunderstandings of Human Evolution.* Chicago: University of Chicago Press.

Gehlen, A. 1966. *Der Mensch. Seine Natur und Stellung in der Welt.* Frankfurt a.M./Bonn: Athenaeum Verlag. (Original work published 1940).

Girard, R. 1982. *Le bouc émissaire.* Paris: Grasset.

Goldstein, K. 1934. *Der Aufbau des Organismus. Einführung in die Biologie unter besonderer Berücksichtigung der Erfahrungen am kranken Menschen.* The Hague: Nijhoff.

Goldstein, K. 1964. Methodological Approach to the Study of Schizophrenic Thought Disorder. In *Language and Thought in Schizophrenia,* J.S. Kasanin (Ed.), 17–40. New York: Norton. (Original work published 1944).

Goodman, N. 1978. *Ways of Worldmaking.* Indianapolis: Hackett.

Gordon, P.E. 2010. *Continental Divide. Heidegger, Cassirer, Davos.* Cambridge (Mass.)/ London: Harvard University Press.

Göller, Th. 1988. Zur Frage nach der Auszeichnung der Sprache in Cassirers *Philosophie der symbolischen Formen.* In *Über Ernst Cassirers Philosophie der symbolischen Formen,* H.-J. Braun, H. Holzhey and E.W. Orth (Eds.), 137–155. Frankfurt a.M.: Suhrkamp.

Grondin, J. 2003. *Le tournant herméneutique de la phénoménologie.* Paris: Presses Universitaires de France.

Handwerk, G.J. 1985. *Irony and Ethics in Narrative. From Schlegel to Lacan.* New Haven/ London: Yale University Press.

Heidegger, M. 1962. *Being and Time* (J. Macquarrie and E. Robinson, Trans.). London/ New York: Harper and Raw. (Original work published 1927).

Heidegger, M. 1928. Ernst Cassirers Philosophie der symbolischen Formen: 2. Teil: Das mythische Denken. *Deutsche Literaturzeitung*, 21, 1000–1012.

Heidegger, M. 1973. *Kant und das Problem der Metaphysik*, 246–268: Davoser Disputation zwischen Ernst Cassirer und Martin Heidegger. Frankfurt a.M: Vittorio Klostermann. (Original work published 1929).

Heidegger, M. 1978a. *Vorträge und Aufsätze.* Pfullingen: Neske. (Original work published 1954).

Heidegger, M. 1978b. *Identität und Differenz.* Pfullingen: Neske. (Original work published 1957).

Hegel, G.W.F. 1979. *Phenomenology of the Spirit* (A.V. Miller, Trans.). Oxford: Clarendon Press. (Original work published 1807).

Hegel, G.W.F. 1991. *Elements of the Philosophy of Right*, A.W. Wood (Ed.). Cambridge: Cambridge University Press. (Original work published 1820).

Henrich, D. 1994. *Aesthetic Judgement and the Moral Image of the World. Studies in Kant.* Stanford: Stanford University Press.

Hobbes, Th. 1996. *Leviathan* (J.C.A. Gaskin, Ed.). Oxford: Oxford University Press. (Original work published 1651).

Hockett, Ch. F. 1960. The Origin of Speech. In *Scientific American*, issue 203, 88–96.

Hombert, J.M. and G. Lenclud. 2014. *Comment le langage est venu à l'homme*. Paris: Fayard.

Husserl, E. 1966. *Analysen zur passiven Synthesis*. The Hague: Nijhoff.

Husserl, E. 1970. *The Crisis of the Human Sciences and Transcendental Phenomenology* (D. Carr, Trans.). Evanston: North Western University Press (Original work published 1953).

Husserl, E. 1983. *Ideas Pertaining to a Pure Phenomenology and a Phenomenological Philosophy,* Book I: General introduction to a Pure Phenomenology (F. Kersten, Trans.). The Hague: Nijhoff. (Original work published 1913).

Husserl, E. 1989. *Ideas Pertaining to a Pure Phenomenology,* Book 2: Studies in the Phenomenology of Constitution (R. Rojcewicz and A. Schuwer, Trans.). Dordrecht: Kluwer. (Original work published 1952).

Jackson, J.W. and P. Costello. 1998. *John Stanislaus Joyce: The Voluminous Life and Genius of James Joyce's Father*. New York: St Martin's Press.

Janz, N. 2001. *Globus symbolicus. Ernst Cassirer: Un épistémologue de la troisième voie.* Paris: Editions Kimé.

Jaspers, K. 1997. *General Psychopathology,* Volume I and II (J. Hoenig and M. Hailton, Trans.). Baltimore/London: Johns Hopkins University Press. (Original work published 1913; translation of the extended seventh edition 1959).

Jong, F. de. 2016. *Symbolic and diabolic forces in criminal law*. The Hague: Boom juridisch.

Joyce, J. 1969. *Stephen Hero*. London: Jonathan Cape. (Original work published 1944).

Joyce, J. 1992. *A Portrait of the Artist as a Young Man*. Ware: Wordsworth. (Original work published 1916).

Joyce, J. 2000. *Dubliners*. London: Penguin Books (Original work published 1914).

Joyce, J. 2010. *Ulysses*. Ware: Wordsworth. (Original work published 1922).

Joyce, J. 2012. *Finnegans Wake*. Ware: Wordsworth. (Original work published 1939).

Juranville, A. 1984. *Lacan et la philosophie*. Paris: Presses Universitaires de France.

Kahneman, D. 2012. *Thinking, Fast and Slow*. London: Penguin Books.

Kant, I. 1965. *Critique of Pure Reason* (N. Kemp Smith, Trans.). New York: St Martin's Press. (Original work published 1781/87).

Kantorowitcz, E.H. 1957. *The King's Two Bodies. A Study in Mediaeval Political Theology.* Princeton (NJ): Princeton University Press.

Katz, D. 1961. *Gestaltpsychologie*. Bazel/Stuttgart: Schwabe&Co. (Original work published 1944).

Klein, M., P. Heimann and R. Money-Kyrle (Eds.). 1955. *New Directions in Psychoanalysis*. London: Tavistock Publications.

Köhler, W. 1992. *Gestalt-psychology. An introduction to new concepts in psychology*. New York: Norton. (Original work published 1944).

Kojève, A. 1979. *Introduction à la lecture de Hegel*. Paris: Gallimard. (Original work published 1947).

Kremer-Marietti, A. 2003. Le problème de la symbolisation chez Cassirer. In *Ernst Cassirer. Geist und Leben*, F. Lartillot (Ed.), 115–131. Paris: Harmattan.

Kreis, G. 2010. *Ernst Cassirer und die Formen des Geistes*. Frankfurt a.M.: Suhrkamp.

Krois, J.M. 1987. *Cassirer. Symbolic Forms and History*. New Haven/London: Yale University Press.

Krois, J.M. 2004. Ernst Cassirer's philosophy of biology. *Sign Systems Studies, 32* (1/2), 277–295.

Krois, J.M. and D.P. Verene. 1996. Introduction. In *The Philosophy of Symbolic Forms*. Volume 4: The Metaphysics of Symbolic Forms (J.M. Krois & D.P. Verene, Eds), ix–xxvi. New Haven/London: Yale University Press.

Kuckenburg, M. 2016. *Wer sprach das erste Wort? Die Entstehung der Sprache und Schrift*. Darmstadt: Theiss Verlag.

Kusters, W. 2014. *Filosofie van de waanzin. Fundamentele en grensoverschrijdende inzichten*. Rotterdam: Lemniscaat.

Kuypers, K. 1972. *Kants Kunsttheorie und die Einheit der Kritik der Urteilskraft*. Amsterdam/London: North-Holland Publishing Company.

Lacan, J. 1961–1962. *Le Séminaire de Jacques Lacan*. Livre IX: Identification. Unedited: Staferla.

Lacan, J. 1964–1965. *Le Séminaire de Jacques Lacan*. Livre XII: Problèmes cruciaux pour la psychanalyse. Unedited: Staferla.

Lacan, J. 1966. *Écrits*. Paris: Seuil.

Lacan, J. 1972. Of structure as an inmixing of otherness prerequisite to any subject whatever. In *The Structuralist Controversy. The Languages of Criticism and the Sciences of Man*, R. Macksey and E. Donato (Eds.), 186–201. Baltimore/London: John Hopkins University Press.

Lacan, J. 1973. *Télévision*. Paris: Seuil.

Lacan, J. 1973–1974. *Le Séminaire de Jacques Lacan*, Livre XXI: Les non-dupes errent. Unedited: Staferla.

Lacan, J. 1974–1975. *Le Séminaire de Jacques Lacan*, Livre XXII: R.S.I. Unedited: Staferla.

Lacan, J. 1975. *Le Séminaire de Jacques Lacan*, J.-A. Miller (Ed.), Livre XX: Encore, 1972–1973. Paris: Seuil.

Lacan, J. 1976–1977. *Le Séminaire de Jacques Lacan*, Livre XXVI: L'insu que sait de l'une bévue s'aile à mourre. Unedited: Staferla.

Lacan, J. 1978. *Le Séminaire de Jacques Lacan*, J.-A. Miller (Ed.), Livre II: Le moi dans la théorie de Freud et dans la technique de la psychanalyse, 1954–1955. Paris: Seuil.

Lacan, J. 1981. *Le Séminaire de Jacques Lacan*, J.-A. Miller (Ed.), Livre III: Les psychoses, 1955–1956. Paris: Seuil.

Lacan, J. 1986. *The seminar of Jacques Lacan*, J.-A. Miller (Ed.), Book XI: The four fundamental concepts of psychoanalysis,1964 (A. Sheridan, Trans). Harmondsworth: Penguin Books (Original work published 1973).

Lacan, J. 1991a. *Le Séminaire de Jacques Lacan*, J.-A. Miller (Ed.), Livre VIII: Le transfert, 1960–1961. Paris: Seuil.

Lacan, J. 1991b. *Le Séminaire de Jacques Lacan*, J.-A. Miller (Ed.), Livre XVII: L'envers de la psychanalyse, 1969–1970. Paris: Seuil.

Lacan, J. 1992. *The seminar of Jacques Lacan*, J.-A. Miller (Ed.), Book VII: The ethics of psychoanalysis, 1959–1960 (D. Porter, Trans.). New York: Norton. (Original work published 1986).

Lacan, J. 1998. *Le Séminaire de Jacques Lacan*, J.-A. Miller (Ed.), Livre V: Les formations de l'inconscient, 1957–1958. Paris: Seuil.

Lacan, J. 2001. *Autres écrits*. Paris: Seuil.

Lacan, J. 2002. *Écrits. The First Complete Translation in English* (B. Fink, Trans.). New York/London: Norton. (Original work published 1966).

Lacan, J. 2004. *Le Séminaire de Jacques Lacan*, J.-A. Miller (Ed.), Livre X: L'Angoisse, 1962–1963. Paris: Seuil.

Lacan, J. 2005. *Le Séminaire de Jacques Lacan*, J.-A. Miller (Ed.), Livre XXIII Le sinthome, 1975–1976. Paris: Seuil.

Lacan, J. 2006. *Le Séminaire de Jacques Lacan*, J.-A. Miller (Ed.), Livre XVI D'un Autre à l' autre, 1968–1969. Paris: Seuil.

Lacan, J. 2011. *Le Séminaire de Jacques Lacan*, J.-A. Miller (Ed.), Livre XIX: … Ou pire, 1971–1972. Paris: Seuil.

Lacan, J. 2013. *Le Séminaire de Jacques Lacan*, J.-A. Miller (Ed.), Livre VI: Le désir et son interprétation, 1958–1959. Paris: Éditions de la Martinière.

Lacan, J. 2014. *Le Séminaire de Jacques Lacan*, J.-A. Miller (Ed.), Book X: Anxiety, 1962–1963 (A.R. Price, Trans.). Cambridge: Polity Press. (Original work published 2004).

Lacan, M.-F. 2010. *Dieu n'est pas un assureur*. Paris: Albin-Michel.

Lapanche, J. and J.-B. Pontalis. 1985. *Fantasme originaire. Fantasmes des origines. Origine du fantasme*. Paris: Hachette.

Le Brun, J. 2002. *Le pur amour. De Platon à Lacan*. Paris: Seuil.

Leclaire, S. 1991. *Rompre les charmes. Recueil pour les enchantés de la psychanalyse*. Paris: Seuil. (Original work published 1981).

LeDoux, L. 2006. *The Emotional Brain*. New York: Touchstone Books.

Lefort, C. 1989. *Democracy and Political Theory*. Cambridge (Mass.): MIT Press.

Le Gaufey, G. 2009. *C'est à quel sujet*. Paris: Epel.

Leguil, Cl. 2012. *Sartre avec Lacan. Corrélation antinomique, liaison dangereuse*. Paris: Navarin.

Lenk, H. 1993. *Interpretationskonstrukte. Zur Kritik der interpretatorischen Vernunft*. Frankfurt a.M: Suhrkamp.

Lévi-Strauss, Cl. (1958). *Anthropologie structurale*. Paris: Plon.

Levinas, E. 1969. *Totality and Infinity. An Essay on Exteriority* (A. Lingis, Trans.). Pittsburg: Dequesne University Press. (Work original published 1961).

Litt, Th. 1926. *Individuum und Gemeinschaft. Grundlegung der Kulturphilosophie*. Berlin/Leipzig: Teubner. (Original work published 1919).

Litt, Th. 1961. *Mensch und Welt. Grundlinien einer Philosophie des Geistes*. Heidelberg: Quelle&Meyer. (Original work published 1948).

Lofts, S.G. 2000. *Ernst Cassirer. A "Repetion" of Modernity*. Albany: State University of New York Press.

Luft, S. 2011. *Subjectivity and Lifeworld in Transcendental Phenomenology*. Evanston (Ill.): Northwestern University Press.

Luft, S. 2015a. *The Space of Reason. Towards a Neo-Kantian Philosophy of Culture* (*Cohen, Natorp, Cassirer*). Oxford: Oxford University Press.

Luft, S. 2015b. The apriori of culture: the philosophy of culture between rationalism and relativism. The example of Lévi-Strauss' *Structural anthropology*. In *The Philosophy of Ernst Cassirer. A Novel Assessment*, J.T. Friedman and S. Luft (Eds.), 381–400. Berlin/Boston: De Gruyter.

Makkreel, R.A. and S. Luft (Eds.). 2009. *Neo-Kantianism in Contemporary Philosophy*. Bloomington: Indiana University Press.

Mann, Th. 1997. *Doctor Faustus* (J.E. Woods, Trans.). New York: Alfred Knopf. (Original work published 1947).

Mann, Th. 2005. *Joseph and His Brothers* (J.E. Woods, Trans.). New York: Alfreds Knopf. (Original work published 1933–1943).

Mauss, M. 1954. *The Gift. Forms and Functions of Exchange in Archaic Societies* (I. Cunnison, Trans.). Glencoe (Ill.): Free Press. (Original work published 1923).

Merleau-Ponty, M. 1962. *Phenomenology of Perception* (C. Smith, Trans.). London: Routledge and Kegan Paul. (Original work published 1945).

Merleau-Ponty, M. 1964. *L'Oeil et l'Esprit*. Paris: Gallimard.

Merleau-Ponty, M. (2001). *Le visible et l'invisble*. Paris: Gallimard. (Original work published 1964).

Meyer, Th. 2006. *Ernst Cassirer*. Hamburg: Ellert & Richter Verlag.

Miller, J.-A. 1999. Les six paradigmes de la jouissance. *La Cause Freudienne. Nouvelle revue de la psychanalyse*. no. 43, 7–29.

Miller, J.-A. 2005. Notice de fil en aiguille. In *Le Séminaire de Jacques Lacan. Livre XXIII. Le sinthome*, 1975–1976, J.A. Miller (Ed.), 189–247. Paris: Seuil.

Miller, J.-A. 2011. L'être et l'un. *Orientation Lacanienne III, 13*, cours n° 12, 8.

Miller, J.-A. 2014. Un réel pour le XXIe siècle. In Association Mondiale De Psychanalyse, *Un réel pour le XXIe siècle*. Paris: Navarin.

Milner, J.-C. 1995. *L'Oeuvre clair. Lacan, la science, la philosophie*. Paris: Seuil.

Millot, C. 2001. *Abîmes ordinaires*. Paris: Gallimard.

Möckel, C. 2004a. *Das Urphänomen des Lebens. Ernst Cassirers Lebensbegriff*. Hamburg: Meiner Verlag.

Möckel, C. 2004b. Hegels "Phänomenologie des Geistes" als Vorbild für Cassirer's Philosophie der symbolischen Formen. In *Hegels "Phänomenologie des Geistes" heute*, A. Arndt and E. Müller (Eds.), 256–275. Deutsches Zeitschrift für Philosophie, Reihe Sonderband, Band 8. Berlin: Akademie Verlag.

Möckel, C. 2009. Kulturelle Existenz und Anthropologische Konstanten. Zur philosophischen Anthropologie Ernst Cassirer's. *Zeitschrift f. Kulturphilosophie, 3*, Heft 2, 209–220.

Möckel, C. 2013. 'Philosophie der symbolischen Structuren'? Zu einigen Parallelen bei Ernst Cassirer und Claude Lévi-Strauss. *Logos & Episteme* IV, 2, 245–267.

Möckel, Ch. 2014. Ernst Cassirer und die Phänomenologie Husserls. Inhaltliche Bezugspunkte, Kulturverständnis und Eigenheiten. *Journal Phänomenologie*, Heft 42, 37–51.

Mooij, A. 1991. *Psychoanalysis and the Concept of a Rule. An Essay in the Philosophy of Psychoanalysis* (S. Firth, Trans). Berlin/New York/London: Springer Verlag.

Mooij, A. 2001. *Taal en verlangen. Lacans theorie van de psychoanalyse*. Amsterdam: Boom. (Original work published 1975).

Mooij, A. 2008. Deux rencontres avec Lacan. *La cause freudienne. Nouvelle revue de la psychanalyse*. no. 69, 200–204.

Mooij, A. 2010. *Intentionality, Desire, Responsibility. A Study in Phenomenology, Psychoanalysis and Law* (P. van Nieuwkoop, Trans.). Leiden/Boston: Brill. (Studies in Contemporary Phenomenology Vol. 5).

Mooij, A. 2012. *Psychiatry as a Human Science. Phenomenological, Hermeneutical and Lacanian Perspectives* (P. van Nieuwkoop, Trans). Amsterdam/New York: Rodopi Editions (Contemporary Psychoanalytic Studies Vol. 18).

Mooij, A. 2018. Psychosis as the Failure of Symbolisation. In *Eidos, A Journal for Philosophy of Culture*, 2/4 (July 2018), 5–14. DOI: 10.26319/4712.

Morel, G. 2008. *La loi de la mère. Essai sur le sinthome sexuel*. Paris: Economica& Anthropos.

Mul, J. de. 2004. *The Tragedy of Finitude. Dilthey's Hermeneutics of Life*. New Haven/ London: Yale University Press.

Mul, J. de. 2010. *Cyberspace Odyssey*. Newcastle: Cambridge Scholars.

Mul, J. de. 2013. Understanding nature. Dilthey, Plesnner and biohermeneutics. In *Dilthey, Anthropologie und Geschichte*, G. D'Anna, H. Johach and E.S. Nelson (Eds.), 459–478. Würzburg: Königshausen und Neumann.

Nasio, J.-D. 1987. *Les yeux de Laure. Le concept de l'objet* a *dans la théorie de J. Lacan*. Paris: Aubier.

Nasio, J.-D. 1992. *Cinq leçons sur la théorie de Jacques Lacan*. Paris: Rivages.

Natorp, P. 2013. *Allgemeine Psychologie nach kritischer Methode*, S. Luft (Ed.). Darmstadt: Wissenschaftliche Buchgesellschaft. (Original work published 1912).

Orth, E.W. 2004. *Von der Erkenntnistheorie zur Kulturphilosophie. Studien zu Ernst Cassirers Philosophie der symbolische Formen*. Würzburg: Königshausen & Neumann.

Orth, E.W. 2008. Ernst Bloch und Ernst Cassirer. Die Kultur als dynamischer Bedeutungsraum des Menschen. *Zeitschrift zur Kulturphilosophie* 2/1, 97–106.

Otto, R. 1929. *Das Heilige*. Gotha: Gotz Verlag. (Original work published 1917).

Paetzold, H. 1994. *Die Realität der symbolischen Formen. Die Kulturphilosophie Ernst Cassirers im Kontext*. Darmstadt: Wissenschaftliche Buchgesellschaft.

Philonenko, A. 1989. *L'École de Marbourg. Cohen-Natorp-Cassirer*. Paris: Vrin.

Plesnner, H. 1975. *Die Stufen des Organischen und der Mensch*. Berlin/New York: Walter de Gruyter. (Original work published 1928).

Porge, E. 2000. *Jacques Lacan. Parcours d'un enseignement*. Ramonville: Érès.

Praz, M. 1970. *Romantic Agony* (A. Davidson, Trans.). London/New York: Oxford University Press. (Original work published 1933).

Rabaté, J.-M. 2003. *The Cambridge Companion to Lacan*, J.-M. Rabaté (Ed.). Cambridge: Cambridge University Press.

Recki, B. 2013. *Cassirer*. Stuttgart: Reclam.

Renz, U. 2011. Von Marburg nach Pittsburg: Philosophie als Transcendentalphilosophie. *Deutsche Zeitschrift für Philosophie*, 59, 249–270.

Rickert, H. 1921. *Die Grenzen der naturwissenschaftlichen Begiffsbildung. Eine logische Einleitung in die historischen Wissenschaften*. Tübingen: Mohr. (Original work published 1901).

Ricœur, P. 1978. *The Rule of Metaphor. The creating of meaning in language* (R. Czerny, Trans.). London/New York: Routledge and Kegan Paul. (Original work published 1975).

Ricœur, P. 2001. *Hermeneutics and the Human Sciences*, J.B. Thompson (Ed. and Trans.). Paris: Éditions de la Maison des Sciences de l'Homme/Cambridge: Cambridge University Press. (Original work published 1981).

Ricœur, P. 1985. *Time and Narrative*. Volume 2: The Configuration of Time in Fictional Narrative (K. McLaughin and D. Pellauer, Trans.). Chicago/London: Chicago University Press.

Roebroeks, W. 2000. *Food for thought. Naar aanleiding van het menu van de Neandertaler*. Leiden: Leiden Univsersity Press.

Russell, B. 1905. On denoting. *Mind*, 14, 479–493.

Safouan, M. 1988. *Le transfert et le désir de l'analyste*. Paris: Seuil.

Safouan, M. 2013. *La psychanalyse. Science, thérapie – et cause*. Paris: Thierry Marchaisse.

Sartre, J.-P. 1966. *Being and Nothingness. An Essay in Phenomenological Ontology*. New York: Washington Square Press. (Original work published 1943).

Sass, L.A. 1992. *Madness and Modernism. Insanity in the Light of Modern Art, Literature, and Thought*. Cambridge, MA/London: Harvard University Press.

Sass, L.A. and J. Parnas. 2007. Explaining schizophrenia: the relevance of phenomenology. In *Receiving schizophrenia*, M.C. Chung, K.W.M. Fulford, G. Graham (Eds.), 63–97. Oxford: Oxford University Press.

Saussure, F. de. 1986. *Course in General linguistics* (R. Harris, Trans.). Chicago: Open Court. (Original work published 1916).

Schilder, P. 1935. *The Image and Appearence of the Human Body*. New York: International Universities Press.

Schilpp, P.A. (Ed.). 1949. *The Philosophy of Ernst Cassirer*. Evanston, Ill.: The Library of Living Philosophers Inc.

Schilpp, P.A. (Ed.). 1966. *Ernst Cassirer* (W. Krampf, Trans). Stuttgart: Kohlhammer Verlag. (Original work published 1949).

Schmidinger, H. 2007. Der Mensch als *animal symbolicum*. In *Der Mensch – ein » animal symbolicum «?*, H. Schmidinger and Cl. Sedmak (Eds.), 9–22. Darmstadt: Wissenschaftliche Buchgesellschaft.

Schwemmer, O. 1997a. *Ernst Cassirer. Ein Philosoph der europäischen Moderne*. Berlin: Akademie Verlag.

Schwemmer, O. 1997b. *Die kulturelle Existenz des Menschen*. Berlin: Akademie Verlag.

Seidengart, J. 2013. Configuration symbolique et réalité physique: objectivité ou objectivation de l'esprit chez Cassirer? In *Sciences et philosophie de la cultures chez Ernst Cassirer*, J. Seidengart (Ed.), 93–111. Paris: L' art du comprendre. (Original work published 1995).

Sellars, W. 1997. *Empiricism and the Philosophy of Mind.* Cambridge (MA): Harvard University Press. (Original published work 1956).

Simmel, G. 2011. *The Philosophy of the Money* (D. Frisby, Trans. and Ed.). London/New York: Routledge Classics. (Original work published 1900).

Skidelski, E. 2008. *Ernst Cassirer. The Last Philosopher of Culture*. Princeton/Oxford: Princeton University Press.

Soler, C. 2011. *Les affects lacaniens*. Paris: Presses Universitaires de France.

Soler, C. 2015. *Lacan, lecteur de Joyce*. Paris: Presses Universitaires de France.

Straus, E. 1935. *Vom Sinn der Sinne. Ein Beitrag zur Grundlegung der Psychologie*. Berlin: Springer.

Strawson, P.F. 1959. *Individuals. An Essay in Descriptive Metaphysics*. London: Methuen.

Strawson, P.F. 1974. *Freedom and Resentment and Other Essays*. London: Methuen.

Tatossian, A. 1997. *Phénoménologie des psychoses*. Paris: L'Art du comprendre. (Original work published 1979).

Theunissen, M. 1991. Melancholisches Leiden unter der Herrschaft der Zeit. In *Negative Theologie der Zeit*, M. Theunissen, 218–285. Frankfurt a.M.: Suhrkamp.

Truwant, S. 2015. Cassirer's functional conception of the human being. *Idealistic Studies* 45, (2), 169–189.

Uexküll, J. von. 1909. *Umwelt und Innenwelt der Tiere*. Berlin: Springer Verlag.

Van Haute, Ph. 2001. *Against Adaptation. Lacan's subversion of the Subject*. New York: Other Press.

Vanheule, S. 2011. *The Subject of Psychosis. A Lacanian Perspective*: New York: Palgrave.

Verene, D.F. 2011. *The Origins of the Philosophy of the Symbolic Forms: Kant, Hegel and Cassirer*. Evanston: Northwestern University Press.

Verhaeghe, P. 2008. *On Being Normal and Other Disorders*. New York: The Other Press.

Vliet, van M. 2013. *La forme selon Ernst Cassirer. De la morphologie au structuralisme*. Rennes: Presses Universitaires de Rennes.

Waelhens, A. de. 1961. *La philosophie et les expériences naturelles*. The Hague: Nijhoff.

Waldenfelds, B. 2006. *Grundmotive einer Phänomenologie des Fremden*. Frankfurt a.M: Suhrkamp.

Waldenfels, B. 2000. *Das leibliche Selbst. Vorlesungen zur Phänomenologie des Leibes*. Frankfurt a.M: Suhrkamp.

Wallon, H. 1949. *Les origines du caractère chez l'enfant*. Paris: Presses Universitaires de France (2e ed).

Welton, D. 2000. *The Other Husserl. The Horizons of Transcendental Phenomenology*. Bloomington/Indianapolis: Indiana University Press.

Widmer, P. 2006. *Metamorphosen des Signifkanten. Zur Bedeutung des Körperbilds für die Realität des Subjekts*. Bielefeld: Transcript Verlag.

Wiesing, L. 2009. *Das Mich der Wahrnehmung. Eine Autopsie*. Frankfurt a.M.: Suhrkamp.

Windelband, W. 1904. *Geschichte und Naturwissenschaft*. Strassburg: Heitz.

Winnicot, D.W. 1965. *The maturational process and the facilitating environment*. London: The Hogarth Press.

Wittgenstein, L. 1963. *Philosophical Investigations*. Oxford: Basil Blackwell. (Original work published 1953).

Zafiropoulos, M. 2001. *Lacan et les science sociales*. Paris: Presses Universitaires de France.

Zafiropoulos, M. 2003. *Lacan et Lévi-Strauss ou le retour à Freud 1951–1957*. Paris: Presses Universitaires de France.

Zimmerman, H. 2005. *Martin und Fritz Heidegger. Philosophie und Fastnacht*. München: Beck.

Žižek, S. 1998. *Die Nacht der Welt. Psychoanalyse und deutscher Idealismus*. Frankfurt a.M.: Fischer Verlag.

Žižek, S. 2008a. *Enjoy your Symptom*. New York/London: Routledge.

Žižek, S. 2008b. *The Plague of Fantasies*. London/New York: Verso.

Žižek, S. 2011. *The Most Sublime Hysteric. Hegel with Lacan*. Cambridge: Polity Press. (Original work published 1988).

Zupančič, A. 2017. *What is sex?* Cambridge (Mass.)/London: MIT Press.

ANNEX

Diagram of the Process of Symbolisation

Three sources/ basis phenomena:*		I-phenomenon/ life, experience	You-phenomenon/ action-reaction	It-phenomenon/ works, objective mind	
Three levels of the human condition:*		intentionality/ corporeality	being situated/ space and time	primacy of language and the Other	
		↑↑	↑↑	↑↑	
Three modes of representation ↓					**Three orders of representation** ↓
imaginary expressive pre-predicative	→			←	imaginary order: myth, religion (art)
symbolic objectifying predicative	→		void being *as* being …	←	symbolic order: language, politics, law, ethics
formalising formal principles, pure meaning	→			←	formal order: science and technology
		↑↑	↑↑	↑↑	
			representation of the real		
		↑↑	↑↑	↑↑	
The real: three domains		Immediacy of life *immanence vitale*	static real brutal reality (*le réel*)	primordial Other *la Chose*	

* Please note: the three levels of the human condition and the three basis phenomena are assumed to run parallel to each other.

Index of Names

Index of Subjects

www.ingramcontent.com/pod-product-compliance
Lightning Source LLC
Chambersburg PA
CBHW031322230926
51848CB00001B/54
9789004373426